ONCE UPON
——— A ———
LOST GIRL

D. L. CASTLE

ISBN 978-1-64028-524-8 (Paperback)
ISBN 978-1-64028-525-5 (Digital)

Christian Faith Publishing, Inc.
296 Chestnut Street
Meadville, PA 16335
www.christianfaithpublishing.com

Printed in the United States of America

ACKNOWLEDGEMENT

First and foremost I thank God for watching over me my whole life and for giving me the courage and faith to share my story. I would like to thank the Christian Faith Publishing team for all of their hard work and support to make my book come to life. Thank you Paul and Brian for walking me through all of the steps. I also thank my amazing husband for his unconditional love and support, especially over the last year when I needed encouragement. You are my rock and the love of my life. To our four beautiful daughters who have always been in my corner and who continue to make me a proud mom. My son-in-laws I adore. My six grandchildren (and counting) who bring me so much joy. My amazing friends; I would be lost without you all. You know who you are. My family members near and far. My adopted family. My church family. My amazing counsellor Susan. And last but certainly not least, my sister and brother who have always been here for me my whole life. I couldn't have asked for better siblings. I am truly blessed. Thank you all.

CHAPTER 1

I caught a glimpse of my mother in the distance. The light was very dim in the room and I felt very warm. I felt as though I could not breathe, and I was sure I was going to die. I had no control over these feelings of dread. I could hear myself screaming when I saw her lying in the coffin, only there was no sound coming out of my mouth. I could feel myself gasp for air, as I turned to run. I had no idea where I was going I only knew I wanted to be anywhere but here. My father caught me and I hid my face tightly in his black suit. I felt helpless at the thought of what I was about to experience. What is happening to me? I hung onto my father and buried my face further into his chest. Then I heard the voice of my thirteen-year-old sister Rose calling me to come and look at our mother. Even back then, I saw the strength in my sister and I admired her courage to walk right over to see our mother. I heard my sister say in a proud and loving tone, "Sis, come here, it's okay, she looks beautiful, she looks like sleeping beauty." As soothing as those words were, I knew she was not sleeping. She was still, she was quiet, and she was dead.

My heart raced to my throat as I slowly turned around. I could not feel myself move, but somehow I made my way over to the coffin. My sister was right. She was beautiful! I could hardly look at her at first, but then I found myself checking the parts of her I knew. I stared at the deep brown chestnut color of her hair, the milky white of her face, and the rich red color of her lips. I wanted to scream, but I was silent. I felt sick inside, and I finally started to cry in pain for my mother. I do not know if any sound came out of me, but inside I was crying my heart out. I stayed with my mother until someone gently led me away. Everything after that is a blur, if people spoke to me I do not remember. I barely remember leaving her and going home, but to this day, I can still feel the loss of breath when I saw my mother lying in the casket and the sting of pain in my throat. I can still hear the thundering of my heart beating so fast, I thought it would come through my chest. Until that moment, I had never experienced such fear and panic as I did on that day. Little did I know this would be the beginning of a lifetime of fear and anxiety.

My sister and I were fortunate enough to go to the visitation for our mother. I had just turned twelve years old a month before. I guess our father thought we were old enough to see our mother. Our younger brother Brad, who was nine, did not have permission to go, and it was a decision we were not happy about. He wanted to see our mother. It was very hard for him to register that she was gone. We had not seen our mother for a while as she was in the hospital and we were not allowed to visit her there. We were very sheltered children. We did not know how serious her condition was, and we did not expect the outcome. We were, however, expected to go on with life as usual and wait for her to come home to us, but that was not to be.

My mother was an amazing mom! She had a wonderful laugh that made you laugh just by hearing her. She showed us and told us how much she loved us all the time. She sent us to Sunday school and would get us to kneel at our bedside and say our prayers every night before she tucked us in. She made sure we spent time together doing family things. We always ate dinner together at the table when our dad came home from work. Speaking of dinner, back then when we didn't like our vegetables, mainly peas, we hid them underneath the table on the inside lip. We were sneaky little imps. Our family was very close from what I remember, but I was very naïve about the world outside of our family.

My mother was a very smart woman. She had a lot of patience with us three children and she always made me feel loved. I remember one time my friend and I were at the plaza spending our big twenty-five-cent allowances. I was about ten years old. You could get a lot of candy with twenty-five cents back then. We were looking at all the candy in the wrappers and wanted more than we could afford. My friend came up with a plan for us to get more candy. The plan was simply to steal the candy. Oh, yes, it was a brilliant plan. I was afraid to steal the candy.

My friend said, "It's easy, I have done it before, I will do it first to show you and then you do it."

I was really scared but I did it. I slipped a few more candy into my jacket pocket and then I went to the cash register and we paid for the rest of our candy with our allowance money.

"Wow, that was easy, but it scared the crap out of me," I said to my friend.

That night in my bed after I said my prayers, I was not feeling very well. I felt sick to my stomach but I finally fell asleep. The next day all I thought about was the candy I had stolen. I was so full of guilt I knew I had to tell my parents. Well, maybe I would start with my dad. My mom was the one who took care of punishments so I thought maybe I should tell my dad first. It took me a while to get the courage to go to my father but once I did I couldn't turn back. I told him I had done something bad and I felt really worried about getting in trouble.

I said, "Daddy, you are not going to like what I have to say, but I have to tell you because I feel sick."

My dad just sat there and listened to me. Then he said, "Okay, honey, it was good that you told me, but now you have to tell your mother."

In my head I was thinking, *What?* I said to him, "But, Dad, why do I have to tell Mommy?"

"I cannot keep this secret from your mother, it is not fair to her and we have to make a decision together on what we should do about this."

So much for not getting a punishment. So, my dad called my mother into the kitchen and he got me to tell her what I did. She spoke to me about stealing other people's property and the repercussions and the outcomes of what could have happened. She talked to me without yelling and assured me that she still loved me.

And then this is what she said to me: "Well, honey, it looks like you have already punished yourself by making yourself sick with worry, and I can tell you feel really guilty about stealing the candy. I think if Daddy agrees with me there will be no punishment this time. I am proud of you for coming to your dad and then to me to admit to us you did something that wasn't a good idea. And, honey, please don't ever do something like that again."

She kissed me and told me to go play. I will never forget her kindness and how she got her point across to me without yelling and making me feel so low. She was an amazing mom.

When I think of it now as an adult, before she went into the hospital she did seem to be sleeping a lot. Some days you would find her in her bedroom reading romance novels. This was back in 1969 to 1970 when the romance novels were a hot commodity. You know the harlequin romance books that always have a picture of the couple in some sort of embrace and they had a steamy name on the front. I read a lot of romance novels myself (in my '40s) and some of them turned my face red. So, to know that, my mom read them really surprised me. I always saw my mom as an angel. She didn't smoke or drink to speak of. She was very polite and kind. And our biggest punishment from her was a spanking on the butt with her soft slipper. But the one punishment that bothered us all the most would be the times she would sit us on a chair. Oh, yeah, that was by far the worst. It is so boring sitting on a chair. At least with the slipper it was quick and done.

As time went on she did not seem as energetic or happy. I wonder sometimes if we would have known her condition if it would have made a difference. But our dad and our relatives kept it quiet from us and the day she passed away was the first time we heard how sick she really was. We were devastated beyond words. Our first introduction about death was the death of our dearly loved mother. My first time seeing a coffin was the day I saw my mother lying in one. Coffins are not my favorite piece of furniture.

Our father decided we were not to go to the funeral. We weren't asked, we were told. You see, back then society was just learning about the importance of asking children how they felt. We lived in a family where children were seen and not heard. You have heard that old saying, "What you don't know won't hurt you." Well, trust me, sometimes what you don't know does hurt you. I found that out many years later.

My aunt from my dad's side stayed home from my mother's funeral and watched me and my siblings. She loved us so much and wanted more than anything to make sure we were okay. She had a family of four and yet opened up her heart and home to us. She loved my mother and was devastated that we had lost our mom. It was a really tough day for all of us and she did her best to keep us busy. When that day was over, our life as we knew it was over too.

We were expected to move on. You didn't dare get angry or that meant you were acting out. I didn't know how to act or be. I didn't know it was okay to cry. Nobody knew what to say to us. So, I tried to move on. I never shared my feelings because I was never asked. Here we were just three young children expected to get on with life. I tried to be as good as I could to please my father, but as time went on he didn't notice anyway. He started drinking and taking antidepressants to help him cope with the loss of his beloved wife, the woman who was his best friend, who took care of the house, and most importantly their children. The mother who kissed us every night and made us feel special with her words of love. The mother who loved us so much, she would do anything to protect us. The

woman who, for the twelve short years I knew her, gave me unconditional love, encouragement, and faith in God. My heart ached for
my mother. Now she was gone, just like that our world had changed.
I couldn't think of the happy times we had as a family, it was just too
painful. I was so full of different emotions that I dared not reveal
them to anyone. I pushed them way down inside of me so they could
never escape and show a side of me I didn't want anyone to witness.

It was November 10, 1970, when my mother died of bowel
cancer. She would have turned thirty-four years young on December
14 that same year. I can only imagine how she felt knowing she was
leaving her three children behind. I'm sure it broke her heart with
worry of what would happen to us. We were her world.

MY THOUGHTS

Not to take anything away from my parents, as they did what
they had to do and felt was right at the time. They were raised in a
different era, and I would not have wanted to be put in their shoes.
I can only say or suggest what I may have done differently in their
situation. It doesn't mean my solutions would have been any better.
When I think of myself not knowing that my mother was on her
death bed and we were not allowed to visit her, it breaks my heart.
I would have loved to hug her and told her how much I loved her. I
would have cried, but she could have cried with me and held me and
told me she was going to miss me but she would always be with me
in spirit. I would have liked to have been told the truth, maybe in bits
and pieces. Just baby steps would have been helpful.

I feel it would have been a good idea to let us children (one at a
time, of course) go and visit our mother in the hospital. We were too
long without seeing her. Children build all kinds of scary thoughts in
their heads as to what is happening in the hospital. There are ways to
make it not look so scary by having familiar things such as pictures, a
blanket from home, flowers, and so on to show the children there are

nice things to concentrate on while visiting the parent. For goodness' sake, at least ask the children if they would like to visit their parent and if the answer is yes then somebody prepare them for it. If the parent is too afraid or upset and cannot function themselves, that is when someone could step forward and give them the help they need. It is not an easy situation for all people concerned but there is always a solution and sometime it is the strangers outside the family circle that are angels in disguise.

Letting us know that our mom was very sick and that the doctors were trying to find a cure for what was keeping her sick might have been useful. Once we got used to that idea, then we could've been told that the doctors were having a hard time making our mother better and she may not be coming home. Not knowing anything at all is just as hard on children as it is on adults. I know as an adult I have heard myself say, "It is the not knowing that is the hardest part," when I am waiting for results of a certain test. I had no idea at all that our mother was so ill. We were so in the dark. Talk about being helpless.

I am not saying we should've been told flat out that she was dying, that would have been scary, but at least prepare us that she was very, very sick and the doctors were trying very hard to make her better. Surely, there was a better way to handle this than to learn about our mom's death sitting on our parent's bed and told simply your mom has died. Talk about a shock. Not that you are ever prepared when someone you love dies, but maybe a bit of preparation on the subject of death could have been introduced to us during the year of our mom being ill, or maybe I am just grasping at anything to have made this hole in my heart feel better.

Last, but certainly not least (maybe it could have been the first thing), I would highly recommend having someone talk to us like a counselor that worked with children specifically. Letting us be angry and sad and talk, talk, talk about our feelings until the talking was over. Surely, someone could have stepped up and realized this was a devastating blow to us children and got us the help we desperately needed. Maybe, just maybe, things would have been different for us in a more positive light. Unfortunately, we will never know the answer to that. I have learned through the years we cannot live in what ifs and maybe. We can only learn from the past and move through to the future.

To have had more time with you,
To laugh and play and read with you,
To hold you tight and share a song,
To say I love you, so sad you're gone.
But, one day when the time is right,
I will see you again in the beautiful light,
I will be knocking on heaven's glorious door,
And my heart will not ache for you anymore...
love you...love you...bye.

And so that first Christmas came and went without my mom. It was very sad, though relatives tried to make it good for us. Nothing was the same. The life we once knew was over. We had no idea what we were about to endure. And so began the bittersweet journey.

Life went on, even though my world had stopped. People were still working, children were going to school, my friends were still playing, and the days went by on the calendar. The world did not stand still for us, the world kept moving. In the year of 1970 when my mom had died, several big events were happening. The Apollo 13 mission launched. The Boeing 747 made its first commercial passenger trip to London. United States invaded Cambodia, ordered by Nixon. One hundred thousand people demonstrated in Washington, DC, against the Vietnam War. The Beatles disbanded. The world's population was 3.63 billion. Popular films were *MASH* and *Woodstock*. Popular songs were "Let It Be" by the Beatles and "ABC" by The Jackson Five. A cyclone in Bangladesh kills five hundred thousand people. And the Nuclear Nonproliferation Treaty goes into effect after ratification of forty-three nations. The 1970s had a lot of incredible things happening in our world, and all of these things I just mentioned happened in 1970. But as a twelve-year-old kid, I was oblivious to any of it. I was only paying attention to one thing and that was the death of my mother.

School was different now; it felt like my classmates were looking at me as if I was strange. Nobody knew how to approach me. I found myself alone, except for my childhood friend. She would hug me and say she was so sorry. We would play together like nothing had ever changed. But, sometimes at night, I would have nightmares and wake up feeling afraid and abandoned. And something that was really strange to me was when one day I either dreamt or I actually saw this beautiful huge bird (which I like to call the paradise bird) outside in my backyard up above the building we lived in. It seemed like it was looking down at me and was there specifically for me. I wish I could remember if it was real or a dream. It reminded me of a peacock only it had so many colors on its wings when it spread its wings. It seemed so real but I was so distraught at that time I really don't know if it was.

I would like to think it was. I know when I saw it I felt happy and peaceful. I never saw it again, only that one time.

As time went on, I don't ever remember talking to my sister or brother about how we all felt. We just seemed to go on with life as best we could. I cannot speak for my sister and brother, but I believe today we didn't know how to express our feelings back then, as nobody took the time to talk to us about how we felt.

Eventually our grandmother (my dad's mom) moved in with us for a while to help my father take care of us. She wasn't with us very long as she took ill and had to go to the hospital. That was scary for me, as that's where my mother went and I didn't feel too good about my grandmother going there. I remember when she left by an ambulance I felt so much fear inside. But although I loved my grandmother I must say she was not an affectionate person. There are two vivid memories I have of her. Once when we were little she let us pick out a cup and saucer to keep, as well as her specially made doll clothes. This was the only time I ever remember her as a loving grandmother. Most of the time, I felt like we were in her way. The other vivid memory is when she screamed at me, "You kids are so bad, it's no wonder your mother died." Her words cut through me like a knife and I kept silent and didn't disagree with her. I thought she must be right, we were bad. I know today as an adult that my grandmother didn't mean those words, we weren't bad, we were three children grieving for our mother, our family, and some attention from our father. But that comment stung inside me for many years.

As I said earlier, shortly after my grandmother came to our house she was taken away by ambulance to the hospital. My grandmother could not take care of us anymore as she had complications in the hospital. She was a diabetic and had taken a bad fall and gangrene set in her leg which had to be amputated from the knee down. When she came out of the hospital she went back to her home and my uncle lived with her. One day when she was feeling better she came to my other uncle's house (my dad's brother) where we were having a family get together. I was up in a tree (as I was a tomboy). My father told me to come down out of the tree and say hello to my grandmother. I was not coming down from that tree. I could see her from a distance in a wheel chair and that was fine by me. I was afraid to see her amputated leg and I remembered the last words she said to me and I was afraid to see her. Eventually my father used his stern voice and I knew I better come down. I wasn't happy about it but I did go see her.

I just stood in the background and said, "Hi, Grammy." That was the last time I saw her.

It wasn't long before she was back in the hospital again as the gangrene had spread to her other leg. She was to have that leg amputated too but she died in the hospital shortly before the operation. I felt guilty that I hadn't been nicer to her when I last saw her. But I was afraid to see her like that and instead of talking about it I just shoved those feelings down. Did I love her? Yes, without a doubt, but she was a tough women and I was never sure how she was going to be with us children. Later on in life, I found out she was adopted by her parents and she came from the United States. Back then you didn't talk about adoption like you do today. I only know that when I found out later in life, I had empathy for her and wished I could have gotten to know her better. But, hey, life doesn't always give you that opportunity, and so I always say to people when they make assumptions about other people that they don't know that person's story. We all have a story and some stories are good and some are not so good and some are downright horrible. My grandmother may have been an angry person because she never knew why her biological parents gave her up, or maybe she didn't get the love from her adopted parents that she needed. I will never know the answer to that, but like I said earlier, I do have empathy and I do see the bigger picture now and have no hard feelings for her. She did the best she could with what she knew and what she had. Love you, Grammy.

The death of my grandmother was a very hard thing for my father to bear. First his beloved wife dies, and then his mother. I was so upset inside because two important women in my life had just died several months from each other. So, here we were alone again. We needed someone to take care of us as our dad was not able to. He was drinking more and had no patience with us. My mom's cousin came to stay with us for a while and tried her best to take care of us. I liked her because she showed me attention, but things fell apart between her and my dad and soon she was packed and leaving us. I was sad to see her go as things were starting to feel a little normal for me and then it fell apart again.

My dad was getting out of control with his drinking. I don't remember any family suppers or family time. It seemed to me that my sister was taking care of me and my brother. She truly watched out for us and tried to take care of our dad too. It was a lot to take on for she was only thirteen years of age. We might have fought a little more than we did before mom passed away, but one thing was for sure and that was the love we had for each other. If anyone lived with us, they would have known we were three broken children trying desperately to get through the very depressing days as best we could. We had no help and everybody had their own lives and families to deal with.

We were alone now with our father. My feelings were mostly numb, but I remember being so full of fear and worried about who would take care of us. I have memories of my father getting angry at us and hollering at us more than usual. One day when we were driving he threatened to put us in an orphanage if we didn't behave. I swallowed his words, and tried my best to be good. The last place I wanted to go was an orphanage, but I never ever thought he was serious.

My father needed help desperately. He chose to get his help from alcohol. The drinking got worse. One night my father was so out of control, I remember hearing the sound of a window smashing. It may have been something else but something woke me up. I had no idea what was happening, I barely remember that night. Many years later as per my sister Rose, she remembers pouring Dad's wine down the sink. Then she took twenty dollars and took my brother and me to one of our mother's friend's house just a block away at the time. I have no recollection of that at all but it doesn't surprise me. For one thing, this would be something my sister would do. She tried so hard to make sure we were safe. And another thing, I was so full of fear that I must have blocked some of that time period from my memory. The next day we went home to our dad and he told us to pack most of our clothes. I thought we were going away for a few days until my dad felt better, but that was the last time I lived with my father. He took us out to the country and dropped us off at our Aunt Maggie's house (my mom's sister), and if he said anything about not coming back for us I truly don't remember. I don't remember the drive to the country where my aunt and uncle lived. And again, as per my sister Rose, during the drive we picked up our cousin as he lived not too far from where we were going. I don't remember that at all. I had no idea what was happening to us. I was full of fear and sadness for my father. Who would take care of him and why were we leaving? There were two things I knew for sure—my mother was taken away from us and our father was giving us up.

I would learn much later in life that our dad had called my mom's sister and brother to let them know he had decided to put us in the orphanage as he just couldn't cope. He had a meeting with them and my aunt Maggie had decided to take us in with her and her family. Here we were, three city kids about to live in the country. I must say that I loved the country as we had spent summer vacations with our mom at her cousin's house in a little town about an hour or so away from where we lived. I have very fond memories of our times spent there with my cousins. And now we were going to live with my mom's only sister (my dear aunt Maggie). My aunt Maggie and Uncle John had eight children of their own. They ate their meals together as a big family. And the best part, there was no drinking! As much as I missed my father, after a week had gone by I was actually happy to be there. For the first time in months, I was a part of a family again that actually took care of each other. I had yearned for the family suppers, the morning chaos at breakfast and, all the things that made a family (without the drinking and fear I felt since my mom's death).

They had a big old barn and a big hill behind it, and they had a big old German shepherd. Their house was way in off the road. There was a little pond where we would be able to skate in the winter. The barn was a place we went often to play hide and seek or have a big sleep over in our sleeping bags. It was a kid's dream to have all this space and play outside when your homework and chores were done. My cousins were very good to us and made us feel welcome, but it must have been a little disrupting to their lives as now they had to share their bedrooms. But I was truly happy and felt safe. You could say I lived with my own Walton family (which was a good wholesome show that came on later in my teens).

Unfortunately, my life was about to take another jolt. After a couple weeks of starting to feel happy, I was approached by my aunt Maggie. I can still feel the numbness and shock as she told me I was to go and live with my uncle (my mom's brother Albert and family). I guess that would've been okay except I was going alone. My brother and sister were going to continue living with my aunt and her family. I felt like I had been punched in the stomach. Several emotions flooded my mind. I felt unwanted and abandoned again. I was devastated. I did not want to leave my brother and sister. I became very angry inside. They say things happen in threes. Well, it was happening to me, I lost my mom, I was separated from my father (his choice), and now I was being separated from my sister and brother (not their choice). I was separated from my family within six months, but it was happening to my sister and brother also. They were now being separated from their sister. It was hard for all of us. My heart cried again only this time I blamed myself, if I would have been a good girl they may have kept me. Inside my head, I was begging not to be sent away. I cried out, "Please, let me stay, I will be good, please." But, my words of pain and abandonment were not to be heard. I didn't know it at the time, but I swallowed all the fear and anger again. Now, I truly felt alone.

MY THOUGHTS

Let me start off by saying I loved my aunt Maggie and uncle John very much. They were amazing people. I have always loved them even when I had to leave their home. My love never stopped for them, not once.

That being said, I still think if you have three children who have just lost their parents (two different circumstances), it is not a good idea to separate them. Yes, I know that it would be very hard to find a family who could take on three children. You would have to really search hard and put the word out and hopefully the government would help the family who so willingly would keep all three children or in our case relatives. The family who takes two children should take all three. Speaking from experience, there is no winner when children are separated.

Maybe, just maybe, if there had of been some help from a good child therapist or counselor to help me (a child) understand why I was chosen to be taken away from my siblings or to help me have some sort of safe place to have a voice. Maybe, if there had of been someone of adult age who would have got me to open up about what I was feeling and let me know what I could do with all those angry and abandonment feelings, just maybe I wouldn't have carried all those feelings into my adult hood. Maybe, my life would have been happier and fuller. But, we can't live in maybe or what ifs. We all have choices to make in our lives. My aunt and uncle had to make a very hard choice, and I wouldn't have wanted to be the one making that choice.

You see, my mom's brother Albert wanted to do his part in helping the children of his deceased sister, and it is totally understandable to want to help. Families want to help the best way they can and when you are grieving the loss of your sister, I can only imagine how distraught you would be. But there are many ways to help, and it is too bad that someone from the outside of the family didn't step in and say, "Okay, this is great that you want to take one of the children but they have lost enough in such a short time, it is not wise to separate them from each other. That would just cause a whole set of other problems for the three of these children. It is very thoughtful of you to want to do this but the children need to be together. But here is what you could do to help. If you want, you could drop by with some groceries once in a while or drop by with used clothing for the kids. Maybe pick them up and take them over night sometimes. Let them know you are there for them, not because you think it is the right thing to do but because you want to do it for the children."

We have to remember that everyone has to live with their choices. All of us at one time or another will make a choice that did not work out so well. And we can spend our life in regret or we can learn from that choice and never make it again. I found out a couple years ago that my aunt and uncle regretted the decision they made in letting my uncle take me to live with him and his family, not because

I wasn't being taken care of but because I should have been with my siblings. I wish I could have spoken to them about the decision they made many years ago before they passed away. I would tell them that they did the best they could at the time with what they knew. I would tell them I have never spoken a bad word about them because I adored them both. I would tell them I will always be grateful for all they did for my brother and sister. They are truly loved and I miss them both. I speak from experience on making choices over the years that were not the best choices and I had to live with the outcomes. Separating three children, keeping two together, and letting the other one go, to me, is still not highly recommended but I do understand their dilemma.

> *And so, I say, see you later for now,*
> *I wish I could stay with you somehow,*
> *I promise to do all my homework and chores,*
> *And stay out of your hair and play outdoors.*
> *Please let me stay, I will be very good,*
> *I will do dishes and bring in the wood.*
> *I guess I will go if that's what you want,*
> *I will still love you my beautiful Aunt.*
>
> *See you later sis and brother too,*
> *I wish I could stay here with you,*
> *I guess I have to go but please don't cry,*
> *Someday we will know the reason why. Love you, love you, bye...*

CHAPTER 2

My heart is now broken into a million pieces. I am broken and empty as I get into my uncle's car with the little belongings I have all shoved into a small suitcase. Clutched ever so tightly to my chest is my cloth doll named Rose-bed that I got from my mom and dad when I was younger. My aunt Maggie and my siblings are standing there brokenhearted as they watch us drive away. I am looking at them through the window and it still brings tears to my eyes. As I said earlier they lived way in off the road and that drive leaving their home was slow and heart wrenching to say the least. My eyes stayed glued to their home until I could not see it anymore, and reliving and talking about that moment in my life is still painful and sad but I can deal with it now. I must say here that I do not remember if anyone else was in the car with my uncle and me. I was oblivious to my surroundings. I may have looked okay on the outside but I was very angry. I was one unhappy child that day, and sometimes I wish I would have hidden somewhere in the house or in the barn and not come out until they said I could stay. But, we were taught to obey our elders and believe they knew what was best for us. Something inside me changed that day, something I lived with for years. I exchanged my sadness for anger, and I had no idea it was happening, it just happened. But the other thing that plagued me was my fear. The last little pieces of the family I knew and loved were taken away from me, and I lived with so much fear but couldn't name it at the time. I was in deep trouble and no one could see it, not even myself.

And now I am living with my uncle Albert and aunt Pattie and their five children (two girls and three boys). I wish I could sound more excited about it but I wasn't happy at all. I really didn't know my uncle and their family except for the times we would all spend weekends together at our grandmother's. I played with my cousins but I didn't really know my aunt and uncle and they didn't know me. Their oldest daughter was getting married that year so now there was a place for me at the table. I had no idea how to act. I was so full of turmoil inside, I just existed the first year. And because I was so angry at being there without my siblings, I didn't make life easy for them. For the rest of the school year, my other uncle, John (where my sister and brother lived), would take us into the city to finish our grades at the same school. He worked in the city not far from the school, which worked out very well. During that time, we would go to my mom's friend Charlene's house up the street from our school for lunchtime and our uncle John would pick us up after his work and bring us home (I would get dropped off at Uncle Albert's house). I was very stressed at this time and not a happy twelve-year-old. We went to a school where it was a rough neighborhood and I remember always rushing to get to Charlene's house because I was afraid of the bullies after school.

This one day I left the school without using the bathroom and by the time I got to Charlene's house it was too late. I knocked on the door and when she opened it up I was just standing there peeing on the mat outside her door. It just came out, I couldn't hold it anymore. I just stood there peeing. Well, I was so embarrassed and her reaction did not help. She hollered at me so loud and I just started crying. She made me clean it up which was fine but she was so rude about it I had a lump in my throat that hurt. To top it all off, she sent me over to my father's house a block away to get an extra pair of underwear and clothes. She made me walk with my dress still on and a bare ass.

Needless to say, I was embarrassed and humiliated. She made me feel like shit.

Another time at her house when she was watching us at lunch, I put the top lid of a pop can on my finger as a ring. You know the little tin thing you push into the can to open it? Well, I twisted it off and put it on my finger, and you guessed it, I couldn't get it off and my finger was swelling. Well, that was a fiasco. There just happened to be a plumber there fixing her bathroom sink and he said he could help me get it off.

She said, "Look what you've done. Now he's going to have to saw off your finger to get it off."

I started to cry and the plumber said he wouldn't cut off my finger and that my babysitter was just kidding. It took me a long time before I would let him take it off. He was able to get it off with no problem, but I was scared to death. I was late getting back to class that day.

I will never forget those two vivid memories. I hated going to her house after that, and I was happy when the school year was finished so I didn't have to go there anymore. But I do have to be fair and say that my babysitter was going through a tough time in her family. She had a beautiful young daughter who had a severe mental handicap and she needed a lot of attention. She also had two boys and eventually she added another little girl to her family. She had just lost one of her dearest friends, my mom. As an adult I admire my babysitter for taking on three more children at lunchtime and at the end of the day. The last thing she needed was more stress, but as a child I did not see it that way. I only knew that I wanted my mom and my family back.

I remember my first Mother's Day without my mom. It was really sad and heartbreaking. A week before the teacher had told the class that we were to write a poem about our mothers for Mother's Day. She came to me and privately told me I didn't have to participate so it wouldn't upset me. I remember telling her that I loved poetry and I would like to write a poem in memory of my mom. If she didn't let me participate, I would have felt like such an outsider. She agreed and apologized to me. I wrote what I thought was the most beautiful poem for my mom. When I read it to the class there was no noise at all. My classmates were so quiet and the teacher was wiping her eyes. I wish I could say I have that poem. But I moved so many times in the years ahead that it was lost forever. The only hope that I have is that she heard me read it to the class and it gave her a big smile and filled her heart with joy from her little girl.

Those are the only memories that stand out for me during that first year at my uncle's house. I truly don't remember too much about the first year. I have some happy and some not-so-happy memories during the following three years. My cousin Sandy and I shared a room together and shared a lot of laughter and I made a few dear friends. I was able to visit my brother and sister as they lived only fifteen minutes away by car. I used to walk or bike over to their house. It always seemed to take forever to get there but I was determined to go. I missed them dearly but as time went on I just shoved those thoughts of sadness down further and further.

My cousin Sandy was like a little sister to me. I enjoyed being with her. She made me laugh. We were stinkers and would get into trouble together. We went swimming a lot at a lake just five minutes away from our house. We walked to the country store many times and went hiking in the woods all the time. We would go to visit my brother and sister and other cousins. We played with other kids on our road, games like baseball and hide and seek. Sometimes we would raid our neighbor's garden and eat their carrots and thought we were so cool, but word got out that someone was raiding gardens in the neighborhood and we had to stop. We were out of the house all the time. We always had something to do outside with our friends. When we had to be in the house we used to take the long cigarette butts out of the ashtray that my uncle smoked and we would smoke them upstairs in our bedroom. We would open the window and blow the smoke out the window. Neither one of us inhaled at the time because we would choke. But we always liked to blow smoke rings out of our mouths for fun. It was too funny as we would laugh at each other and just thought it was innocent fun. These were happy memories because of her.

But, every now and then, I would miss my father's presence in my life. I waited for him to call me, but the calls were very few. When I did talk to my father, he would say he was coming to see me and I would wait but he wouldn't show up. I would bring my little suitcase back up to the house. I would look out the window with excitement in my heart waiting for my father to come and spend time with me. Sometimes, I would wait outside at the end of the yard and as the time went on the excitement I felt in my heart would turn to sadness and I would have a sick feeling in my stomach. It was a huge letdown and I would feel so unwanted and abandoned. I felt so hurt and angry inside but I wouldn't talk about it, I just kept shoving those feelings away.

The anger can only hide for so long, and eventually I acted out in different ways. Once I was so angry inside, I took the few albums I had of my family (Mom and Dad and my siblings) and burnt them in the outside garbage can, which is something that I have regretted all my life. Needless to say, my aunt and uncle were not impressed. Another time, I was being teased by my cousin Cane and he made me so angry I dug my nails into his chest and scratched him all the way down. I felt so bad that I did that to him but I put on this stubborn face and acted like I didn't care. The sad thing is, neither my uncle's family nor mine saw this as an emotional problem or an underlying problem, we all just figured I was being a brat. After all, I was being taken care of and had a roof over my head, which is a lot more than some children have today. But that wasn't the problem. I was very thankful for the food and shelter I had, but I was so unhappy deep inside and there was no one around that could figure that out.

I didn't know how to communicate and I left them in the dark many times. Coming from a background where kids were seen and not heard kept me from opening up to my family. We never talked about how I felt or how angry I was living with my aunt and uncle without my sister and brother. I did not feel like they wanted me there. I felt they took me in as they thought it was the right thing to do but I needed more than that. I felt I was a burden to them and just another mouth to feed and clothe. I wonder sometimes if I would have opened up about how I was feeling if things would have been different. Instead I just kept shoving it down and took what I could get from their family. It was not a good outcome for any of us. These were the feelings I had. It doesn't mean my aunt and uncle felt that way.

During the times I would go to see my siblings, I got to meet some really nice kids who lived in my sibling's area. They became good friends to me during high school and that made driving the bus in to high school most enjoyable. This one girl and I had the same name and we hit it off quite well. She was always joking around and laughing and we were little buggers when we got together. We hung out together quite a bit and if I am correct she was the first one to get me to inhale a cigarette. And I also believe she laughed her head off as I choked my lungs out hiding behind this big cement block on the school grounds. We were trouble together but it was all innocent trouble. We would make fun of our one teacher because he was so cranky and almost got caught passing a note to each other with a very rude picture of our teacher drawn up as a creature. I was sent out of the room that day but I deserved it as I was laughing and not paying attention. When the two of us were together, we were always getting called out for talking and disturbing the class. We couldn't even look at each other without laughing. We would go to this little country church for youth gatherings and we (and when I say we, I mean she) would pull pranks on the minister. It was all in fun but the poor minister had his hands full with us. I loved going to that little church because the minister made all of us youth feel wanted and loved. These were very happy moments in my early teens.

Eventually, when I was fifteen (almost sixteen), I got myself a job in town at a grocery store, working in the meat room. The manager of the meat room only lived about a ten-minute walk away from my uncle's house. I was told about the job from a girl at my high school named Mary who was working there at the time. I worked on Friday and Saturdays at the beginning and had a way to and from work with my manager. I became very good friends with Mary and with her family. Sometimes I would stay at her house and we would go to work together. We became inseparable, and soon I was spending a lot of time with her. We would go skating on the lake in the city and that was where I met my very first real boyfriend. By this time, I was sixteen.

As a sixteen year old girl my hormones were all over the place. Not only was I emotional I also had this sadness in me that I kept shoving down inside. Sandy and I were hanging with different friends and finding ourselves on different paths. I was spending more time in the city with my boyfriend and working on the weekends. This boy was so good to me and I fell head over heels for him. He was tall, dark, beautiful Lebanese decent and handsome with a huge heart. I finally felt as though I belonged and I felt loved and needed for the first time in a very long time.

The only downfall was the fact that my uncle didn't seem to like this boy. I suppose as a parent he didn't trust a fifteen-year-old boy around his sixteen-year-old niece. He did have long hair but most guys wore their hair long in the '70s. However, this boy never gave my uncle any reason not to trust him or like him. He was a very respectful teenager and wasn't a troublemaker by any means. And most importantly, he treated me very well.

Unfortunately, because I was late getting home one night by about fifteen minutes (or probably a half hour), my uncle didn't want me to see this boy anymore. I was devastated. I was not about to give up this love that I had so desperately needed and wanted. We had an argument and I cried my eyes out. But, like I said, I was not about to give up this boy. I didn't think my uncle would ever let me go out with David again so I did the only thing I thought I could do. I decided to run away. I found myself packing a small suitcase of clothes and leaving early for the school bus the next Monday morning. I only had a small suitcase which meant I didn't have room for my prized possession which was my cloth doll named Rose-bed. I was upset to leave her behind but I had no choice. I figured I could pick her up another time but that never happened. I don't know what happened to my doll but it was gone forever. Well, that was it, I was leaving and I wasn't going back. My cousin Cane got on the same bus as me for school and he never said a word about the suitcase I was carrying. He was a good guy and he just let me do what I had to do. I found myself at my father's door looking for a place to stay. At this time in my father's life, he had remarried to a much younger girl (six years older than me) and they just had their first little boy. He did not have the room for me but he said I could sleep on the couch for a few weeks until I found another place. My uncle Albert and my cousin Sandy came in to get me to come back but I was very stubborn and would not go. I was sixteen then and I thought I was old enough to make my own decisions. I thought at sixteen I knew everything and I was almost a grown-up after all and I knew exactly what I wanted and that was to be loved. You couldn't talk to me once I made up my mind. I was not going back. I felt really bad for my cousin though because I knew we would miss each other. But I made my choice, that was it and it is sad to say but I never looked back.

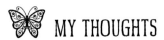 MY THOUGHTS

First and foremost, I love my aunt and uncle. They are my family and I will always love them. They had a lot going on in their own lives and it wasn't easy dealing with a very angry twelve-year-old girl. I guess the one word I think of when I think of my aunt and uncle is *communication*. There really wasn't any, at least none that I could see. It always seemed there was miscommunication between us. Let me be clear, not just on their part but on my part as well.

One example I can remember was one late afternoon when my cousin Sandy and I were playing with our friend. Her mom said she was going into the city to the mall. One of us could go with our friend. Sandy and I both wanted to go and neither of us would budge on who would go. Sandy went into the house very angry at me and I waited while our friend asked if both of us could go to the mall. Our friend said we both could go. I ran to our house to tell my cousin we could both go but just before I opened the door I heard her yelling to her mom that she hated me and wished I never came to her house. She didn't want to share her bedroom with me anymore and she didn't want to share her friends. She said a few more things but I was so hurt and upset I just started running and I ran to the end our road and started hitchhiking on the main road. I was so angry and hurt, I didn't know where I was going, maybe to my father's, I didn't know.

Of course along come our friend and her mom pulled over and said, "What are you doing hitchhiking? Where are you going?" I explained to my friend and her mom what I had heard Sandy say and that I was running away. They calmed me down and said I should come with them to the mall and the mom would call my aunt and tell her that I was safe with them. My friend's mom called my aunt Pattie and told her I was with them and my aunt was furious with me for not asking if I could go to the mall. When my friends mom got off the phone she said my aunt was really angry and it sounded like she didn't believe I was running away. All I knew was that I was in trouble.

'When I arrived home I knew my aunt and cousin were upset with me. From their view it would have looked like I just went to the mall with my friend. But that was not what happened. And so my aunt talked to both of us and we were to apologize to each other. I don't believe that I ever told my aunt or cousin what I heard in the shed. I felt like I had to take the blame and accept that I was in the wrong. That is one small example about communication with me and my uncle's family. And again, I am not blaming them for I could have insisted for them to listen to me too but I didn't. I always shoved my feelings down. Again, as I said earlier, we all just thought I was being a brat, we never saw the underlying problem. I guess my advice to anyone who is taking in a twelve-year-old girl who has been separated from her family within a year to make sure there is a lot of communication. This is a big deal for any family to take on especially when the child does not want to be there without her siblings (as in my case). Yes, I was very lucky that I did not have to go to an orphanage, and for that I am truly thankful. But there should have been outside help, again, such as a therapist. Mind you, there are good therapists and not-so-good therapists. It's like anything, you have to search until the child feels safe and trusts the person they are talking to. This may take time but the end results may outweigh the sad outcome of the child carrying all this anger and panic with them into their adult life.

As I said earlier in the first chapter I believe being separated from my sister and brother should not have been an option. A big part of me wishes that my uncle Albert did not feel like he had to take one of the children in order to be there for his sister. Another part of me wishes he would have helped his sister by contributing in other ways like food, clothing, and visits. But that did not happen, and I have no idea how things would have turned out if I would have stayed with my siblings. I only know that I wish I could have had the chance to find out as I was a very lost girl for a very long time in my life. That being said, I do want to make it perfectly clear that I do not blame anyone for my choices and mistakes in my adult life. My uncle and aunt did not have any influence on my decisions. The circumstances and the lack of knowledge back then were a big factor in the direction I took. A person could drive themselves crazy if they concentrated on the "what ifs" or the "I should haves." What happened to me happened and I choose to move forward and learn from my mistakes. If my words can help anyone in a similar situation like this, then I would be forever grateful that my pain was not in vain. And I do thank my aunt and uncle for all that they did for me. We were all going through our own stuff but I will always love them.

And just so I don't end this chapter on a sad note, I would like to share with you a happy childhood memory. This memory makes me smile and fills my heart with love.

When I think back to my childhood days before my mom passed away, I can recall many times of getting together with our relatives at my grandmother Ada's house (my mom's mom). She lived in the country with my great uncle Chuck and had a long, bumpy dirt driveway to her house. She did not have running water and we had to carry pails of fresh spring water from the well up to the house. There wasn't a washroom in the house so we had to use the outhouse that was built just down the hill not far from the house. And of course there was no electricity, so you read by oil lamps at night. You always had the best toast in town as she cooked from a big old wood stove.

During the summer holidays, we would spend time at our grandmother's house. Almost every day we would walk the hot black road to a lake called Wood Lake. The water was clear and refreshing. After a long time of playing and laughing in the water, we would lie on our towels in the hot summer sun and dry off. Then we would pack up our things and walk back to Gram's house. As a kid, I would never have thought of that as relaxation and peaceful. I only knew it gave me a sense of happiness that I would long for later in the years to come. We shared walks in the woods, climbing trees, and building forts. We shared picnics and going down to the big beach (just several miles away) that took your breath away it was so beautiful. And, my dad took us fishing whenever he could. Ah, those were the days, the days of innocence. It was years later when my grandmother finally got electricity and her first television. She finally got indoor plumbing and running cold water. She never did get hot water so you still had to take what we called then sponge baths. It is amazing to me that even though she didn't have all the modern necessities in my early childhood years, spending time at my grandmother's house were some of the best days of my life and I wouldn't trade them for anything. I can only hope that my grandchildren will have happy fond memories of visiting me (their nanny). But one thing is for certain, my children and grandchildren would be appalled if they had to use an outhouse.

Whether we have experienced a happy childhood or one filled with abuse or neglect or whatever the case maybe to remember a time when our hearts were filled with love and happiness is something no one can ever take from us. Hold onto those special moments, even if they only lasted a moment, because those are the moments that will help us to believe there can be happy times again. We ourselves can make those moments happen if we trust in ourselves and others along the way. Life is too precious and short to live in the dark past of our life. Somewhere along the way there is light. We just have to look deeper and it will be there. For me it was my grandmother Ada's house.

CHAPTER 3

I never thought I would be living with my dad again, but here I was living with him and his new family. This was a big deal for me. I hadn't been with my father in years, and so I was a little timid about staying there with them. I really didn't know his wife that well and I wasn't around when their son was born. I remember when I saw their son (my new brother), I thought he was so cute and innocent. I was actually concerned about how his life would be with my dad and my stepmother. I knew they loved him but I really wasn't sure what type of life he would have. My stepmother wasn't exactly motherly but she did the best she could. My dad was much older and at least he had some experience but he still drank. I knew it was not my responsibility to worry about them though and so I decided that they had enough on their hands and they didn't need me crowding their life. I talked to my boyfriend and he said he was going to ask his parents if I could stay with him and his family. I wasn't too keen on this idea but I felt so scared of what was going to happen to me that I agreed to his suggestion.

And a couple weeks after I stayed at my father's small apartment my boyfriend David did ask his parents if I could live with them. I don't know how he did it but he got them to agree to me living with them. They were such a beautiful family. David has two adorable younger sisters and two amazing brothers. Number one reason I felt safe was because there was very little drinking to speak of. I felt safe and wanted. I was very happy there. My relationship with David was like something out of a fairy tale (at least in my mind it was). We would go for long walks and talk for hours. We used to go to a very big park where there were several lakes just ten minutes or so from his house. We would go there early in the morning and watch the sunrise. We had a lot of fun skating at our favorite lake and just felt we would live forever like this. David loved to play the guitar and he taught me how to play a few songs. I was never as good as him. We were just two innocent kids who had the world by the tail. The music was good in the '70s and that's what we were into, well that and a few drinks and for him it was weed. I guess we weren't that innocent.

When I had lived with my aunt and uncle in the country and I needed to go into the city (because I knew a lot of people on our road), I would wait at the end of our road and hitchhike. I would not recommend this today but back then it was a normal thing to do and I would pick and choose who I would put my thumb out for. Well, this one time my friend Mary and I decided we wanted to go to another city about an hour and a half away to see our friends. Mary was not keen on hitchhiking at the start of the highway but I assured her it was okay. Every time I would put my thumb out she would stop me and I would say, "Mary, we aren't going to get anywhere if you keep putting my hand down and not putting your thumb up!"

She would usually answer by saying, "I can't help it. I don't want to hitchhike. What if we get in with a crazy person?"

Of course, I was older and I was used to hitchhiking so I saw no harm in it what so ever. She finally agreed to do it but barely put her thumb up as she stood behind me. We finally got a ride from a guy who was driving a big transport truck and it was quite a feat to get inside the cab. The guy looked normal to me and although I was a little nervous I was glad to get off of the highway. He talked away and was actually very nice and said he didn't want us girls to hitchhike and that it wasn't safe. He was going to the same city we were and we were happy to ride along with him. By the time we got out of the cab, even I knew then that hitchhiking in the country and knowing most the people you got in with was different than hitchhiking in the city on a very busy highway. I believe that was the last time I ever hitchhiked.

By the time I got home that day, my boyfriend was livid. He actually put me over his knee and decided I was to get a spanking for every mile it was to the other city. He put up such a fuss that I promised him I would not hitchhike again. I believe he only got about twenty spankings in. Obviously he didn't hurt me but he got through to me. And of course you know I am going to tell you not to hitchhike ever. It is one thing to be a male to hitchhike if you have no choice, but it is another thing if you are a female. Please don't put yourself in that situation. There are many ways to get around today and hitchhiking is not one of them. You have no idea who will pick you up. It could be someone very nice but it could also be a psycho path. Unfortunately, in our world today, we need to be so cautious about strangers and as sad as that is, it is a fact. I am a very trusting person and I love to meet people but I also know that I cannot take a chance and put myself in a situation that I cannot get out of. I was young and foolish when I hitchhiked and I am very thankful that I never got in with a dangerous person. So, please don't think it could never happen to you because it could and we need to be smart and safe.

When I was seventeen, I received a call from one of my friends telling me that our mutual friend was in the hospital. She had been shot accidentally by her brother when he was cleaning his rifle. Needless to say I was shocked by this news and went to see her with my friend. She looked very pale and weak and I felt so bad for her. As we were talking she reached over and pulled her blanket away and exposed her wound for us to see. I lost my breath and went down hard hitting the floor with the front of my head! I woke up to a nurse above me with smelling salts under my nose. All I said was "Please help me. I've never fainted before!" I was so embarrassed when they put me in a wheelchair. I had to go to the emergency downstairs. Yes that's right, I fainted and my poor friend survived a gunshot wound! Note to myself; let people know right away that I am a fainter!

School wasn't going so well for me so I decided I wanted to quit school and work full time at the grocery store. I went to see my father and asked him if I could quit school and work full time at my grocery store job. I could not focus on school anymore and most of the girls who were in my class always made me feel like an outsider (except for my few dear friends). I mean, look at what I was doing. I had run away from my uncle's home and now I was living with my boyfriend and his family. I was the talk of the classroom, or at least that is how they made me feel. So, I decided in all of my sixteen and a half years of experience that I needed to quit school. This was also around the same time that I told my dad that I started smoking. (Yes, I know smoking is bad for you but back then it was normal and no one worried about dying or letting someone else die from our dirty habit.) Remember it was the '70s and it was all about "Peace, man" and "Relax, have a cigarette or a joint." And my dad said I could do whatever I wanted. I think I could have asked him for anything as he probably felt so guilty for giving up his three children. So, I quit school in grade 11 and never got my grade 12 diploma like all my friends and family. No diploma, no prom. Not recommended! To all the young people out there who are even contemplating quitting school, "Don't do it. You will regret it!" I regretted it and all my friends graduated without me. My siblings graduated and I didn't. I missed out on the best years of school and I will never be able to talk about the prom. Please listen to me, finishing high school and getting your diploma is very important especially when you want to get an interview for a job. Stay in school!

And now I must say on the flip side of that: if you don't finish high school, at least go back to school down the road because it is never too late. Don't ever give up on yourself, you are worth the effort to try and make your dreams come true. Remember that you are worth it! You rock whether you finish high school or not but finishing high school gives you more opportunities. Every one of us, no matter where we come from or what has happened in our lives, is important and special. Keep moving forward and you will be so proud of yourself. And whatever you do try not to live with your boyfriend and his family at a young age like sixteen. You know how your parents try to tell you something for your own good and you think they just don't want you to be happy? Well, trust me, they really are telling you these things for your own good!

Living with my boyfriend made it easy for us to be intimate. Not an ideal situation to put ourselves in. David was my first love and he meant everything to me and he was the first boy I made love to. I was smart enough to get on the pill but the pill was not strong enough for me and I did in fact become pregnant. I was in tears the moment the doctor said I was with child. But, when I told David, he was so kind and loving. He said we would work it out and be okay. We told his parents and that was fun, NOT. But after a few weeks of them being very upset with us, they seemed to accept it, but we all knew our lives were about to change. Several months later (five months pregnant), I started to hemorrhage while in the washroom and I screamed for David saying that I couldn't stop bleeding. He opened the door and looked at me with fear and the next thing I know I passed out. I remember waking up in the hospital hooked up to an IV with a blood transfusion. David was sitting beside me holding my hand and crying. I was very weak and was later told I lost the baby and I was very close to losing my own life. It didn't really hit me that I almost didn't make it as I was more concerned about the little boy we had just lost. I was happy to see my aunt Pattie had come to visit me. My sister came to see me too and I felt like the black sheep of the family but she was just so glad that I was okay. I really gave them all a scare. As for losing my baby boy, I was devastated and felt sadness swimming around me. I cried and cried until I couldn't cry anymore.

After I lost our baby boy things got stressful between David and me. Remember we saw each other every day as we lived together with his family. We were just two young people living together at such a young age, twenty-four hours a day, seven days a week. It didn't help matters any that I started getting jealous when David would go to school and be around other girls. I wasn't treating him very nice and I accused him of wanting to be with someone else. I pretty much drove him crazy. A month later, David and I broke up. Well, to be honest, he broke up with me. Things were becoming too strained on us, especially him. I became too attached to David, I smothered him and the poor guy couldn't breathe. I was heartbroken when we broke up, but something inside of me became very cold. I think that was when I decided I was sick of people I love leaving me and I shoved more anger down inside.

This is probably the time in my young life that I started drinking a little more. Sure, I drank some with my boyfriend, but nothing serious. All the kids were smoking pot those years in the '70s. And the one time that I decided to try pot with David it didn't turn out so well. I guess I could share with you my first big introduction into smoking pot when I was with David. I didn't smoke pot like everyone else. I know this will sound funny but I would take the joint and pretend I inhaled but I never inhaled. I had it down to a science and this way I didn't have to feel left out. But this one night I decided I would try it with him. We had just smoked a couple of joints between us sitting in an enclosed car with the windows up. I remember going into his house at curfew time and it hit me like a ton of bricks. I went to get a drink of water and the glass I was holding seemed like it was disappearing while I held it. It freaked me out. I was so high I couldn't function and it scared the heck out of me. I started to feel really big and everything around me felt small. I went into the bedroom I shared with his sister and I started to freak out. I kept telling David to help me and that I was feeling scared shitless. I told him to slap me in the face and bring me down but of course he wouldn't even think of hitting me. Thank goodness his sister wasn't home that night.

David was so high I was freaking him out, but he was used to being high so it was easier for him to ride the wave. I told him not to leave me so he suggested that we go watch TV. His parents were in bed. Thank goodness! I lay on the couch and he lay on the floor beside me. But when I would look down at him it looked like there were spiders coming out from his hair and I watched them float up to the ceiling. I started crying and so he sat beside me and just held me until I fell asleep. The next morning his mom woke us up and was she upset with us! I was not supposed to be lying with her son on the couch. Why wasn't I in bed? We told her I was sick through the night and I didn't want to be alone. We think she believed us, but not likely. David didn't like what happened to me so he went to speak to the guy he bought the pot from. The guy was laughing and asked him if he had a good high because it was laced with some other drug. I really don't remember the name of the other drug. David was pissed at the guy for selling him something that was laced and especially when it freaked me out. They had an altercation and I believe that was the last time he bought from him. That was fine with me because I had no intention of doing it again and I realized then that I could say no and not worry what my friends thought. If they were my real friends, then they would accept the fact that I just didn't like to smoke pot. I hope you enjoyed that little bit of information. What can I say I was a wild child of the '70s.

As I mentioned earlier I became very good friends with Mary from my high school. She is the one who helped me get my first job at the grocery store. And when I was with David I had introduced Mary to one of his friends named Justin (who eventually became her husband). We all hung out together and we were all the best of friends. Well, we had been friends for almost two years now, and when David and I broke up Mary was there for me through all the crying and tears. At first I went to my dad's house again. He had moved to another apartment building closer to Mary's part of the city. But when I went to my dad's place, they were having a hard time and I was just another mouth to feed. And not only that, I started to feel really depressed and lost. I was so consumed with the loss of my relationship to David and I really felt like I was going to fall apart.

I couldn't sleep and I was so full of fear. When I talked to Mary and she heard how lost I was, she decided to ask her parents if I could live with them. I was almost eighteen and because I had a job at the grocery store I was able to pay them board. Not that it was very much, but it made me feel good to contribute something. I was so thankful they let me live with them and because they had known me now for a while as Mary's best friend they actually liked me. So, I jumped into my new life and fit right in with Mary and her loving family. All the depression I had been feeling was pushed aside and shoved down because I was loved and given a mom and dad to love.

Three weeks after David and I broke up, a friend of Justin's had asked me out to a Kiss concert. I was hesitant at first but I was so hurt from my breakup with David that I said yes. And wouldn't you know it, as soon as David found out I was going to a concert with someone, he came to see me at Mary's house. He asked me to take him back and said he made a mistake breaking up with me. I was so confused that I told him I had to think about it. I went upstairs and talked to Mary and she told me if it was her she wouldn't take him back but it was my decision to make. I didn't know what to do, but a piece of me was still angry at David for breaking up with me and I had already said yes to this other guy about the Kiss concert and I didn't want to let him down. So, I told David that I did not want to get back together and that I was going to the concert. I knew I hurt him but I was stubborn and didn't trust that he may break up with me again. Needless to say, I went to the concert with Richard. He was such a fun guy to be around. He was very respectful and caring and I had a great time with him at the concert. Although we missed some of the concert because he became ill (found out later it was drugs). We took him to the nearest hospital in a city we were unfamiliar with but we had to make sure he was okay. Once he was looked at and given the okay to leave, we headed back to the concert and enjoyed the rest of the night. We dated for a couple of months and I really liked him but it just wasn't working for us. We were better friends and so we broke up and still hung out as friends.

My best friend Mary and I would go to the same park that David and I used to go to but it was okay as we rarely saw David there. We kept very busy so I wouldn't think of him. We would walk from the east end of our city over to the north end of the city where our park was. It was always a laugh and always a fun time when we did this. We would take turns carrying her 8-track (yes, I said 8-track) and listen mostly to the Bee Gees. We would sing and laugh and just have a grand old time. We wore bell bottoms and mid drift tops. We had the best times together. You've got to love those mid '70s.

I started to tell you that I didn't drink a lot but after my boyfriend and I broke up I started to experiment with alcohol more. What I really mean is that I started trying the different types of alcohol that were out there. Mary and I started off with lemon gin. Too funny! But it was a light drink and we mixed it with seven-up. We eventually went to vodka and then rum. We really were innocent back then. We could only afford a pint which wasn't a lot but we would buy a bottle and split it between us. It was just enough to give us a glow on. We had a lot of laughs and innocent fun. We didn't drink to get drunk we drank to get a buzz on. We still had to go home and open the door of her parents' bedroom (knock first) and tell them we were home. That was very hard trying to fool her mother when we had to act straight and all we wanted to do was laugh. We always had a few words to say to each other about who was the most sober to be the one to knock on her mom's door and say, "We are home now, Mom," and just hope and pray she didn't turn the light on or ask us many questions. It makes me laugh today but not back then. Her mom meant business and I did not want to ruin my chances of staying there.

Mary's family became my family. They became a huge part of my life and still to this day they consider me as their adopted daughter and I consider them as my adopted family. Her sisters and brothers became my sisters and brothers. I was and am so blessed to have them in my life. They treated me as one of their own. I had a curfew and chores. Sometimes my adopted mom would speak to me in

French, forgetting I did not speak French. Let's just say by the time I left their house I could understand a few French words.

I continued to work and I dated a few guys (one at a time, not together). Each relationship lasted several months. We all hung out together and I was rarely alone with my dates as Mary and I were inseparable. If you dated me, you dated my friends but we had a lot of innocent fun. We went to a lot of concerts and hung out at beaches or the lakes. Her boyfriend Justin was very good to me and he always made me feel welcome wherever they went. Poor guy, I was always the third wheel when I wasn't dating.

Then out of the blue I met this one guy who I thought was very nice. I gave him my phone number and we went on a couple of dates. But the third date was a nightmare. He asked me to come to his apartment and watch movies. I thought that was innocent enough so I said sure. When we got there unbeknownst to me there were three other guys sitting on the couch watching a movie. He introduced them to me as his roommates.

He then casually said, "Well, I guess we could watch a movie in my bedroom."

Alarms went off in my head and then I thought, okay, maybe I am just panicking for nothing. So, I said, "Okay, sure, no problem."

We went into his bedroom and there were no chairs to watch TV from. The only spot that was available was the bed. The TV was on his tall dresser and was pointed right at the bed. I was hesitant at first and then he apologized about there being no chairs and said there was nothing going on and I believed him. Next thing I know we are sitting up on the bed and about ten minutes into the movie he leans over and kisses me. I respond to him with a short kiss and then turn my face to watch the movie. The next thing I know he pulls me down the pillow and goes for my shirt. I am saying no to him, "I don't want to do this! We are supposed to be watching a movie!" He is ignoring me and I am feeling really scared and he says it will be okay. I am still saying no and now panicking and actually scared the other guys (I didn't know) would come in and join him. I have fear in my eyes when he looks at me and he still says, "It's okay, I know you want to." By this time I am pushing him away harder and telling him to get off me and I don't want to do this. He can't get my shirt off as my hands are holding it tightly and so he just goes for my pants. I am still saying no but he is not listening to me. He got my pants halfway down my legs and the next thing I know, he was having his way with me. It was over quite fast. I lay there still and quiet now and felt sick to my stomach. I am ashamed I let this happen and feel really dirty. I am very angry and hold in the tears that want to come down my face. I pull up my pants and very coolly tell him to take me home. He asks me if I want to finish watching the movie.

I say, "Are you fucking kidding me? Take me home now!"

When I leave the bedroom, I do not look at the three guys sitting on the couch. I am ashamed of myself for coming there in the first place. He drives me home and before I get out I tell him what he did to me was wrong and I never want to see him again. I go into the house and take a shower and cry. Then I don't tell anyone that night because I am so ashamed that I let him get away with it. I was afraid and didn't stand up for myself back then.

The next day he showed up at my work with a bouquet of flowers. I couldn't look at him or talk to him. When he left my work, I threw the flowers in the garbage. Then he called me later and apologized. I told him he was a pig and to never ever call me again. He insisted that he felt bad and he thought I was just being shy and that's why he didn't stop. He wanted to know how he could make it up to me. I told him he could never take back what he did to me and it was over. He then became angry at me and said it wasn't over. He kept calling me at work and at home for several days. I wouldn't take his calls. Then he had one of his buddies call me from a different phone and he said to me, "I hear you're a whore." I hung up the phone and felt sick to my stomach.

MY THOUGHTS

Where do I begin? I want every woman or man to know that no means no! The word "no" does not mean yes, it does not mean maybe and it does not mean okay. It means simply no! It doesn't matter if you are yelling the word or firmly saying it. There is no different meaning for the word "no." It is what it is. My downfall was that in order to watch his television you had to watch it from the bedroom. But just because we were in a bedroom does not mean that I wanted anything else to happen. Some may say that I put myself in my own position. In a way I did because I didn't speak up and say, "No, that's okay, let's go out for a walk instead or do something else." I let myself be put in that position, but I did not deserve to be raped! But I started second guessing myself. Was he right? Was I to blame for what happened to me? Should I have screamed, would it have made a difference? Should I have fought him harder? I felt so ashamed of myself and eventually I told my best friend Mary.

After a long discussion, I decided to just drop it as now I was afraid of him. Did I make the right decision to let it go? What if I decided back then to charge him and make him pay for what he did? And would he pay? It would be my word against his. It would be a he said, she said deal. And did I really want to put myself through all those questions and shame I would feel on the stand. I don't know, I will never know. What I do know is that I lived with the decision I made at that time and I cannot go back and change it. I can be proud of myself for voicing to him what he did to me was wrong and he was a pig. And one thing is for certain I cannot live in "what ifs" or "I should haves." That will only make me sick and he would have control over me. I chose then and I choose now to let it go and give it to God so I can be free of the shame and disappointment I had of myself.

I never saw him again and I heard a couple years later he was murdered and the police suspected it had to do with drugs. I was shocked when I heard of his death but not surprised. I would never wish a death sentence on anybody, but that was where his life went. He made some very bad choices and he had to live with the consequences.

So, please be careful out there when going out on dates. Until you really feel comfortable with the person do not put yourself in a situation that you cannot get out of. Life is too short to put ourselves in harm's way. We need to watch out for each other and let our friends know when someone may be bad news. At least, then we can feel good that we said something to keep our friends safe. My story could have turned out a lot worse. I could have fought him harder and ended up being beat. I will never know because of fear. And I am just one of many women who are taken advantage of and put in a situation where just saying no doesn't mean shit to a man who has no morals or values. And this goes for some women too who have taken advantage of a man. It goes both ways. "No means no" for all sexes. Anyone who does not give their consent to someone who wants to have sex with them can charge that person with rape if that person proceeds to have sex without consent. It is not an easy road to go down when you are charging someone with rape. You have to be willing to open up your life in public and that can be brutal on your self-esteem. There are women who have been raped and beaten up and told they will be killed if they say anything. The victim lives in fear and then walks away and blames themselves. We are worth so much more than that. We were not put on this earth to be sexually assaulted by someone who thinks they have the right to do this to women or men.

If something like this has happened to you and you didn't give your consent and the person still took from you, this is called rape. Seek help, don't go through this alone. Talk to someone you trust and talk to a counselor before you make a decision. You have to be the one who makes the decision on what steps you want to take, whether you want to charge the person or let it go, you have to make sure you will be able to live with your choice. I didn't charge this guy out of fear and shame but that was my choice. Everyone's situation is different and what might work for one person may not be good for another person. But, again, I must stress that seeking help is very important as this is not something anyone should go through alone. Help is there if we ask for it. The last thing we want is for this to happen to another innocent victim but we have to do this carefully so we can be safe too. I pray that anyone who has ever been raped will look to God for courage and strength and for guidance on what would be the best course of action for such an appalling act toward women and men.

CHAPTER 4

After several months of not dating and feeling like crap because I didn't talk to a professional and I just wanted it to disappear, I decide to get out there again and to trust that all men are not like that. After all, my first boyfriend David was nothing like that so I knew there were good guys for me to date. So, I date a really nice guy named Ted who I met through some of my friends, and we really just become good friends. I guess I still wasn't ready for anything more. We hung out a lot and enjoyed the same things. Ted drove a Volkswagen and it was really cool. I bring the car up for one reason. This one time when we were driving down the highway and listening to music all of a sudden on the news they announced the death of Elvis Presley. It was August 16, 1977, the day Elvis died. I would be nineteen years of age two months later. We were both shocked and I started to cry. I loved Elvis and his music and he was too young to die. We drove over to our friend's house and just talked about Elvis and his music. That was always a big memory for me when I was dating Ted. But sometimes you just know that it isn't going to work with certain people as you are better as friends and that's what basically happened between me and Ted. I realized Ted and I were better friends than boyfriend and girlfriend. And when we broke up we still stayed friends and that was a good thing. I did not want to hurt him as he was such a sweet guy so I broke it off before he became too close to me.

Just before Ted and I broke up, my one adopted sister, Lindsay, and I moved into the basement of my other older adopted sister. Amanda. We were only there for several months or so but we had fun while we lived there. It was all new to us and we did the best we could to pay the rent and have some groceries when we could. We didn't pay our sister Amanda very much to live in the basement but we both weren't making great money either as times were a bit tough. But, we liked being out on our own and so we made it work. It was our first taste of independence from our family. This would be the beginning of independence without our parents and once we were out of their house we never looked back.

I guess I should add in here at this point of my story that I always felt a sad and depressing cloud following me. Most times I could ignore it. Sometimes it would try to take control over me and I would be down for a couple days and then I would move through it again and continue on. I always felt like I was running from something but I could never put my finger on it. I would always have the same occurring dream of myself running from something and just before the something would go to grab me I would take flight and fly. Those dreams haunted me for a long time after my mom passed away. I had no idea what was in store for me later on in my life and if I had of known I would have kept running.

During the mid to later '70s, the music was amazing. I went to a lot of concerts during my later teens such as Kiss, Supertramp, Nazareth, The Stampeders, and Trooper, to name a few. The music in the '70s was awesome to say the least. Here are just a few of the top names in music when I was listening to record players. You may know some of the following names: James Brown, Alice Cooper, Stevie Wonder, Neil Young, Rush, Elvis Presley, Meatloaf, Beach boys, Steve Miller Band, Barry White, Joe Cocker, Fleetwood Mac, Deep Purple, Queen, Elton John, BTO, Boston, and oh my goodness the list goes on and on. Great music!

Eventually, I am at this STYX concert and I meet one of Mary's distant cousins. When we leave the concert, it is so busy and we are all squished together and Mary's cousin Jack can see that I am stressed out and he takes my hand and leads me out of the concert. I thank him for helping me get through the crowd of people and he just says no problem. He bummed a ride home with us in Justin's van. Jack asks me for my number and I don't give it to him as I just met him and was unsure. Mary assures me he is a good guy and so I give him my number. He calls me a few days later and we start dating. This goes on for a couple months and then we become very close. We hung out with a lot of different people and he was a social butterfly. He was not shy and could talk to anybody. Jack made me laugh a lot. In the midst of starting a new relationship, Mary and I were going to Florida for a week with a couple of other friends from school. This was a really big deal for me and a great opportunity. My friends were in the last year of high school so they were eighteen and I was nineteen years old. The trip was put on by the school and they had it set up that every day you had something to see and do. I was so excited and my friends helped me out with some of the money so I could go. It was my first time on an airplane and it was a big 747 jet. All I thought was, "Wow, look at me, I'm someone important!" We were young and had the time of our lives on that trip. It was everything we dreamed of and more. I was old enough to buy these tropical drinks and beer which my friends were grateful for. We made great memories and felt so grown up. That was my first taste of life outside of my small city.

When it was time to get on the plane and come back home, it was bittersweet. When our plane landed in our city, we were met by our boyfriends and I actually missed Jack. We were together all the time now and eventually we fell in love. But for the first year I did not realize that he has a drug problem. I knew he did weed, but everyone did weed in the '70s except for me. Remember my spider episode with my first boyfriend David, how it made me paranoid and I didn't like the feeling of being out of control? Well, apparently,

I didn't learn from that episode because one time my new boyfriend Jack and I went to his brother's house and they were doing hash through a bottle. He talked me into trying it. He said it was a different high and I would like it. It had been several years since I tried the weed so I thought okay I will try it. That was a bad choice for me. Everyone was fine except me. No surprise there! We were watching a show on animals at a zoo. I felt like the animals were coming out of the TV and running toward me. Yup, I was freaking out again. Did I not learn the first time? Nope had to go through it again to show me I didn't do well with drugs. Again, I had to lie down and Jack stayed with me as he felt bad I was freaking out. That was the last time I did any sort of drugs. Ever! But as I started to say earlier I didn't know that Jack had a drug problem and was doing other drugs as well. I started to notice more and more that he was acting out of sorts and not always happy as he usually was. But what can I say I was in love with him and just carried on. I guess I should have paid more attention to his behavior.

I had quit my job at the grocery store and worked at a few other places during our time together. I worked at a department store and I liked it well enough. I bring this up for two reasons; one because this is when Jack bought me an engagement ring and asked me to marry him. I was a happy girl and even though I still had a cloud that followed me and made me feel down I had something wonderful to look forward to. And the second reason I bring this up is because this is where I was working when I got a call from my friend Mary telling me that my uncle Albert's son had passed away. I was devastated! How could that be? He was very young and was married with two small toddlers. He was in his early twenties. I remember feeling so sad for my aunt Pattie and uncle Albert and my cousins. Did I mention he was in his twenties and had two small girls? Just devastating! I left the store immediately and went home to get all the details. I was told that he had an aneurism. This was the first funeral I had ever gone to where the parents had lost a child (in this case their son). It was horrible to hear my aunt cry. It was heart-wrenching, to say the least. My uncle Albert held it together as best he could for my aunt but he was devastated and the grief on their faces was haunting. I felt so bad for them and for my cousins. I also felt bad that I hadn't been to see them in a long time. I was too into my own life to take the time to go visit them. I regretted that for a long time. I grieved for my cousin and his family by myself and decided that one day I better go visit them.

Well, it wasn't long before I decided that I didn't want to work downtown anymore. This was a time when jobs were plenty and I wanted to try something different. And the one job I got that I really loved was being a flight attendant for a small central air flight at our city airport. My sister Rose had worked at the airport in one of the offices. She called me one night telling me there was an opening for a flight attendant with a new airline that just flew to area's around our province for the business people. There was a man from the states (Texas) who bought an old German airplane and had some people from our province run the operation. I went for the interview but never thought I would get it. I had to learn CPR and have a little bit of training but other than that I was offered the job. I was ecstatic! There were two of us who took turns flying. Our pilot and the one flight attendant were married. We all got along very well. We would fly to all the small cities in the province and we also had to go to Bangor, Maine. I loved flying. After we dropped off all of our passengers after takeoff, I was allowed to go up to the cockpit and enjoy the flight from watching out the pilot's window. We also had a champagne flight to Nova Scotia which was so much fun. A car company chartered us for a trip to Nova Scotia and I served them champagne on the flight. I was having the time of my life. Meeting new people and making people feel comfortable on the plane. It was a dream job to me.

But sometimes all good things must come to an end (at least that is an old saying I used to hear growing up). One day we were landing in a small city and as we were landing our pilot pulled up all of a sudden with no warning. Everyone gasped and looked back at me. I was taught if I didn't know what was going on in a case like that just apologize to the passengers and make them feel safe. My speech went something like this: "Attention, ladies and gentlemen. We apologize for the abrupt pull up when trying to land. It looks like the runway is busy at the moment and so we will be circling the airport for a few minutes. Let me assure you that everything is okay. Please make sure your seatbelts are fastened and we will be landing shortly. Thank you." I said this with a big smile on my face and acted like this happens all the time. No big deal. But it was a big deal! We circled that airport for twenty minutes, and let me tell you, it felt like an eternity. I would get on the speakerphone again and say, "Please bear with us, it shouldn't be much longer." I was scared to death. I wasn't allowed to go to the cockpit to see what was going on as it would disturb our pilot and he just kept beeping the speakerphone by my station to tell me to keep letting our passengers know that we would be landing shortly.

Finally, after what seemed like a very long wait, we landed. When everyone was safely off the plane, I went to the cockpit, and when I opened up the door my boss was soaked from sweat and he looked like his life had flashed before him. He told me that the wheels would not come down and he was told to circle around and keep trying to get them to come down. We were lucky we had enough gas to circle as many times as we did. I could feel the blood drain out of my face. I couldn't believe that we almost had to have an emergency landing. I never really thought about that ever happening. It was a surreal experience. I would hope that I would have been able to help the passengers if we had to have an emergency landing as best as I could. My training would have to kick in and just go with it. But I was quite happy that we didn't have to experience that happening. I thank God for keeping us safe.

Unfortunately, we had to get a lift back to our city airport in a small airplane and rain and lightning started. The plane we were in was rocking like crazy and I thought for sure we were going to die. But we made it safely home to our airport and I could have kissed the ground when we landed. I don't really know what happened to the German plane after that. There were rumors that they were trying to get parts from Germany but were not having any luck. Then I was called a week later and was told they were not going to fly that plane anymore and I was out of a job. To be honest with you, I could have gone on to pursue the flight attendant career with another company, but that episode scared me so bad I decided flying was not for me. They say you should always get right back up on the horse, so to speak, but I let the fear take over and couldn't shake it at the time so I walked away from a very good career.

As I said earlier (before I interrupted myself), I started noticing my boyfriend Jack acting different and out of sorts more and more. We had a few arguments here and there, usually about his where-abouts. But this one time when we were both going out separately with our friends I could tell he was upset about something. Mary's boyfriend Justin was dropping Mary and me off at a dance and Jack was hanging out with Justin. On the way to the dance bar Justin picked up an old friend of his who was also going to the same dance bar and gave him a lift to the bar. Justin introduced us to this friend of his and his friend said to me, "Hi, aren't you a cute little thing." I just smiled and said thank you. Jack looked at me and slapped me in the face. I was completely shocked by his behavior as I didn't see that coming. The friend said, "Hey, man, that wasn't called for!" and Jack just looked at him with anger and said, "Just remember she's my girl-friend." When I got over the shock of the slap I was pissed right off. I got out of the van and didn't look back or say good-bye. My friend Mary didn't know what to say, we were both shocked. That was the beginning of odd behavior from Jack.

By this time, I had moved out of my adopted sister Amanda's basement and moved into a small house (that my friend's mother owned) with two of my girlfriends. We lived beside a school and just up the street from a police station. One night Jack came to my house apparently all high on something strong and he was accusing me of something ridiculous. He said I was having an affair on him and I just laughed at him and told him not to talk so foolish. I could tell by the look of anger on his face that something wasn't right. He seemed to be looking right through me instead of at me, if that makes any sense. He seemed out of it but I let him come in and started a normal conversation like any other time. I asked him if he wanted a drink of something but he said no. He seemed to be agitated by something and I just ignored the look of anger on his face. The next thing I know he starts hollering at me and accusing me of having an affair again and he was not going to take it. I tried to talk to him in a calm manner but he was not calming down. We argued for about twenty minutes, and the next thing I knew he goes into my cutlery drawer and gets a bread knife. Within seconds he has the knife at my throat and is threatening me my life. It seemed like we struggled for a long time. I got away from him and ran into my bedroom. He comes at me like a madman and has me pinned on the bed with the knife at my throat. I am screaming at him to stop, and with all of my strength I hold the knife away from my throat, then the knife finally falls behind the bed. I quickly reach behind the bed and I grab the knife and hollered at Jack to calm down and sit down. He finally sits down, puts his head in his hands, and starts crying and says he was really scared at how high he was and he really thought he was going to kill me. I told him to calm down he didn't hurt me. I then told him to get off the drugs or we were over. I had enough of the bullshit with drugs. He says he needs air and leaves my apartment. I let him go to cool off, expecting him to come back in a few minutes.

About fifteen to twenty minutes later, a knock comes on my door and I think it is Jack but it is a big policeman at my door. He says that my boyfriend Jack is at the police station and was asking to be arrested for attempting to kill his girlfriend, me! Oh shit, are you serious? The officer was not in a good mood as he said it's not every day that a man comes into the precinct to admit to attempting to kill his girlfriend. I assured the officer I was okay and that we just had a bad argument. He asked me several questions about Jack and wrote several long notes on his pad. He said he had to check the apartment to make sure there was nothing going on. He checked the apartment (as I said, I shared the apartment with two other girls, one girl was out and the other was at the other side of the house sleeping in her room) and found nothing out of the ordinary. He said he would go back to the police station and talk to Jack and then he would be driving Jack home. He then told me to lock my door when he left. Wow, it seemed so surreal to me. Was this really happening? I did not sleep for several days after that.

To be honest with you, I really didn't think Jack was going to kill me that night. Yes, we did struggle for the knife and it took all my strength to hold it an inch from my throat, and, yes, he did seem very angry, but I was so naïve about bad drugs I just thought he was messing around. A couple days later I realized that he wasn't joking around, and I thank God for giving me the strength to knock the knife out of his hands. When I think of how it took all my strength to push the knife away from my throat and how he was a lot stronger than I was, I truly believe someone was watching over me that night. This was my first wake-up call about the drugs he was taking. It was getting seriously dangerous.

So, I had a huge decision to make. Do I let this go and it may happen again and I may not be so lucky or do I break up with him until he gives up the drugs? We broke up for a while! I felt Jack needed to get his act together and get off the drugs. We kept in touch and he assured me he was not doing bad drugs and getting himself together. We both started dating again during that time apart and we were still friends. As a matter of fact, one time when I was dating a nice guy named Tom, Jack dropped by to say hello and sat down and played cards with us. Jack was just a really friendly guy and liked meeting new people. You never knew when he would just show up out of the blue. It was awkward sometimes but I found it funny too. I am sure Tom didn't think it was funny though. Eventually I stopped dating and just hung out with my girlfriends for a while.

My best friend Mary and Justin were getting married, and Mary asked me to be her maid of honor and also to live with her for a month or so before the wedding. Mary and Justin found a really cute apartment in a house, and so Mary and I set up the house and lived together before her marriage to Justin. Let me just say that we had a blast. We were so happy to get the chance to do this as we were so close and never had the opportunity before. Mary was always so good to me and I was going to miss living with her after she got married. We were more than friends, we were sisters, and living with her for that short period of time will always have a special place in my heart.

As luck would have it (or not have it), because Jack and I were both in the same wedding for Mary and Justin, we saw each other a lot. Mary and her sister Lindsay had a double wedding and it was a huge event. It was so beautiful and magical and the whole wedding made me wish Jack and I could make things work out. We both got caught up in the wedding and really thought we could make the relationship work. Eventually he even went out west to find work and get away from everything. It wasn't long before he got a basement apartment and talked me into coming out west. Just before I went out west I found out I was pregnant by doing one of those home pregnancy tests. I had missed two of my pills one week because they made me feel sick sometimes and that is what happens when you miss your pills. I was two months pregnant when I flew out west with a suitcase and a dream. But that dream turned into reality.

As I said earlier, Jack got us a basement apartment in a house of someone he met who worked where he worked. This guy was very trusting and kind to Jack and me. But I hated the big city after three weeks and wanted to go back home. I was always alone as Jack was working and I was so home sick. I did not want to have our baby away from home. But Jack didn't have enough money to get both of us home. Then one day he came home and he told me to get packed because we were going home and come upstairs to our land lord's floor. I asked him where he got the money for us to go home and he told me he got it and not to worry about it. I was so happy and so I got packed and went up with him to the guy's apartment as we were leaving through the front door. But then Jack went into the guy's bedroom and took some money from underneath this guy's mattress. I stood in the doorway of this guy's bedroom and asked Jack what he was doing. He told me he was just borrowing some money from the guy and was going to pay him back. He assured me the guy would be okay with it as this guy had shown Jack where he kept his money and had told Jack one time if he ever needed money he could help him out. But I did not fully believe this story. I was not impressed and we argued for about twenty minutes. Jack told me that he would pay the guy back as soon as we got home. I was still not satisfied but Jack said he was going home and I better come or I would be left alone. I thought he was bluffing but I wasn't sure at this point so I told Jack he had to leave the guy a letter saying he was desperate to go home but not to worry he would pay him back every cent. Jack wrote the letter and then we left for the airport. I felt sick to my stomach leaving, knowing we were using some of this guy's money, but I desperately wanted to be home and I trusted that Jack was telling me the truth and would pay him back. And then again on the plane Jack told me not to worry that he would definitely pay the guy back and everything would be okay. To this day, I do not know if Jack ever paid back the money as he would always tell me not to worry and he was taking care of it. Even though I felt guilty for a long time I trusted Jack was taking care of it. Meanwhile I was about to have a baby soon and I needed to take care of myself.

We didn't want to get married until after our baby was born. I was not going to get married because I was pregnant no matter what anyone said. We stayed with Jack's parents when we first came back from out west and then we found an apartment where we could live and raise our child. I loved the old-fashioned apartment we lived in. It was an old Victorian home that the owners had turned into two apartments. We lived on the second floor. The apartment had tall ceilings, lots of crown molding and it was just a very nice place to raise a baby. We set up the baby's nursery and just waited for things to happen. We didn't have a washer or dryer to do our clothes so most times I would do our clothes in the big claw style tub we had.

I thought it was a good idea at the time but it became very hard bending over the tub and wringing out the clothes in my condition. I would be exhausted after doing our laundry. I would also go pick up a few groceries and carry them home from the store that was a couple blocks away. Sometimes, Jack would go to pick up some groceries and I would be so thankful. But most times, Jack had somewhere to go so I did a lot of taking care of the home with not much help from him. But I was living in denial about his drugs again. I suspected he was doing them again but I wanted this to work. I wanted a family.

In the midst of getting ready for my baby's arrival, my sister Rose had a baby shower for me. On the day of my baby shower my water broke but I did not have any pain so I did not go to the hospital until the next day. My baby shower was amazing. All my relatives were there at my aunt Maggie's house (where my sister and brother grew up). I felt so loved and I appreciated all they did for me. My sister was always making sure I was okay and the shower was more than I could have asked for. I was truly overwhelmed with love and it felt good to be with my family. I never realized how much I had missed my mom's family until I was sitting amongst them at my shower. They hadn't changed at all except a little older like me. We laughed a lot and talked about the days when we were young and hung out together. My heart was so full of joy and love that day.

The day after my shower I went into labor. I was having bad contractions so Jack and I went to the hospital. I should have gone the night before but I wasn't due for three more weeks, I thought I was fine. I found out that my adopted sister Lindsay was down the hall from me. She had come in the night before and gave birth to her first baby girl. I was so happy to know she was in there and her baby was doing great. But I ended up having complications with our baby's birth and almost lost her. They had to prep me for a caesarian and when they took me to the operating room they had me on all fours like a dog so I could save my baby. The cord was wrapped around the baby's throat. Before they put me under, I quickly asked

God, "Please do not let my baby die, please don't let me lose this baby." I was so afraid I would lose my baby.

When I woke up I felt for my stomach first thing and could not feel any stitches. I was high and told the nurse they did a really good job and quickly said in a panic, "Where is my baby?" The nurse brought over my baby and said they didn't do a caesarian after all as the doctor was able to release the cord and bring her out with forceps. That's right, I had a beautiful baby girl. It took me a few minutes to register that she was a girl as I really thought I was having a boy. But when it finally registered she was a girl I was thrilled beyond words. They laid her across my stomach and when I saw her I was stunned by how beautiful she was. She looked like a little angel. She was my girl and I was over the moon in love with her. I named her Charlie. She was actually named after a female star on a TV show that I loved growing up.

I thanked God for saving my baby and I knew from that moment on I would be the best mom I could be to her. I would protect her from harm and I would always love her. I would never ever leave her. She was my everything at that moment and she would continue to be one of the best gifts I could ever have in my life. I was twenty-one when I gave birth to Charlie and she was a wonderful birthday present a week later.

We took Charlie to my almost in-laws the first week. I was very nervous at the beginning being a new mom. His parents were very helpful and they loved their granddaughter very much. Charlie was their second granddaughter. Jacks brother and sister in law had a beautiful three year old daughter named Lynn. She loved holding Charlie and treated her like a little sister. She was so good to her baby cousin. And just a side note; Charlie and Lynn became very close friends who have an amazing relationship today. I went through the mother blues that week. I was constantly crying and Jack had no idea what to do with me. Then once we got the first week in we went back to our apartment. I was in heaven and thought my life may finally be on a good road. But after we started the family life Jack got cold feet. He was always out and eventually I realized I had to face the fact and accept that he was doing the drugs again. We started arguing all the time and the tension was really bad. But whenever I looked at my baby girl she gave me such joy and peace. After some long conversations with Jack I realized, he was not going to give up the drugs no matter how convincing his lies were. I did not want our daughter to grow up in this kind of atmosphere. It just wasn't getting any better. Not only did I know he was doing bad drugs again but there were rumors from a few good sources that he was cheating on me. So, I made a decision to leave Jack and once that decision was made there was no turning back for me. I could take a lot but once I made up my mind there was no way to talk me out of it. Charlie was just five months old when I left to live with a good friend of mine, Emily, and her daughter. I also got myself some help from welfare so we could survive. It was embarrassing for me to go to get help but I did it for Charlie so she didn't have to do without anything. And let me say one thing I always made sure Charlie had whatever she needed and then if there was any money left over I would treat myself, which didn't happen very often.

 ## MY THOUGHTS

At this point in my story, I would like to talk about drugs. It is not my favorite subject but it played a very important part of the breaking up of my relationship with Jack. It cost him dearly as he was not in his daughter's life as much as he could have been. The drugs took a lot away from him and it was devastating to witness. He missed out on so many amazing times with our daughter and he would live to regret it.

Smoking pot when we were young in the '70s was not considered bad. It was illegal but most people would just be so mellow and get the munchies. It was all about "Peace, brother," "Relax, man," "Enjoy the ride," and so on and so on. Except for the few of us who were paranoid and couldn't relax, the rest of the people who smoked pot were fine and easy to deal with. It was actually so much better than watching someone who was violent when they drank alcohol. The worst thing about smoking pot was it made you so mellow sometimes that you could become lazy. I have never known anyone in my group of friends that ever became violent from smoking pot. In today's world I am not sure what pot is like. I have no idea so I cannot give an honest opinion. What I can make you aware of is that some pot can be laced with something else and that is when it can become very dangerous. I know from experience of the time I tried the pot with David and it was laced. So, if you are thinking of trying pot make sure that the source you get it from is very reliable. Remember you are taking a chance when you try any sort of drugs as you have no idea whether or not they are laced with another substance. We have to be so careful nowadays as there are people out there who don't give a shit about us they just want to make money off of us. If you were to over dose on something do you really think they care? Selling drugs is a big money making industry and people get rich off of selling it.

My concern is more with the hard drugs. The drugs that make you hallucinate and make you give up on life and everyone who cares about you. These drugs don't care for anyone and take every drop of humanity from you because they can. These drugs fool you into thinking life is better for you when you have no one to answer to. The drugs that literally take your life because they have the control over you, and you have no control. These drugs are nonnegotiable. My best advice to anyone who is thinking of taking any of these drugs is to think about dying a slow and painful death or a fast and senseless death. That is what you will get when you go down this road. You will get nothing but an eventual death. My second thought on this is to never go down this road and if your friends want you to come down this road then they are being selfish and just don't want to be alone on that road. Turn around and walk away, just walk away, because turning to drugs to help you cope with life is the wrong path, period. Talk to someone that you trust and someone who loves you or if you cannot talk to any family members then seek help through your doctor. There is help out there for all of us for any type of hard situation. Drugs are not the answer to live a good life. Reaching out is the answer. We all have a choice to make and we have to live with our choices. There is so much information out there today than there was when I was growing up and we are very lucky to have the resources we have. You are important and you are loved. You are worth so much more than drugs. Please just walk away, just walk away.

Did I have friends who got into heavy drugs? Yes, I did, and that is why my heart goes out to anyone who is watching a loved one go down that road. I can feel the pain and anger that I know a parent, sibling, friend, or spouse goes through when they can't get through to their loved one. It tears a family apart. The person you once knew as a gifted loving child is taken away from you in the matter of weeks just because of that one try of a hard drug. "Oh, it's okay, I will just try it this once, I am not stupid I won't get addicted." That is how it all begins, just once, and it has you by the throat and then you say, "Well, I will just have it one more time." And boom! It has you right where it wants you. And that is not taking into consideration the money factor. That just causes a whole new set of problems. When the drugs take hold of you, guess what? You will do anything to get the money for them. It is a sad hard fact that drugs will take you apart little by little until there is nothing left to take. Please, please, walk away from drugs, just walk away.

Okay, now that I have shared my thoughts on not going down the road of drugs, I still believe we can change our lives around. Where there is a will to stop the drugs there is always a way. Help is always available for us if we reach out for it. Don't ever give up on making your life better even if you go a couple steps back. We are worth the fight to live our lives without drugs. I believe that God loves us and there is nothing too big for God to help us with. But we have to be willing to do the work. Unfortunately, when you go down the road of doing drugs you can be sure it will be a hard road back but it will be worth it in the end. God bless all who struggle with drug addiction. May you have the courage to give yourself a drug free life.

CHAPTER 5

Charlie and I were now living with my good friend Emily and her daughter. We were barely surviving but we had a lot of respect for each other and helped each other the best we could. We always made sure our daughters came first. Jack would visit every now and then with our daughter. He would sometimes want to get back together but I would say no because of the drugs and I knew he was seeing someone else. This was a very hard time for me as I still loved him but I knew I could not take a chance with him. Even when he visited me he was high and I couldn't take the lies. One night after a long day of frustrations, I went to bed early and just cried myself to sleep. I was beyond upset I couldn't stop crying and I opened up my life to God. I prayed and prayed to him to show me where my life was headed. I begged him literally to let me know that he was listening to me and to somehow show me what was in store for me. I fell asleep after what seemed like hours of crying out in such turmoil and only woke up when Charlie cried the next morning for her bottle. Later that day, I remembered having a dream the night before that I didn't quite understand but I felt so at peace. I was so relaxed and felt okay but I couldn't understand why I was so calm.

After dinner that day, Jack came over to see Charlie and he was high and instead of getting angry I just accepted it and we visited our daughter together. I would not let him see her alone though. We were in my bedroom with her and everything was going well until he asked me to get together with him and let us be a family. He missed me and our daughter. I explained to him that I could not put Charlie in jeopardy. He was furious with me and decided that he wanted to take Charlie to see his mother. We argued and I tried to talk some sense into him and said I would bring her to see his mother the next day. He did not agree and hit the dresser with his fist. I stood there for what seemed a very long time and then said to him, "Okay, you can take her to see your mom. How about you spend time with her for a few days?"

Jack looked at me for a few minutes and finally said, "Well, I am taking her for good. To be honest with you I want her to live with me and my mom and family. I mean it, I am not bringing her back."

I stood there again and just looked at him and then I remembered my dream and the peace that I felt and I wasn't afraid.

I told him, "Okay, you can have her."

Jack looked at me stunned for a few minutes and then he said, "Okay, I will take her. Get her dressed."

"No, you get her dressed. You might as well start now. If you want her then you get her dressed."

It was winter and I gave him her snowsuit and packed a bag with diapers and her clothes. My friend came into the room and asked me what was going on as she heard a bang. I told her everything was fine and that Jack was going to take our daughter to live with him and his family. She looked at me as if I was crazy and lost my mind. I assured her that everything was fine and not to worry. Everything was under control. I went out to the living room and told her that he wasn't going to take her.

She said, "He's dressing her as we speak, he is taking her!"

I put my hand on her arm and smiled and said he will not take her trust me. She just shook her head and was very upset with me.

I went back into the bedroom and he had her dressed. He picked her up and said, "I am taking Charlie and she is living with me."

I said, "Yes, that is what you said and I am not stopping you. Charlie is now your responsibility."

He started to walk toward the living room and when he got to the door my friend was ready to explode. He just stood there and looked at me. I just calmly stood there on the outside but was now shitting on the inside.

He walked over to me and handed me my girl and said, "I can't do this. You take her. She needs to be with her mother."

I took my baby girl and held her close to me and said good-bye to Jack.

My friend just looked at me and said, "How did you know he wouldn't take her?"

I told her I didn't know but I felt that God would keep her safe and I went on faith that he wouldn't take her.

My friend said, "What would you have done if he went down the stairs with her?"

I looked at her and said, "He wouldn't have made it down the stairs. I would have grabbed Charlie and he would have had to get the police involved because I would never give her to him, ever!"

My friend just looked at me and smiled and said something like, "Wow, that took a lot of guts."

I said, "No, just faith that God was not going to let anything separate me and my daughter."

That was when I realized that God's dream would happen even though I didn't know what it meant. And I will tell you here in this part of the story that the three things I saw in my dream did in fact happen and I only remembered them as they were happening to me. It was really the most bizarre feeling. It didn't make sense to me at the time but it made perfect sense afterward.

Eventually, Emily was moving on in her life and moving to another apartment and I had to find another place for me and Charlie. Remember Lindsay, one of my adopted sisters who I lived with in the basement of her sister Amanda's house. Well lucky for me that Lindsay offered me a room in her home and so I accepted.

It was bittersweet to leave my friend Emily and her daughter as we had become so close but we both knew it was time to move on and I knew Charlie and I would be safe at Lindsay's home.

So, here I was with my daughter Charlie living with my adopted sister Lindsay and family. I felt so bad during that time because I didn't want to be a burden. I was also trying so hard to be strong and still accept that Jack was not going to give up the drugs. He would visit our daughter once in a while when he was not stoned. But he wasn't consistent. I felt so bad for Charlie, especially as I watched Lindsay and her husband Daniel enjoy their young daughter Mackenzie together as a family. Mackenzie and Charlie were just twelve hours apart. Life is funny. Lindsay was very good to me but her place was small and I felt bad because that meant Charlie and I took up more of their space. I felt like a burden even though I knew she wanted to give me a place to stay. She made sure I felt welcomed and said I could stay as long as I needed. We shared a lot of good talks together and laughter. We did well together but it was stressful too. Charlie was not sleeping the best at this time and I felt we were invading Lindsay's space. Eventually, I felt it was time to move on. I put the word out that I was looking for a place to live and of course my best friend Mary (Lindsay's sister) said we could live with her. She and her husband Justin didn't have any children yet and they had an extra bedroom I could use.

I accepted Mary's offer. She was also very good to me. She wanted to help me and her godchild Charlie out. I stayed there with them for several months and it was very good. At this time, some of our good friends started going to church (so random) and would tell us how it was changing their lives and helping them cope with things. So, we started to go to church with our good friends. It was good at first because I was so lost and didn't know if I was coming or going. We went to a lot of outside church functions and some of my friends changed their lives around for God which was beautiful to see. We even got tickets to go to see Elvis Presley's stepbrother speak in another city two hours away. His name was Rick Stanley, and he was one of three stepbrothers Elvis had when his mother married their father. Rick was five years old when Elvis came into their lives and his life was changed dramatically. Unfortunately, he got himself addicted to heroin but eventually met a wonderful Christian girl who he later married and he gave his life to God after Elvis's death. Rick Stanley was called a born again Christian and we were so excited to hear what he had to say. It was so amazing, I felt like I was getting my life on track. I got the courage to go up front and have someone put their hands on me so I could give up smoking. It was just like you see it on TV. I still remember to this day smelling smoke when the guy put his hand on my forehead and I fell backward into my guy friend's arms, remember Richard? He was there with a bunch of us and he came up front with me to stand behind me. It was so crazy to even do this. But the even crazier thing was that I didn't want a cigarette. I didn't smoke for about five months. To be honest, this kind of stuff freaks me out but I just wanted to see if it would work and I can't answer what happened to me but I truly did not want to smoke at all. I had no cravings what so ever. I only started again because I made a bad choice to start again.

But then something happened at one church that really bothered me. There was a special function going on at this church in our city and so a bunch of us went to check it out. When we were praying all of a sudden people around me started to talk really loud and fast and I couldn't understand a thing they were saying. It really bothered me because I didn't like not knowing what they were saying and it scared me too. Then I started to feel like I wasn't good enough to go to church if I couldn't handle everything I was learning and that I was unworthy of love and how could God love me when I made so many bad choices in my life. I felt like the church we were going to expected me to be perfect. I eventually stopped going to church and started questioning my life and how worthless I felt. I was really down on myself. I had a really rough time with this.

I do have to say here that I have nothing against different churches and religions, whether they are Baptist, Pentecostal,

Anglican, Muslim, Catholic, United Church, or Mormon churches. I believe they all have one purpose and that is to teach us to love God and be the best person we can be. But I also believe that we all need to find the church that best suits us as individuals. Whether it is a Catholic Church, Anglican, United Church, or any of the churches I mentioned above. We all have to be where we feel loved and safe. A place where we feel we are forgiven by God and are worthy of his love and where we do not feel judged for our past mistakes.

For a long time, I walked away from every church possible. I decided I could love God but I didn't need to go to church to be a Christian. I would pray here and there but I did not want the church to be my playground. I guess I had gone to way too many different churches and was very confused about a long of things. But I finally made the decision that I could be a good person on my own and God would be with me every step of the way, church or no church.

In the meantime, it wasn't too long before I got on my feet again and decided that I was still very blessed to have my little girl. But it was time to move on and let Mary my adopted sister have a life with her husband. So I moved on again. I was a very lucky girl to have so many friends and adopted sisters. Especially good friends and sisters who would do anything for me and make sure my daughter and I had a place to live. It wasn't too long before I moved in with my other adopted sister Amanda (I know this is too funny but remember my adopted family, well, they had five daughters and two sons). So, I moved in with my oldest adopted sister Amanda and her daughter. She had more room and I could sleep upstairs with my daughter. It worked out perfect. We had a lot of laughter together and helped each other out with great advice (just as with my two other adopted sisters, Mary and Lindsay).

During this time, I would work part time at a restaurant/bar to make ends meet along with the welfare I was receiving. I became friends with more girls and I started to go out more. I knew Charlie was safe with Amanda and so after I would put her down to sleep I would go out with my girlfriends to this one bar where my one friend

Justine worked. I loved to dance and this was a great release for me. The only problem was that I started to drink a lot more. I was always a two- to three-drink person as I always needed to be in control. But now I was drinking a lot more and found myself wanting a relationship again. I wanted to be with someone who would love me and Charlie and give me the family I wanted. Needless to say, this was not a good idea to look for someone good when you are drinking. At least it wasn't for me.

I found myself dating again but the guys who would ask me out always turned out to be only interested in one thing. I was so oblivious at the time because of the drinking I thought the guys I went out with were good guys. Even though I would date one guy for several weeks or a couple months they always turned out to be into drugs or something else. I did not want to be alone but I didn't want to be with a loser either. I had my daughter to think of. My adopted sisters were all with someone nice, I wanted that too. But again, the drinking was not helping my situation and my choices were not getting any better. I felt so lost and alone and desperately wanted to be loved and have someone love my daughter as much as they loved me. I had this ridiculous idea in my head that if I had a man in my life I would be much happier. That may have been true in some ways but I had to be happy with myself first before I would ever find the right person for me. Don't get me wrong, there are a lot of fantastic guys out there, but trying to find one when you are drinking usually ends in disaster at least that is how it was for me. I am speaking from my own experience.

During these times, I would see my blood sister Rose once in a while, and it was always great to see her. We would spend time talking about old times and then about what we were up to then. She was always my number one supporter. She always showed me love and was always bringing Charlie and me treats of some sort. She loved her little niece. She would fill me in on the family and let me know I was loved and missed by my aunts, uncles and cousins. We were very close and had an amazing bond that stayed with us through our whole lives. We still have an amazing bond together and try our best to get together when we can. After I would see her during my crazy years of trying to find a man I would miss my mom's family and would try to make a point of going out to see them.

And actually, when Charlie was about ten or eleven months old, I took her out to visit my aunt Pattie and uncle Albert and we spent the night. There was something that I didn't tell you about living in my aunt and uncles house after my mom died and dad gave us up. Okay, here it is, this will sound very strange to some people and maybe not so strange to others. But, there was a ghost in my aunt and uncle's house. And, yes, I said ghost. Now, I know what you are thinking, okay, this broad is out there. You see, when I lived there, several strange things were always happening. There were cupboard doors opening and closing, drawers opening and closing, the feeling of someone standing beside you or rushing past you. When either my cousin Sandy or I had to do the vacuuming we both would cringe because every time we were vacuuming under the beds we both would think there was someone beside us or behind us.

My aunt Pattie woke up one night to see a ghostlike being standing at the end of their bed. It scared her at first and she quickly woke up my uncle and told him she just saw a ghost like figure standing at the end of the bed. My uncle Albert thought she was seeing things and told her she was imagining things. But in the meantime, we would all be in bed and my uncle would tell my aunt Pattie to go downstairs and tell their son to stop all the slamming of the cupboard doors and she would tell him nobody was downstairs we were all in bed. He would go down and sure enough no one was there. And I was told by my cousin many years later that my uncle finally saw the ghost like being one night in bed.

As I said earlier, this one time when Charlie was ten or eleven months old we went to visit my aunt Pattie and uncle Albert and spent the night there. I was fine at first and ignored the fact that I could feel a presence in the bedroom. Because my daughter was fussy that night I went down to get a bottle ready for her. I took Charlie with me to keep her quiet as it was late at night. I got the bottle ready and went into the living room and sat down on the couch to feed her. Charlie was crying louder at this point, and so I put the bottle in her mouth. The next thing I know I feel like someone is sitting on the other end of the couch and Charlie pushes the bottle out of her mouth and starts smiling and looking in the direction of the end of the couch. I froze. I couldn't move for a couple minutes and she kept smiling and then giggling. This freaked me out because she wasn't looking at me at all, she was looking past me. And she had just been crying hard for her bottle for the last fifteen minutes. I finally got the courage and jumped up, walked upstairs and into the bedroom, turned on the lamp, and kept it on all night. Was this really happening or was it my imagination? I know it wasn't my imagination! And my cousin told me years later my uncle Albert found some old keys in the back yard one time when he was digging to make more room to do something he was working on. I don't remember what it was for, may have been to make the well bigger or when they added on to the house. But whatever he was doing, as per my cousin he found these very old keys and brought them into the house to show my aunt. They didn't realize right away but later on they noticed the spirit was gone. There were no more cupboard and drawers opening and shutting. There were no more feelings that someone was behind you or brushing past you. Life was now quiet in their house. Some people say maybe the spirit was looking for those keys. I say anything is possible.

I know I interrupted my story again. As I was saying before my ghost story, I was feeling alone and desperate to find someone to love me and Charlie and make us a family. I was on a mission and my main focus at that time was to find a boyfriend and father figure for my child. That was all I was concerned about. Wow, I wish I knew then what I know now. That would have been the last thing I would have worried about. But, there was no stopping me. I was young and foolish. I thought there was someone out there for me and I was determined to find him. The problem was I was looking in all the wrong places and that would lead me to trouble.

Then my adopted sister Amanda was getting back with her husband and he was moving back into their house. It was for the best that I leave so they could work out their marriage and I was really happy for them. And I was lucky again as my best friend Mary and her husband Justin had moved into a bigger house and invited me back to stay with them. By this time, Mary and Justin had a beautiful baby girl. Jack and I were the godparents and having a godchild meant the world to me. I was truly honored when Mary asked me to be her daughter's godmother.

I loved living with Mary and Justin but when I think of it today I don't feel I was very responsible at the time. I was always daydreaming that some wonderful guy was going to sweep me off my feet and love me and Charlie and give us a home of our own. I could stop bouncing Charlie and me from home to home. I am glad that she was just young enough to not know the difference and was happy wherever we were as long as we were together. My friend Mary did so much for me and my Charlie (her godchild) and I wish today I would have been more responsible and had more of a clear head. I was so wrapped up in finding a man that I didn't think about myself and how I was acting. I know I cannot go back and change how I was now but I do regret my actions. Mary deserved so much more from me.

As I said, Mary was so good to me and Charlie and I was so grateful but I was so lonely and I kept thinking I was getting too old and who will want me anyway. This was a major downfall for me. I was only twenty-two or twenty-three. I dated a few guys when I lived at her house but nothing serious as I usually met them when I was drinking. I had a real pity party going on at that time in my life. My poor friend Mary still stuck by me and just wanted me to be happy. I found myself praying again but not going to church. I would talk to some wise older people who I knew that went to church and they would make me feel better and would let me know that I was loved.

But I always felt that I had this huge grey cloud over my head and I couldn't get myself on track.

Then a couple months later, my one friend Justine asked me if I wanted to move in with her and her daughter. Her mom and dad owned the building and we could live upstairs in this huge apartment that had three bedrooms. She was single and so was I, and I felt that maybe it would be a good idea to let my best friend Mary and her husband Justin enjoy their daughter and be alone for a change. So, I accepted her offer and Charlie and I moved in with her. Justine was the friend who worked at the bar. We helped each other with our daughters. We took turns cooking and cleaning. It worked out very well. Her mom and family lived downstairs and were always very kind and helpful. Whenever we had to go to work at the bar her mom or one of her sisters would watch the girls. We were very lucky to have her family right there if we needed them.

But there is one thing I regretted when I lived there and that was the fact that I was drinking too much. Not because of anyone else, just because I was lonely and the crowd I hung out with all drank a lot and so I did too. I knew Charlie was home safe as I would always put her to bed before I left the house and I always came home to her at the end of the night. People seemed to like me because I was funny when I drank. It was fun at first. But then when I drank too much I would become sad and talk foolish. I would say things like, "Nobody likes me, I am not good enough to be someone's girlfriend," "Look at me, what do I have to offer?" I would have a pity party all by myself. It was not a pretty sight. And I always ended up with someone that I regretted later.

During the time I lived with my friend Justine, I did something that is still hard to talk about today, especially because of who I am today and the obstacles I have overcome. So my only concern about sharing this part of my story is that people who I know and love will not look at me differently. I hope that will not be the case but I must say here that I have forgiven myself and most importantly God has forgiven me.

I was living on welfare and working part time at a bar to make ends meet. I had made sure that Charlie had everything she needed. At the end of the month I had very little money to spend and so I never bought anything fancy. My friends would give me hand me downs and they were like new so I never wanted for anything really. I never had to worry at the bar if I needed a drink, we were all good friends at the bar and drinks came easily. But one night one of my friends and I were in the mall and she had told me to wait for her and she would be right back. When she met me about twenty minutes later I noticed she was wearing a really nice long sweater.

She looked at me and said, "Let's go for a walk around the mall," and so we did.

I asked her, "Where did you get that sweater?"

She proceeded to tell me, "Well, I lifted it from the store."

"What? That's crazy. How did you do it so easy and not get caught?"

She told me what she did and I was amazed how she didn't flinch at all about it. It was like she had done this before. I told her I would just die if I ever got caught and I told her I had taken candy from a store once when I was about nine years old and I felt too guilty to ever steal again. But wouldn't you know, after she talked to me about how easy it was to do and she had never gotten caught, the bad part of my brain fought with the good part of my brain and I decided I needed to take something to prove to her I wasn't afraid. Well, as we sat in the mall and watched people go by, I had a struggle with the good girl on my one shoulder and the not-so-good girl on my other shoulder. Well, needless to say, the not-so-good girl won. I went into the grocery store and I had a long white cotton coat on that had huge pockets in it. I swung my purse over my shoulder and walked around the grocery store for about ten minutes and then I took something. I walked out of the grocery store with something well hidden under my coat. I saw my friend and told her we needed to leave the mall because I had taken something. When we were outside the mall and down the street, my friend asked me what I took. I reached into my coat and pulled out a coconut! I stole a big coconut! My friend stood there and laughed and laughed.

"What the hell did you steal a coconut for?"

"Well, we may be hungry later!"

And later that evening when we were walking home from a bon-fire we were at (no word of a lie) we were singing a lot of songs from that era and we started singing, "Put the lime in the coconut." And all of a sudden, we both looked at each other and said, "Coconut!" We got the coconut out of my coat and sat down and tried to open it by hitting it on the ground and after a long time of trying to open it we got it opened and enjoyed a few pieces of fresh coconut.

Now that doesn't sound too bad when I tell the story about the coconut you may think, Oh, that was innocent or maybe not. But the fact that I got away with it means I may try to take something else. About three weeks later, my friend said she was going to get a nice pair of jeans at one of the popular stores. I thought she meant she was buying the jeans but, no, she was going to steal a pair of jeans. I was welcome to come if I wanted or not, it didn't matter to her. I thought about how nice it would be to have a new pair of jeans. I didn't like the idea of stealing them but I was curious to see how she would do it. So, she told me how she would do it and it involved putting one pair of jeans on underneath a baggy pair of pants she would already have on. I tossed the idea around and around in my head. Out came the two little people on my shoulders again and they argued back and forth in my head. Don't do it, do it, don't do it, do it. You need the jeans, you don't need the jeans. And so on and so on. Finally, I said I was going to do it. Let me just say I was scared shitless. Guilt was written all over my face and it took me a good five minutes in the change room to come out with the new pair of jeans under my pants. My friend told me to get the look of guilt off of my face or we were going to get caught. I put a smile on my face and took the other jeans to the lady and said they didn't fit but thank you, have a nice day. Out the door I went and about two blocks away from the store I started to hyperventilate. I was so scared and felt so sick to my stomach I knew this was not for me. I was too scared to take the pants back to the store because I wasn't sure if they would press charges and I immediately thought of Charlie and how I could lose her. Needless to say, I never stole anything else in my life again. I never told my friend that I was done stealing, I just never did it again. Then, about two weeks later, one of our friends got caught stealing at the same store we were in and she was charged and had to go to court. That was it for me for sure, and I believe my friend was done too. It just wasn't worth it. I thought about what would have happened to Charlie if I had gotten caught stealing the jeans. I was so ashamed and felt so bad that I had put myself in that situation but most of all that I had put Charlie in that situation. It could have gone really bad. It wasn't worth the new jeans at all. I realized the moment my other friend got caught that I was a very lucky girl and I would never jeopardize myself or my daughter ever again by doing something so dishonest. I thank God for helping me to walk away from a path that would have made me lose everything important to me. I truly believe God or my angels were getting in my head and steering me in the direction of honesty.

MY THOUGHTS

From my experience on stealing something that did not belong to me, I can truly say I am not that person. I was never meant to be that person, and I am so thankful that part of me is long gone. Let me just say too that it really isn't worth it. I have learned to do without most of my life and I managed to have a good, honest life. I was taught as a young child growing up by my dear mom that I was not to lie and not to steal. Those were the two things that she instilled in me and the times I was a lost girl I momentarily forgot them. The good news is that I remembered through the love of God that following a positive path was much more rewarding in the end. This is not to say that I was a perfect walking person because I was far from it.

I continued to make mistakes but I did walk away from a path that could have taken me down an ugly road of criminal activities. Thank God that was not the plan that God had for me. So in wrapping up my thoughts on stealing something that does not belong to us, think of the consequences of our actions, think of the many people it affects, think of how you would feel if someone stole something important from you, we always have other options, we do not have the right to steal anything that is not ours in the first place, stealing something is dishonest and can turn into stealing bigger things. And for anyone who is thinking of stealing something, trust me, it is not the way you want to live your life, you deserve to walk an honest and healthy path. You are worth so much to yourself and others. Be true to yourself and others and watch your life become richer.

CHAPTER 6

I was still down on myself and had the "poor me" attitude and "who's going to want to be with me." I had really low self-esteem. If I had only known that it would be a good idea for me to go to a counselor or therapist to find out why I felt the way I did, maybe I could have made better choices. I regret not getting help at that time. But when you are in that state you don't think of the sensible things to do. At least I didn't. Eventually I met some really nice girl friends through my roommate and we would all get together and go out to this one park in the summer and have bonfires. We would all take turns getting wood for the fire. We would always meet our guy friends and new friends out at these bonfires. There was a lake there too and we would just drink and listen to music and have fun. It all seemed so innocent at the time but when I think of it today as much as it was fun it was dangerous too. This was a well-known park and we were lucky we didn't get busted for abusing the property by breaking down trees and bushes for our bonfires. Not a smart idea.

As I said earlier, I started drinking more than usual and I dated the wrong type of men. As long as someone was interested in me and made me feel wanted then I would go out with them, always thinking maybe this guy's the one. It never worked out that way. In the midst of all this my ex Jack would show up once in a while to see our daughter. At this time, he had been seeing someone for a while and they were getting married. I remember the day they got married because that was the day I finally let him go from my heart. Now it was truly over for us.

Going to the bar became the thing to do at that time in my life. One time when a bunch of us were sitting at a table a couple of guy friends came and joined us. There were a couple of new guys joining us who knew our guy friends. I watched this one guy and I actually felt sorry for him. They were making fun of him because he was stuttering when he talked. I found out later that he didn't have a stutter problem except when he drank heavily. His name was Carter. We saw each other a few more times and we always seemed to be the ones without a steady boyfriend or girlfriend. Somehow we ended up dancing together one night and then we just became an item. Eventually I let him come home with me one night from the bar. We were all looped up. Carter met my daughter the next morning and he immediately took to her. Whenever we went for walks he would carry her on his shoulders. When he wasn't drinking, I saw a guy who was very kind to Charlie. I knew I was taking a chance but he seemed genuinely smitten by Charlie and a couple months later I thought maybe he was the one. I kept ignoring the drinking at first because I just wanted to be loved and I knew he loved Charlie.

Then one night at the club something happened that would change my thoughts on drinking. I was drinking single Tia Maria and milk. I would get up dancing with my girlfriends and was having a good time. My drinks were always on the table when I came back from dancing and I would drink them. I do not know to this day which one of my so-called friends was getting my drinks but they were getting me double Tia Maria with milk and vodka. I did not know there was Vodka mixed in my drinks. I would be so thirsty from dancing I just kept downing the drinks. I do not remember leaving the club. At all! I only remember bits and pieces of that night. Carter showed up at the bar and brought me home in a cab. Charlie and I were spending the night at my older adopted sister Amanda's house. Charlie was sound asleep, thank goodness. When I woke up the next morning I was so shocked at what I saw. My clothes were on the floor wet and puke all over them. The big mirror that sat behind this small rocking chair was smashed on the floor. My head was pounding and I didn't have any idea how I got home. I was devastated. Carter told me I was totally out of it when he brought me home. He helped me up the stairs as I was all over the place (I was lucky I didn't fall down the stairs) and he stayed with me. Apparently, I fell backward down into the rocking chair and the mirror behind it broke into pieces. Carter had been drinking that night too but luckily for me he wasn't loaded like I was. He helped me up carefully so I wouldn't get cut from the broken glass. Then I started puking (which was a good thing in one respect), but I also fell onto the bed and wet my pants. After that he undressed me and put me to bed. But what scared me the most was the fact that I couldn't remember how I got home or anything after that.

I truly believe he was meant to be there with me. When I think of what could have happened if he wasn't there, it scares me. I could have fallen back into the glass but he was there to get me up off the chair. I could have choked on my throw up but he was there to help me be up and not on my back. He made sure I was okay. I will always be thankful for that. I also truly believe this was my wake-up call from God to look at how things were going in my life with the drinking. From that day on, I told myself if I was to drink, it would have to be one to two drinks or no drinking at all. And most importantly, I was to get my own drinks. I can honestly say that I have never been in that shape ever again. I was very cautious when I drank and my drinks were fewer and fewer. I am not a drinker to even speak of today. My friends will usually say to me "ones not going to hurt you." But, I am so turned off of alcohol for several reasons and I do not need it or miss it. I have just as much laughter and fun without alcohol. That episode was the last time I ever got pissed drunk, and as I write my story that was thirty-three years ago. I was twenty-four.

The next time I went to the club a few of my guy friends were teasing me about how drunk I was the last time they saw me. Then they started making up outrageous stories. I was devastated because I didn't know if they were just getting me going or really telling the truth. My girlfriend Justine said they were just trying to get a rise out of me. My guy friends were not exactly sensitive people or honest people. The people my friend and I hung with were not exactly saints. But they always watched out for us and you didn't mess around with any of them.

One of our newest guy friends eventually told us he had just gotten out of prison just about a year before he met us for murder. What? Yes, that's right. He was sixteen or seventeen when his girlfriend had been raped and beaten by someone and he got a shotgun and killed him. Obviously, that is a short version of what happened but that was all I was ever told. That was shocking to hear. But, he took a chance in telling us. He said he didn't have any friends and he considered us his friends. So, he watched out for us and treated us pretty good. He was older than us, maybe in his mid to late thirties. He never did tell us his age but he looked young. He was out on parole and he had to keep his nose clean, which he did.

It wasn't long after the drinking episode that I started thinking maybe it was time to move on again. I loved the apartment I lived in with my good friend Justine and she and I became very close. We had made a lot of good memories and respected each other. Her mom and sisters were very good to Charlie and me. We watched out for each other's child. Her mom was like a grandma to Charlie and treated her very well. But, something was telling me it was time to settle down and move out on my own and start being an adult. No more partying. Charlie was getting older (she was two years old) and things had to change. And honestly, as much as I knew Carter loved Charlie, his drinking was starting to get to me too. I noticed he was drinking more and more. I didn't want that to be a part of my life anymore. So, I decided to break it off with him. He was not happy at all about my decision and would search me out every couple days and try to get me to take him back. He would tell me he was going to quit drinking and that he missed me and Charlie. I really felt bad for him but I told him I needed time to think.

During all this time, I would see my adopted family and they too were very good to me and Charlie. I was a lucky girl. I had the best of friends and a dear family who loved me as their own. My sister and I would see each other when we could and that always made me happy. I didn't see my brother Brad as often as he went out west for a while to work. But when I did see him, it was as if we had always seen each other. We got along very well. The three of us were still close and that was important to me. But I always felt like the black sheep of the family. Where was my life going? What was I doing to help myself? What the heck is that cloud that keeps following me?

So, I moved again! First, I moved in with my sister Rose for a little while until I could find myself my own place. It was nice living with her. We hadn't lived with each other since we were twelve and thirteen. She treated me and Charlie very well. We were spoiled. I liked her apartment. It was small but it was welcoming and every-thing was brand new. You also had to be buzzed in to get into the building which made me feel safe and it was clean and in a good area. I loved living with my sister Rose. I always looked up to her and wished I could be more like her. She accepted me flaws and all and always had my back.

I looked for work but it was hard to get work when you didn't graduate (stay in school). The only jobs I could usually get were in a restaurant or bar. When I was living with my sister she went away for two weeks on vacation. During those two weeks, my ex Carter tried to get back with me. Eventually I gave in and we got back together. Also, my dad and my stepmom and my two young brothers stayed with me and Charlie as their apartment was being fumigated. My sister just happened to be on vacation for the two weeks and I felt I should help them out when they called for a place to stay for a week. We were pretty cramped but we made it work. And while I was liv-ing with my sister my cousin Sandy came to visit me there and she even gave me a new haircut. I hadn't seen her in a while and I was so thrilled when she came to see me and Charlie. When my sister came home from her vacation I was so happy she was back. I missed her. But as I watched my sister and how independent she was I realized that I needed to be independent too. She didn't need her sister and niece to take care of. She needed to enjoy her apartment on her own and I did not want to be a burden. She deserved better from me. And so I decided I needed to get a place real soon as I needed to be independent and start fresh. I moved out of my sister's place and I rented a big apartment above a restaurant just on the outskirts of downtown. I was very grateful for my sister's constant love and support no matter what and being with her that short period of time gave me the courage to finally get my own place.

I finally had my own place and I felt so grown up. Charlie had her own room and there was a big yard in the back. The only downfall of this apartment was some days all you could smell was food cooking but it was an okay price to pay and it was worth it to finally have my own place. I was so happy. Carter moved in with me as it just made sense because he was there all the time anyway. He tried to stop drinking but he was having a hard time. His drinking was starting to scare me at this time as he was getting verbally abusive and saying very mean things to me. Our relationship was really falling apart. But he would always apologize the next day and promise not to drink anymore. That would last several days and then it would start all over again.

During this time, my dad would come and visit with my younger brothers from his second marriage. It was nice to spend time with my father and my brothers. They lived in a small town just outside my city. I was lucky if I saw them once every couple months or so, but I treasured those moments when I saw my father. I missed him so much. Of course, I always felt nervous when he would spend the night and drink with Carter but once I knew dad was sleeping I could go to sleep.

Before too long, Carter and I started to fight more and more. The verbal abuse had graduated into destructive abuse. What I mean is not only was I verbally abused, but he started to throw things and break things. I decided I did not want him drinking anymore and I wanted him to leave. That was enough of this craziness! I already had a cloud of sadness and fear following me I did not need this treatment from someone who said they loved me. But just when I decided to make him leave for good I found out I was pregnant. When I first found out I was pregnant I was so upset. How could I bring a baby into this world when I didn't want to be with the baby's father? It wasn't fair to this child. I did not know what to do. I was so lost. I wasn't sure if I wanted Carter to be a part of Charlie's or this new baby's life anymore. But I had to tell him I was pregnant and when I told him I was pregnant he was thrilled and I knew there was no way I could get him to leave now. I told myself that maybe because I am pregnant Carter will stop drinking and we can have the happy family that I always wanted.

I was scared to have a second child and not know how things would work out but I never once thought about life without this baby. This baby would be loved and taken care of just like my first daughter. I started to feel like things would work out and tried really hard not to worry. We would be okay. So, I still worked part time and made our place a home as best I could. I would get excited when I would touch my belly and watch it grow knowing I was carrying a precious baby inside me. I loved this baby so much and I was thrilled that Charlie would have a sibling. Charlie and I would sit together on the couch and talk about the new baby that was coming to live with us. She would touch my belly and say, "I am going to help you with the baby, Mommy, and I am going to feed it and bathe it." Charlie was so excited to know she would have someone to play with. As far as she was concerned it was her baby. Those moments with Charlie were the moments that kept me going. I had to keep it together for Charlie and the new baby to come.

When I was at the end of my third month going into my fourth, I started to get cravings. This was funny to me because I never ate ice cream (except when I was a little girl). But one evening I felt like having ice cream so I asked Carter if he would go to the store and get me some ice cream. The nearest store was a good fifteen-minute walk but he was happy to go. I waited and waited for Carter to return and soon my craving went away and before I knew it the time was 11:00 p.m. Where the heck was Carter and where was my ice cream? I went to bed pissed off like anything! I thought to myself, "If he thinks he is just going to take off like that and not come home, he has another thing coming!" I was livid and seething at the mouth. Being pregnant and seething is not pretty.

The next morning around ten I received a phone call from him and guess where he was? Jail! Yes, jail! He apologized and said he would explain everything later and asked if I could come down with clean clothes and meet him at the court house. What? What is happening here? I got dressed and asked my friend to watch Charlie while I went to the courthouse (yeah, that was fun). I arrived at the courthouse and was so embarrassed and angry. I had no idea what was going on. I gave someone his clothes and then I sat in the courtroom waiting for him to be brought out. When he came out he looked remorseful but I was so angry I just wanted to know what the heck was going on. Well, if I was mad the night before, it was nothing compared to how angry I was when I heard the charges. He denied the charges to me of course. The charges were assault and break and enter. I was in shock. This can't be happening. Oh, it was happening all right, and it wasn't a good story. You see, instead of going to get me my ice cream, Carter took a detour and decided to go to a party instead. But the party he was trying to get into was being held by someone who did not like him. But that didn't stop him from pushing his way through her door. He assaulted the girl by putting both hands on her breasts and pushed his way through and wouldn't leave. Someone called the police and had him arrested. There may be a little more to this story but that was the gist of it.

What the heck do I do now? I have him telling me he didn't touch her but there are witnesses that back up her story. Son of a gun, are you freaking kidding me? He ended up getting eight months in jail and probation (out of those eight for good behavior and a pregnant girlfriend at home he got out in six months). The jail was out of town and was not easy to get to. Great, just flipping great! Only those are not the words I used. I was not feeling the best as I was still getting morning sickness. I thought I had a cloud over me before, now my cloud just got bigger.

While he was in jail he would call me when he could and say he was sorry. He said this was it, he was never drinking again and he was going to change for me and our children. He told me so many happy ending stories and I believed him, hook, line and sinker. I thought with him going to jail this must be the thing that would change him and if I stayed in the relationship this long I might as well stay the six months and reap my reward at the end of this.

Needless to say, I felt trapped. I felt hopeless and I felt so alone. But amidst all this, I did start to pray again. I can't remember exactly what I prayed but I believe it was mostly that Charlie, and the new baby and I would be safe and taken care of. At night I would lie in bed and read my bible and try to comfort myself. I was so depressed and I tried so hard to be up with Charlie. But some days I would find myself hollering at her for the most trivial things and then I would hold her and say I was sorry. I felt very bad for Charlie as I was not in a good emotional state. At one point for one tiny little second, when I was having a bath I lay in the tub and I thought, "What would it be like to be dead?" I scared the shit out of myself when that thought crossed my mind and I started crying and praying. The last thing I wanted was to be dead and I could never leave Charlie and the little one coming into my life. That was the one and only time that I ever had that type of thought in my head. It is actually hard for me to admit that I ever had a thought like that but if I am telling my story then I have to be honest and tell the things that are important. I was a lost little girl inside and every now and then something would trigger that little girl that lost her mother and family in such a short period of time. Being pregnant and my hormones all over the place, it was very hard to keep myself sane especially when the father of my baby was in jail. Yes, I had to pull myself together for my children and make things work. So, after the tub episode, I pushed all the fear and anger down inside again so I could be there for my children.

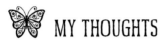 MY THOUGHTS

Well, this should be good. The thoughts I am going to share with you is how not to find a man when you are lonely. Yes, I am chuckling as I write this down on paper. I am just going to put it out there and hope in some way this will give you some good thoughts to think about or at the very least a good shake of your head.

How not to find a man? Well, for one thing, try not to follow my route. As you can see, it is not a successful route. Was there any fun along the way, maybe a little but not enough to warrant my way of finding a man. First of all, from my experience trying to find a man when you are lonely and think a man will take all your problems away, not a good idea. Why did I always think I needed a man to make me happy? I believe it was because I didn't love myself enough and didn't know that I could make myself happy because of my low self-esteem. I didn't need a man in my life at that time I just thought I did. And maybe, just maybe, not having my father in my life made me desperately want my daughter to have a father. My girlfriends gave me more happiness than the kind of men I went out with when I was drinking. And please let me say right here, I am not bashing men (I love and respect most men). I am only bashing the ones who took advantage of me when I was drunk and knew I could not make a good decision while in that condition. But on the flip side of that, I did put myself in those situations. I was the one drinking more than I should have. But in the big picture there is really no one to blame and it won't make things better to blame someone else or even myself for that matter anyway. It won't change a darn thing!

But please try not to be loaded when looking for a man. Try hard to be sober if you can. Most times when we are drinking what we think we see really isn't there. And most times if we are drunk the guys who check us out think they can get somewhere. So the best advice here is not only should you not drink and drive, but try not to drink and date. It would be different if you met a guy somewhere when sober and you go out for a dinner date and have a glass or two of wine, but starting out drunk does not go very well. And most times when you say yes to a date with someone you met while being drunk you can bet your sweet life that when you see him the next day for your date you will wish your friends had of stepped in and saved you from yourself.

I know these are only two ways on how not to find a man but they are the two ways I made mistakes with. Let me tell you if I could go back and change some of the ways I handled things this would be one of them. I wish I had more self-esteem back then and I wish I relied on myself more than I did. I really had this ridiculous idea that I needed a man to take care of me and my little girl. Wow, was I wrong about that idea. I was already taking care of my little girl I just needed to take better care of myself. I just didn't have the tools at the time. So, do I beat myself up for the choices I made in the men I went out with? Not now. Not ever again. I lived with guilt and shame over these guys for many years. I felt like I was such a bad person to be drunk like that out in public. Yes, I know I was young and immature, but it didn't help the way I felt about myself. I went about things head on and always had this hope that this one would be different. When I think of the times I spent making myself look like a fool, it can still get under my skin. I can still feel bad in a heartbeat, but then I remember that I forgave myself long ago and that God loves me and his son forgave me when he died on the cross to save our sins. When I remember this, I am able to hold my head up and be proud of the person I am today and have been for many years. Loving myself did not come easy, but God helped me love myself through the program of Al-Anon (stay tuned for that chapter, it's good stuff) and the counselors I opened up to. I thank God for saving me from myself. I was drowning and couldn't get back to the top where I belonged and wanted to be. Of course, in the next chapter, you will see I was still floating through life. I didn't learn all this good stuff until later.

CHAPTER 7

For the next six months, I would have to take care of everything and do the best I could for Charlie and me. I was not one of those girlfriends who whined about her poor boyfriend in jail. Carter deserved to do time in jail for his actions. I had no sympathy for that whatsoever. My concerns were for Charlie and the baby on the way. I worked part time and I provided us with food and shelter, which were the two most important things we needed at that time. I was lucky that my adopted sister Lindsay and her family needed a place to stay for a month or so and it felt good to be able to pay them back for helping me a couple years earlier. It was good to have company with me for a while. I wish I could say I was happy though when they lived with me. I was pregnant and cranky. I felt so bad that I wasn't in happy moods when they lived with me. It had nothing to do with them, they were great, I was just so stressed out from working and having to go out and see Carter in jail that I was miserable. He kept bothering me to bring Charlie out to see him. He said he missed her so much that he was heartbroken. So, I gave in and took her out against my better judgment. Let's just say I never took her out there again. It was one thing for me to be frisked and humiliated but to have my innocent daughter put in that situation. It broke my heart. How did I get to this point in my life?

Then because of good behavior, Carter was let out early as I was to give birth in one week. He was on his best behavior and I thought maybe jail was the best thing for him. He was excited for me to have our baby. My due date came but no baby yet. Then two days later, my water broke and I was in labor. This time I was able to see my baby be born which meant the world to me. There were no complications and when it was time to push I was ready. By the third push my baby was born. I asked the doctor "what did I have?" and they told me I had a baby girl. They brought her to me and Carter and I fell in love with our new little one. Here she was, my beautiful baby girl, and she was so innocent and she needed me. I knew without a doubt that I would love her and protect her and never leave her. Now Charlie (who was three and a half) had a baby sister and I couldn't be happier. I was excited to take my baby girl home to start a whole new life together with her sister. I named her Ava.

Carter was to bring Charlie the next day to meet her little sister Ava but that did not happen. I never heard from Carter until the following day and I was so hurt and sad that Charlie had to wait another night before seeing me and her new sister. Carter had gone out to celebrate Ava's birth and of course he looked like he was still feeling good when he came to see us. I never said a word because Charlie was with him and I did not want her to see us argue. So I focused all my attention on trying to get Charlie to see her new baby sister. She would not look at her new sister at first. She was more concerned about me and she got up on the bed and hugged me. Finally, she wanted to meet her sister and we let her hold her on the bed beside me with me helping and she was excited. I told her she was a great big sister and she could help mommy take care of her. Eventually she warmed up to the idea and I was so in love with my two girls. I never said anything to Carter about the day before as I felt it was pointless now.

At first things were okay. We had a schedule to be followed and we did our best to take care of the needs of both girls. I was surprised to see that Carter was keeping to his end of the bargain. We started to get along better and there was no drinking to speak of. But just when I thought things were going good it all fell apart just like that. I was busy with Ava and Charlie. Carter started going out again and started drinking. He would come home loaded and we would fight. Things would get broken and I found myself so unhappy. This was when he started throwing objects at me again. It started off with a mug or glass and then it would be whatever was in his sight. He would just throw it at me and if I didn't get out of the way fast or duck something would hit me. I lost more and more dishes.

One night he had gone out drinking and I had enough of waiting up for him so I had locked the front door downstairs so he couldn't get in and I locked and barred the back door too. I figured if he couldn't get in he would just go back to wherever he had been all night and I could get a half decent sleep. The locked doors didn't stop him. He just kept yelling and banging on the door. I wouldn't give in and the next thing you know he breaks the window in the bottom front door and opens the latch. He was really angry with me and I was afraid he was going to hurt me.

I ran to the back door and looked in the small porch for a stick and found a piece of wood. I was so afraid I thought if I threatened him with a piece of wood he would back off and go to bed. I was sick of Carter thinking he could just do what he wanted and get away with it. He came toward me in the kitchen like a big bear about to attack me and I told him to get out. He laughed at me when he saw the piece of wood I had. I told him not to come near me or I would hit him with the wood. He came at me again just as angry as the first time and didn't stop and I plowed him in the side of his hip and he backed off. He was pissed that I hit him and he came after me again and I hit him again. Finally, after a few heated words, he went and crashed on my bed and passed out. I threw the piece of wood out into the back porch. The next day when Carter got up he complained of a sore back side. He asked me if I hit him and I denied it. I was so scared I thought I better lie. And to tell you the truth the night before when I dropped the piece of wood back where I found it in the back porch, I felt so bad for even picking it up in the first place. What the hell was I doing hitting him with a piece of wood? What is happening to me? I was becoming violent, to protect myself. Little me, I weighed 95 pounds and Carter weighed 185 for sure and was solid muscle. But never in a million years did I ever think that I would ever be hitting him with a piece of wood. I was so ashamed and knew I had to do something or one of us was going to be hurt.

Things were a mess in my life. I didn't know who Carter was anymore, and worst of all I didn't know who I was becoming. I knew he had a drinking problem but I never saw this violent side of him before. And here I was now getting violent myself. I started to worry how things would ever work out. I felt so trapped. My girls were my life and their mother was hitting their father with a piece of wood. How would I ever be able to raise them on my own? Then I realized I was raising them alone anyway so why not move out closer to my adopted family and raise the girls out of the city. So, I looked for an apartment and found the perfect place on the east end of town, more in the country area. There were only three apartments in this big house, and the apartment I was in was on the main floor. I told Carter he was not coming to live with us as I could not take the drinking and his behavior anymore. I told him it was over.

This new place was heaven. I was away from all the bullshit and it was so peaceful where we were. The apartment wasn't huge but it was just right. It had two bedrooms and a big kitchen and a good size living room. There was a trucking business next door but I didn't mind at all. Our closest neighbors were just across the road. And best of all, there was a beautiful babbling brook just down in the back yard. There was a picnic table there and the area was surrounded by tall trees. It was so peaceful. I loved it there. It felt like home to me.

As I said earlier, I told Carter he wasn't coming with us as I couldn't take the drinking and I didn't feel like I loved him anymore. He was quite upset and told me he would make me love him again and to please give him one last chance. Eventually he wore me down and I agreed to give him this one last chance as he begged me to let him move in and said he would get a job and show me he could change. And lo and behold, he did get a contract job through unemployment that was for several months which was a start, and you have to start somewhere. He actually liked the job and during those months he acted like a whole different person. We bought some nice furniture and made our place very homey. He didn't drink and even though he had some mood swings he did pretty well. Maybe just maybe he could change. I even decided it was time to quit smoking. I was so proud of myself and I did pretty well during those months. Also during those months, we started hanging out with his good friend's brother and wife. They didn't drink and they had three kids of their own. We had some really nice times together and we even went out to beaches and would have so much fun with the girls. We would go to their house and hang out and I really got to see a happy and kinder side of Carter. His friend was a very good influence on him and his friend's wife was absolutely beautiful in every way. When we were with them I had the best times with Carter and our girls. It was so nice to see this side of Carter and it made me fall for him again.

After several months, we decided to get married and started making plans for our wedding. Everything was moving so fast now that he wasn't drinking. And one of my aunts on my dad's side (Aunt Marcy) had decided that she wanted to help us out and said she would have the reception at this beautiful old club house where she worked and lived. She was so excited for me and wanted me to have a nice wedding. She even got me a secondhand wedding dress and hat with a veil that was so pretty that I was so thankful she was helping us to afford to get married. During the time that we were getting things all organized and ready for the May wedding Carter's job was up. What is it they say again? "All good things must come to an end"? That is when things started to change again.

The drinking started again and the binges started. He would come home a couple days later after drinking and we would fight and it just became a cycle. I did not know how to stop this cycle.

I didn't understand his need for alcohol. But I did understand my need for smoking again. I picked a bad time to quit smoking was all I could think of. Needless to say, I didn't start smoking a pack a day again but I did smoke one cigarette a week during that period. I would pour a bath and smoke a few puffs while the steam of the hot water would mask the smell of smoke. Carter never did catch on that I was sneaking a cigarette at least once a week or maybe he did and just never told me. I don't know what difference it made anyway as he still smoked.

I hardly went anywhere during that time but one day we decided to visit his family who lived in the downtown area. The four of us hopped on the bus and actually had fun riding the bus with the girls. His parents lived on the second floor of an old house that housed several tenants. I could tell when we got there that his dad had been drinking so immediately I had my guard up for the girls. Carter had taken the girls in the living room to play with his mom and siblings and his father was sitting in the kitchen close to the fridge. Carter's father asked me to get him a beer and I thought it was strange that he would ask me when he was sitting right there by the fridge but I decided to just say politely, "No problem." I went to the fridge, opened the fridge door, and leaned in to get the beer off the bottom shelf, and that is when I felt this hand grabbing the back side of my butt to the front of my crotch. I quickly turned around ready to tell Carter to knock it off and who was standing there but his dad with an evil smile. You can't even imagine the look on my face and the dropping of my jaw in complete shock and disgust. I was so pissed off, but more than that I was so shocked that I couldn't even speak to him. I passed him the beer and walked in a daze into the living room. Carter asked me what was wrong and I said, "I'm not feeling well all of a sudden, I don't want to stay too much longer." He never questioned my answer and it was as if he knew something must have happened in the kitchen. We were going to let the girls stay for the night earlier when we first got there but there was no way in hell my girls were going to stay there now or ever! When we got home and the girls were playing together I told Carter what happened. He was very angry and embarrassed and totally understood why I would never go there again and that the girls would never be babysat by his mom and dad. End of discussion!

We were getting closer to the wedding and my aunt Marcy had everything almost done. And then the week before the wedding I started to panic and I decided I had to call her and call it off. I couldn't go through with this, what was I thinking? I picked up the phone several times that week to call my aunt Marcy and then I would just hang up. I couldn't call her and call if off now. That would be awful. How could I do that to her? She was so good to me and she was so excited for me. She was so important to me and I loved her so much I couldn't change my mind and lose her love for me. I know now that I could have called her and she would have done anything to make me happy. I just didn't have the courage or heart to call it off. So, I told myself to go through with it. I have two daughters with two different fathers and who is ever going to want to be with me anyway (at least that is what I always heard from Carter)? He would say, "Who would ever want you when you have two children from two different fathers?" He started saying these remarks after we had been together a couple of years. I also became very self-conscious about my body. In the summer, I wouldn't wear shorts or short dresses. I would always wear pants or a long dress. He would say to me, "You may have a pretty face but look at your body. Your legs are so skinny!" Sometimes when you are told something enough times you start to believe it, and I accepted that he was probably right. So I thought this is my lot in life. I made my bed now I am going to lie in it. And maybe, just maybe he will change. He changed for several months, maybe he can do it again. He just needs a good job. I kept talking myself into getting married. And the next thing I know, I am walking down the aisle to get married.

When Carter was working and things were going well I wrote a song that I was going to sing to him at our wedding. My neighbor across the street played the guitar and I asked him if he could help me to put music to my lyrics. He did come up with music to the lyrics and we practiced this song as a surprise for Carter to be played on our wedding day. Well, since things were not going so good and I felt so trapped and unable to call off the wedding, I did not want to sing this song to him at our wedding. I felt like a fraud singing this beautiful song that was written when he wasn't drinking and when I thought we would be okay. But I sang it to him because my neighbor had practiced so much with me and took the time to write the music for the lyrics. I did not want to disappoint him. So I sang it to Carter and he loved it and thanked me and said it was beautiful. And if I am not mistaken I could have sworn I saw tears in his eyes. For a few minutes, I actually thought marriage may work out for us. I am such a sucker for romance.

Every girl dreams of a beautiful wedding and a romantic honeymoon. That's just the way some of us hopeless romantics are. In my case, my wedding was a disaster. First, it poured buckets on us. Some people say that's good luck, I say it doesn't matter if there's a blizzard or hot sun if your marriage is going to work it will work, the weather has no bearing on a marriage at all. Of course, that's my opinion only. So, we started out with buckets of water (no exaggeration), and that was probably the best part of the day! Next, the only thing Carter had to do for our wedding was to book us a room at the hotel we had our reception at. He told me he did. You know I am going to tell you he didn't. We go to the desk and there are no suites available, we have to take the cheapest room in the place. Fine, I am tired, let's just get to our room. It is now two thirty in the morning. I am exhausted, we are to meet our friends for breakfast at the restaurant at nine the next morning, but of course I am expected to do my wifely duties in the bedroom. Two hours later because Carter is so drunk, he can't perform but is determined to. So, I gently say to him, "Can we please go to sleep and take this up in the morning, I am really exhausted."

Next thing I know he jumps up and kicks the lamp on the nightstand. Of course it doesn't go anywhere because it is nailed to the desk (that part was funny). The shade goes flying across the room. He is getting dressed and leaving me there at the hotel because I want to go to sleep. I jump out of bed and I had to beg him to get back into bed and we can continue. I tell him I was wrong and I am sorry in order to keep peace on our first night of marriage. How's that for romance? My marriage was doomed!

We didn't go on a honeymoon right away because we really couldn't afford it. But a couple months later we did go to a really nice town a couple hours away and tented with a bunch of our friends for three days. Our good friends watched our two girls and we knew they were safe with them and their three children. But while we were on our short honey moon it was not what I expected. Half the time I didn't know where Carter was. It was really a good drunk on his part and I was so embarrassed and I knew my friends were upset with his behavior. The weekend went by so fast and I was not a happy camper, no pun intended.

Shortly after our wedding, I worked full time at a bar serving food to the customers. My cousin Sandy had gotten me the job because she knew I needed money. Carter watched our children. One of us had to work. And let me say that I appreciated that Carter watched our girls. He loved the girls and was good with them, but the only downfall was that he gave them whatever they wanted. When I would come home at night I was tired. I worked long hours on my feet and I just wanted to come home to a hot bath and a happy family. I missed my girls during the day. This one night I had worked extra hours and I was truly exhausted. When we went to bed of course Carter wanted sex, but I got the courage to tell him I was going to sleep and that he definitely wasn't deprived. He didn't take that very well and the next thing I know his foot flies over my head by inches and hits the wall! Yes, he actually kicked a hole in our wall just inches above my head! I was so scared I calmed him down and then again agreed to have sex. Sex was always a big deal with him. He expected sex at least once a day or he would say I wasn't normal. The problem was I was tired, not that I wasn't normal.

One time when I was at work he came to my work with a friend of his and sat over in the corner where it was hidden. He watched me for an hour or more without me knowing he was there. I was very friendly to my customers and my coworkers and I felt good at my job because I was liked. My cousin and I would laugh and sing to the music that came on in the bar. But the friendlier I was to people, the more he got angry, sitting there drinking beer. Then I finally noticed him and I almost fell to the floor. I knew he was mad just by the look on his face and I knew I was in trouble. I walked over to him and his friend and said, "Hi, this is a nice surprise. Who is watching the girls?" He told me the girls were fine and were with our neighbor's daughter. I said, "Oh that's good, glad you could come and see where I work. As you can see I do very well for tips because I treat people very nice." Yeah, he wasn't buying it. All he saw was me flirting with the customers in his mind but that was not happening at all.

It is time to leave and we get a taxi with his friend and are driving home. I do not say anything because I am scared of what he will do. Then he looks at me sideways and slaps me in the face.

His friend grabs his arm and says, "Come on, man, don't be doing that."

I don't say a word. Tears are running down my face and I know we are going to fight when we get home. And we did, he didn't want me to work there anymore. But I told him we needed the money and I wasn't quitting. I told him I liked my job and I have to be nice to my customers if I want to get good tips. He finally agreed that maybe he was over reacting and I could stay at the job. Plus I told him that he would miss out on the really good food I would bring home from work for dinner at a great price. I guess you really can get through to a man through his stomach. Just kidding, I have to have some sort of relief and that would be through humor.

Remember the guy friend I had who was in prison. Well, I hadn't seen him for a long time. Ever since I had moved to the country area of the city and was married and out of the bar scene, I never knew that he had ended up back in jail. It wasn't for anything big but because he had broken his parole he had to do some time. Well, apparently, he decided when he was on a weekend pass he wanted another day or so of freedom. Apparently, there was a warrant out for his arrest and guess where he comes to visit when he is heading back to jail? Yes, Carter and I. I had no idea at first what was going on and then he told us what was happening. He was getting his father to drive him back to the prison to turn himself in and it was a couple hours away. He wanted my husband and me to come for the drive so he could visit with us on the way. I started to panic once I heard all this. I was so afraid the police were going to come to my door and take me away and my girls would be taken away from me for helping a fugitive! I told my husband he could go but I was not going anywhere. I had two little girls to think of. Well, my friend and my husband insisted I go. I kept arguing with them. My friend wanted to catch up on our lives but I did not want to leave my girls. Carter pretty much said I was going and that was it and I was to get the babysitter from across the street. When he had that look on his face I knew better than to argue.

Well, let me tell you, as much as I liked my friend, I was not happy. We drove back to the prison with him. There were no seats as it was just a working van so we sat on the floor and there were a couple of our old friends in the van when we got in. They were all drinking and carrying on. I felt sick to my stomach the whole way there. It felt like hours and hours of driving but it had only been about two and a half hours. But all I could think of were my two little innocent girls and what would happen if the police stopped the van. How would I ever live with myself if we had to go to jail? I was in panic mode the whole ride there and back. I felt so unsafe and scared that something bad was going to happen for sure. Finally, his dad let him out not far from the prison and he was to walk to the gate and turn himself in. We said good-bye and all I thought about was getting home to my girls. The drive back couldn't happen any faster. By this time, Carter was half in the bag and he was useless and of no comfort to me. We finally got home and I broke down. My legs were like jelly when I came into the house. Our babysitter left and the only thing that gave me comfort was when I went to see my girls who were sleeping safe and sound. All my fears and anxiety were gone and I was never so happy to be home in my life.

If I had to choose which of the abuses scarred me the most it would be the emotional abuse. As I said earlier, he would tell me I was so skinny which made me feel very self-conscious in shorts or a dress. He would tell me nobody would ever want to be in a relationship with me because I had two children with two different fathers. There were other uncalled for words he would say to me but these two things bothered me the most. I always felt like I had nowhere to go. Who would want me, I felt like damaged goods. Of course, later on in my life, I realized this was his way of controlling me and keeping me where I was.

The physical abuse was not only hurtful but humiliating too, depending on what he did. There was one instance where I had made pork chops one night for supper, and the next night we had a different type of pork and he complained about the supper. He was so upset when I argued back with him that he poured a cold bucket of dirty water right over my head (I had mopped the floor earlier that day and didn't dump the water yet). I felt like I was a piece of shit as far as he was concerned and I was so humiliated and my girls witnessed this act. As was said earlier, Carter was a very big muscular and tall man. He was very strong and I was very weak. And every time he fought with me he would leave and go drinking for a couple of days and then return home saying he was sorry. This became an unwelcome pattern.

I hid a lot of what was happening to me in our marriage and before our marriage as I was ashamed of what was going on. I was living in a constant nightmare filled with violence and fear. I watched as my husband would kick in our furniture. One time he kicked in the back of our new couch set. Brand new and he ripped it up. He smashed a beautiful, old-fashioned antique mirror who was from an old relative of mine to pieces. Anything that meant something to me was broken. But when I think of it today all of the furniture he destroyed and all the things he broke could have been me that he was taking his anger out on. In the big picture, I guess I was lucky that he didn't beat the shit out of me like he did everything else.

The only time it was peaceful was when he was gone on his binges. Then I would laugh and play with the girls and sometimes I would get the nice ladies upstairs to watch them while I went to work. My spirit inside was gone most of the time and I was so depressed half the time the only thing that kept me going were my two girls. They needed me and I needed them. But things were getting worse by the minute.

One time when Carter and I were arguing and he was having a drinking withdrawal, he became angry at me and he punched me in the face. My lip swelled up right away and he pulled back to hit me again, but then he must have seen the fear and surprise in my eyes and he walked away. I think I saw a look of remorse on his face. That was the one and only time he hit me in the face. Maybe it was because he always liked my face which was the thing he praised me on, well my face and my butt. Whatever!

I was thrown over a table and pinned up against a wall one time when my dad and step-mom were sleeping in the next room. I had gone out with my neighbors for her husband's birthday. While I was gone my dad and step-mom dropped by and decided to spend the night. I only had two drinks when I was out but because I came home with a big smile on my face he thought I was up to something. When I opened the door to come into the house he grabbed me and pushed me up against the kitchen wall, squeezed my face with one hand and told me to take the smile off my face or he would take it off for me. Then when I only smiled more he pretty much picked me up and threw me on top of the kitchen table. Let me tell you that hurt my back. The table was one of those old-fashioned chrome ones. Again, because my parents were in the next room and I knew he was freaking out, I had to calm him down and give him sex.

There were many fights and arguments over money being spent on booze and on his two- to three-day binges away from home. I knew he was cheating on me because I would hear rumors. I was actually hoping he would leave me for one of his affairs. Our fights would leave the house in a mess because he would throw things and knock things over. He was always threatening me. But I got very good at ducking and that would piss him off. I guess I had very good reflexes. Thank goodness because some items would hurt. Sometimes I would go lay down with the kids when he was out drinking and when he would come home I would lay quiet and hope he would just go to bed. But, he would always hunt me down and I would follow him to bed so he didn't start a fight or wake up the girls.

I found his friend sitting out in his car one time in the pouring rain. I thought that was strange because the guy had just called on the phone for Carter. I told him Carter would be home shortly and he said okay and hung up. I didn't know he was sitting out in his car at the time when he made the call. I put on my coat and ran out to his car and told him to come inside for a coffee. He kept saying no that's all right. I insisted he come in as it was cold outside. He finally agreed and came inside while I made him a coffee. As he drank his coffee I asked him why he didn't just come to the door and come in and wait, and he told me that Carter had told him and all his friends they were never to come to our place if he wasn't home. And if any of his friends called for him on the phone and he wasn't home they were to hang up and not talk to me. What? That is ridiculous! What the hell did he think was going to happen? I was so upset that he would even think that I would do anything behind his back with his friends. I was so disappointed in Carter and I told him he had no right to tell his friends something like that. How could he not trust me? I never gave him any reason what so ever not to trust me. And then it hit me, I wasn't the problem, he was the problem. What the hell was he doing when he was out of the house on his binges for two to three days? He was the guilty one!

It was shortly after this argument and one day after a terrible fight, that left the kids hiding in the big walk in closet, I sat crying and thinking about my children. Is this what I wanted my children to think was a happy marriage? I always thought if you were married you stayed no matter what. I had made vows in a church in front of witnesses and God. But, when I thought about my girls and what they were being subjected to, it made me so sad for them. This was around the time that I started to think it was time to get him to leave for good. I just had to come up with a safe plan. A couple days after this episode my friend Mary was having a bachelorette party at her house for our friend and she was making it a sleepover. She invited me and I wasn't sure about it. I didn't go out too often but I decided to go and Carter was to watch the girls and I would be home the next day. Mary's husband Justin went over to stay with Carter and the girls.

The next day, when I went home Carter was gone and Justin was watching the girls. I questioned him and he told me Carter went out drinking. "Are you fucking kidding me?" It hit me like a ton of bricks! "The one time I go out and he leaves our children to go drinking." I saw red and that was it. It was one thing for me to me abused but I would be dammed if my children were going to be treated like that. Carter didn't come home for a couple days but when he did something deep inside of me surfaced and I stood up to Carter and told him to leave. I had packed all of his clothes and put them outside on the step. Of course, he left for a few days thinking I would let him back. But every time he came back I would tell him it was over. I was never going to take him back. That worked for a couple times and then he started to get angry and tried to force me to take him back by saying things like, "No one will ever want to be with you, look at you, pretty face but no body." Or he would remind me again and say, "You have two girls with two different fathers, no one else will be with you." But that didn't work this time, and I knew it would never work again.

I got the courage over and over to keep saying it was over and once I made up my mind that was it. There was no turning back. Let me just say here that when I got married I said it was forever and I didn't believe in divorce. I believed that you stayed together and worked things out. I didn't just get up one morning and say I didn't want to be married. This was a very big decision for me and I didn't take it lightly. Some people would say to me, "You must be really happy you are out of that marriage," "You must be having much better days." Yes and no was my comment. Just because I made this decision of ending my marriage didn't mean it was easy. I still grieved for the marriage and the family we had. When I said my vows on my wedding day I meant them. But that all changed when I thought about living the way we were for the rest of my life and letting the girls think it was okay. I wanted my girls to have a chance at a good life and see that not every marriage was like ours. They deserved to see what I saw with my mom and dad, a loving and respectful marriage.

MY THOUGHTS

Let me first say it was a real struggle when I was writing this chapter. I had several nightmares and sleepless nights for a couple of reasons. First being my two daughters. I had started to write this book ten years ago, and back then I still wasn't ready to go through with it. I felt my children were still too young to know about the abuse. Today I am in a good place in my life and I am ready to tell my story. But the last thing I want to do is hurt my children or anyone else who is connected to this story. But something kept prompting me to carry on because it was important to let others know there is help out there.

I also have to say another reason I struggled with this was because of Carter. My dreams would be of him finding out that I was writing this book and telling the truth about the abuse and he would come and get me and hurt me. But I don't want to live in secret anymore and I want to share my story to let people know they are not alone. Also, as you will read further in the book, I came to a place in my life where I could forgive him and also forgive myself for my part in our relationship. I am also not writing this to disrespect my ex by any means that is why I am using fictional names. But I have a message to get out to others. I have been silent long enough. I am doing this for others to see that they are worth more than they know. We are all worthy of love and respect. We deserve a chance for happiness and to be the person we were always meant to be. So, amidst the sleepless nights, I would walk away from my story for a day or two and sometimes a week and ask God to be with me when I continued on. Just a side note: my strength and my courage come from having faith in God and I do not have to see God in order to believe he is with me.

My true hope for Carter is that he found happiness in his life. It has been about twenty-seven years since I last saw him and we were both very angry at that time. As I said earlier, I have forgiven him and myself for my part in our relationship. It took a lot of work but I was ready and I wanted to forgive him. Once you forgive someone you are free from the anger you keep inside but it doesn't mean you forget. I have a beautiful daughter because of Carter and I will always be grateful for her. I choose to look at the good that came out of our relationship and the knowledge I have learned along the way. But I also feel I need to give someone else hope and encouragement.

So why do we stay in relationships that are abusive? Why do we allow our children to witness the abuse? Even when we have put them to bed trust me they can hear what is going on. Why do we think it is our own fault that we are abused? Why, why, why? These are just a few of the questions I have heard from others who say they would never allow a man to control their lives. It's not that simple to answer especially when there are kids involved and you don't think very high of yourself. Sometimes you feel you are lucky enough to get someone who wants to be with you. And sometimes you feel trapped and where will you go. How will I get enough money to make sure we are okay? Sometimes we think maybe it will get better or maybe it isn't that bad. We beat ourselves up until we just think it is easier to stay where we are. We don't know how we will make it financially alone so we give up and take what we get. We stay in the marriage or relationship and become a victim. It is usually the fear of what will happen that keeps us frozen and unable to move forward. It is a very scary and sad place to be.

The only ones who leave are those of us who hit a breaking point and say enough is enough, I don't care how I will survive but I will and when I do I will be so proud of myself. Is it scary? Oh, heck, yes! It is scary and it is tough. But what a feeling of freedom and your self-esteem starts to get better (not right away though) and you believe that you are worth it and if you have children then you know you are giving them a great opportunity to live without abuse. But don't ever think it will be a walk in the park or a piece of cake for you will be just fooling yourself. Every situation is different. What may work for one person may not work for another person. Again, I must stress depending on the situation it is better to be dam well sure you have a good plan so someone doesn't get hurt. That is why I will not give advice. What I will do is try to let people who are being abused know that there are options and to give you encouragement. It is good to know we are not alone and people do care what happens to us and for me personally just knowing that God is with me is very comforting.

You would think it would be much easier to leave if there are no children but that's not true for everyone especially those of us who have low self-esteem. How do we end up with guys like this (or even woman who are abusive)? Well, a wise counselor told me once that I didn't pick these men, they actually picked me. I asked why and her answer was that these people looked for women who are kind and shy and very nice. Women who wouldn't say boo to anyone. That did describe me at the beginning of my relationship. Add drinking a lot at the beginning to that list and I am your gal.

You know we all have a voice and we all have choices. When you are in the middle of the abuse you do not see that clearly. I became very quiet and secretive about my abuse until the very end when I decided to get out of the marriage for the sake of my girls. Although I left for the sake of my girls I also got out because I didn't like the person I was becoming. Sometimes when the fights were going on I wanted to hurt him like he hurt me and that scared me. I was not brought up to hurt anybody and deep inside I did not want to hurt Carter. Remember when I hit Carter with a piece of wood? That bothered me for a long time even though I was protecting myself. I had to get out before one of us was seriously hurt. It's not an easy road but it is possible.

CHAPTER 8

In this chapter, I want to give you a little information on the statistics in Canada and the United States concerning abused women. I went on the internet and found a few websites that were very informative on this horrible existing subject and that is where I retrieved by sources.

The first website I found was from the BWSS which stands for Battered Women's Support Services/The Violence Stops Here. Did you know that globally the most common form of violence experienced by woman is physical violence inflicted by their intimate partner? An intimate partner is basically a spouse or boyfriend you are intimate with. On average, every six days a woman in Canada is killed by her intimate partner. Woman aged twenty-five to thirty-four years old are three times more likely to be physically or sexually assaulted by their spouse than those aged forty-five and older. And, it is so sad that every year in Canada an estimated 362,000 children witness or experience family violence.

I found out more information on the website from the Canadian Women's Foundation. This amazing group fund more than 450 emergency shelters across Canada. They also help woman to rebuild their lives after escaping violence through interest free loans and other programs. And thankfully they fund counseling for children who have witnessed violence to help them heal and prevent them from becoming victims or abusers themselves. I was shocked to hear that 83 percent of all police-reported domestic assaults are against women.

What does the Canadian Women's Foundation say about moving women out of violence? They say to learn about emergency services in your community, such as your local women's shelter or sexual assault center. Search online or consult the front pages of your telephone directory.

Something interesting that I found was Statistics Canada did a survey of women over the age of eighteen across the country for "Violence against Women." The survey was one time only. They found that half of all Canadian women have experienced physical or sexual abuse. Also, another Statistics Canada study found out more than 3,300 women stay in shelters on a given night to escape abuse. This was based on surveys filled out by most of the approximately six hundred residential shelter facilities in Canada.

According to the Native Women's Association of Canada, two to three aboriginal women are reported missing or murdered each month, and the suspected numbers that go unreported are even higher. In the Canadian Woman's Foundation, it was reported that as of 2010 there were 582 known cases of missing or murdered aboriginal women in Canada. In 2011, from the eighty-nine police-reported spousal homicides, seventy-six of the victims (85 percent) were women. I was so shocked to hear all these numbers. One number is too many! This is so devastating. And just two weeks after I wrote this information I saw on the news that the Liberals are going to lead an investigation into the missing and murdered indigenous women. The RCMP found in 2014 nearly 1,200 documented cases of missing and murdered aboriginal women and girls between 1980 and 2012, a number that exceeded previous public estimates. What the hell is going on? Why wasn't this looked into many years ago? These numbers are horrible! The news said the liberals are starting with what they call Phase 1 which is where a special group of selected ministers are to spend the next two months consulting with families of missing, murdered indigenous women in Ottawa (August 2016). Phase 2 will be in the spring of 2017 and it will be the actual inquiry itself. Hopefully by the time you read this there will be answers given to our indigenous families. Thank you to those who are finally looking into this very sad and disgusting affair.

In the United States, from the National Domestic Violence Hotline website, I found the statistics about the abuse on women. They said their statistics have been compiled from various sources. On average, twenty-four people per minute are victims of rape, physical violence, or stalking by an intimate partner in the United States, more than twelve million women and men over the course of a year. They also reported that one in four women and one in seven men aged eighteen and older were victims of severe physical violence by an intimate partner. From 1994 to 2010, four in five victims of intimate partner violence were female.

So why don't we just leave? As I said earlier it is not that simple. I spoke about fear of what will happen (what would my husband do to me) and low self-esteem as my reasons. But there are more reasons we are afraid to leave such as: Believing abuse is normal, embarrassment or shame, still loving your partner, cultural/religious reasons, language barriers/immigration status, lack of money, and disability (being physically dependent on their abusive partner). Whatever the reasons, you can believe they are real. So what can we do to help? The Canadian Women's Foundation did suggest the following ways we can help:

If someone is in immediate danger and you know this for sure call 911 or the emergency number in your community.

Put her safety first. Never talk to anyone about abuse in front of their suspected abuser. Unless she specifically asks for it, never give her materials about domestic abuse and never leave information through voice messages or emails that might be discovered by her abuser. However, abuse thrives in secrecy, so speak up if you can do so safely.

If she wants to talk, listen. If she doesn't, simply tell her she does not deserve to be harmed and that you are concerned for her safety. Ask her if there is anything you can do to help, but don't offer to do anything that makes you uncomfortable or feels unsafe.

If she decides to stay in the relationship, try not to judge her. Remember, leaving an abuser can be extremely dangerous. Sometimes, the most valuable thing you can offer a woman who is being abused is your respect.

CHAPTER 9

At the time I kicked Carter out of the apartment, I had a tape of Whitney Houston's music and I played this one song over and over. The song was very powerful for me and those words gave me courage to keep going. There were a lot of good lyrics in this song but there were several lines that really stood out for me. They were: "I believe the children are our future, teach them well and let them lead the way, show them all the beauty they possess inside" and "Because the greatest love of all is happening to me, learning to love myself, it is the greatest love of all." Every time I heard these words I would tell myself that my children and I deserved better. I had never thought about loving myself. It was such a new idea for me. Also at this time in my life I still had trouble believing I was loved by God because I felt I wasn't good enough to be loved.

Carter didn't make it easy for me though. He didn't give up. He had married me for life and that was it. His friends would call to talk me into giving him another chance but I would politely tell them that I was done with the abuse. He made it hard for me to go to work because he would tell me he was going to come there and hurt me.

I started to lose more and more weight and couldn't sleep. My friends across the road were worried about me. They would get their daughter to watch my girls and have me over for a game of cards or just a cup of coffee and chat.

One night when I was there we were playing cards and my friend's nephew was there playing cards with us. We hit it off and it felt good to be with my friends if only for a little while to take my mind off of my messed-up life. Their nephew had stuff going on in his life too and we became friends and talked to each other whenever we saw each other about our dilemmas. One night he came over to my house and we played cards and talked. The reason he came to my house was to tell me he was moving away to get work and asked me if I would write him. I said, "Yes, of course. I will miss you." Then he kissed me and I realized he liked me. We kissed for a few moments then I stopped him and said, "That is all I can give you right now." He was okay with that and we said good-bye. I was to see him off a few days later but I was unable to make it. I was sad to see him go but I knew I had too much on my plate to be in another relationship.

I wish I could say things were getting easier after that but they weren't. I eventually had to leave the home I had come to love. Carter would not let me be alone or happy.

He would come to my house and start fighting with me, I would tell him I was going to call the police and have him arrested and he would pull the phone out of the wall. He would try different tactics to get me to take him back and I wouldn't give in. I just wanted to be alone with my girls. I didn't want to be with anyone just myself. I had enough and I needed to find myself. But Carter would not leave me alone. If he couldn't be with me then nobody could. One time when he came over we fought and then he involved Charlie and whispered something in her ear. The next thing I knew they both got down on their knees and begged me to let daddy come back and I was livid! I told Charlie to get up off the floor and hugged her and told her to go into her room. I proceeded to tell Carter to never use the girls to plead for him ever again. He got mad and pushed me and I glanced over at the block of knives that were on the counter and for one insane moment I thought if I stabbed him this could all be over. Then I snapped out of it and told him to leave. He left and I was so thankful. I broke down and cried and asked God to help me.

Another time Carter came to the house and my best friend Mary was at the house. He kept harassing me to take him back and I kept telling him no. I eventually started screaming at him and it wasn't pretty. I had enough and I grabbed the closest thing to me which was a small plant and I shoved it in his face. I actually started to laugh and my friend was just standing there in shock and then he got up and pushed me into the big picture window. I lost my balance, but I stood there and wouldn't back down. He was embarrassed and humiliated and I didn't care at the time. I was done, and I mean done! When I tried to talk to him nicely I never got anywhere and when he started saying rude things to me this time I lost it and made myself look like a crazy woman. And you know what I was a crazy woman at the time. I didn't know if I was coming or going and he would not stop coming to my house and push me and push me to take him back. So, I lashed out at him and it felt good to push that plant with all its dirt in his face. Of course, later on in the day, I felt bad but not at the time.

I knew now that I couldn't live in my home anymore. It was time to leave and keep my girls and me safe. I asked my friends/ neighbors across the road if I could keep some of my stuff in their basement until I got a place of my own and they were more than happy to help me. Just a side note, I had received a good tax credit back that year and I had bought a beautiful heavy wooden bedroom suite from my friend's sister Tatiana as her and her family were moving. It was beautiful. It had a big long dresser, two side tables, one tallboy dresser and the bed had four beautiful, thick bedposts and headboard. It was quite new and I was so proud to have something nice again that I paid for by myself. So, my neighbors were awesome to keep this bedroom set and all the rest of my stuff in their basement for a while.

I moved in with my adopted parents and they helped me with the girls. I had to quit my job as I was living in fear of my life. I went to the doctor and he put me on antidepressants. I did not want to go on them but I was such a mess I needed help. I was on them for two weeks and I was worse. All I wanted to do was sleep and I was so depressed I couldn't even take care of my girls. My adopted parents were worried as I was not able to function. My adopted sister Mary talked me into going to the doctor about these pills and he put me on another pill. I was not happy about the pills at all but they were better than the first batch. I went to live with Mary and her husband Justin again and eventually I was able to function and take care of my girls the best I could. Mary and Justin were so good to the girls. She was and always will be a blessing to me.

During these weeks of depression, I received letters from my guy friend (my neighbor's nephew). He would call me when he could and we would talk about our lives. He was coming to visit his family and wanted me to come and see him if I could while he was here. It was only a short visit to pick up more of his stuff and then he was back to work. I decided to go and see him at his brother's house (my old neighbors). It was great to see him. We went downstairs in his niece's room so we could have privacy and talk about what I was going through. Then he held me and told me everything would be all right. The next thing I know we are making love. This was not planned, it just happened. I needed to be held and told I was beautiful and that everything would be okay.

Eventually we just sat and talked. Then all of a sudden, his niece flew into the room and tells us Carter was walking up their driveway.

"What? Are you freaking kidding me?"

Well, what are the chances of that? Pretty good, apparently! We hid in the big closet for what seemed like forever because we both knew what would happen if he saw us together. An hour or so later, his niece came down and said he was gone. I would not come out of that room until an hour after that as I was scared to death. My friends said he just wanted to see how they were and stopped by to say hello. What? I was so spooked I thought I would throw up. My friend held me while I cried.

Eventually my friend had left and I felt so alone. It was nice to have a male friend who would listen to my problems and care so much about what would happen to me and my girls. I knew in my heart I was starting to fall for him. But I really didn't know much about him. I had to let go and just get my life together as best I could. He was living far away and the chance of us being together was next to impossible. So, I tried so hard to make things work. I felt like I was such a failure and a burden to my adopted sister Mary. She was so good to us and I was so appreciative for her huge help to us. But I was still afraid that Carter was going to win this battle and I was losing more weight and not eating very well. I was a mess. I couldn't go to work because I lived in fear every day. I didn't know if I was coming or going. I tried praying and praying but I felt my prayers were not being heard. And if they were I wouldn't have noticed as I was so consumed with fear. But I know today without a doubt that God was with me every step of the way. I know today that he carried me.

Speaking of God carrying me through this time in my life, I would like to share with you my most favorite poem of all time, Footprints. I cried the first time I ever read this poem.

One night a man had a dream. He dreamed he was walking along the beach with the LORD. Across the sky flashed scenes from his life. For each scene, he noticed two sets of footprints in the sand; one belonged to him, and the other to the LORD.

When the last scene of his life flashed before him, he looked back at the footprints in the sand. He noticed that many times along the path of his life there was only one set of footprints. He also noticed that it happened at the very lowest and saddest times in his life.

This really bothered him and he questioned the LORD about it. "Lord, you said that once I

*decided to follow you, you'd walk with me all
the way. But I have noticed that during the
most troublesome times in my life, there is only
one set of footprints. I don't understand why
when I needed you most you would leave me."*

*The LORD replied, "My precious, precious
child, I love you and I would never leave you.
During your times of trial and suffering, when
you see only one set of footprints, it was then
that I carried you."*

The author to this poem has always been known as "Unknown Author" but the author was found out to be Mary Stevenson who wrote it in 1939.

I finally went to my doctor again and we had a long talk. I told him I had to leave my home that I loved so much and my job as I was afraid Carter would come there and hurt me (as he kept threatening me that he would). I told him I was living in fear. My doctor asked me if I knew anyone that lived outside of our province where I could go live for a while and get on my feet and get counseling. I told him my sister Rose lived in another province but was living in a College dorm as she was studying to become a nurse. Then I told him one of my adopted sisters had moved to another province with her family and maybe I could go there. But I didn't want to leave my home and my family and the kid's family. Why should I be the one to leave my town? I started to get angry and he settled me down. He told me it didn't have to be forever. I could just go live with my adopted sister for six months or so or even get an apartment through welfare's help and at least get away and get on my feet. At least I would have family there. And maybe get some counseling which would help me to get stronger.

So I went home and shared the doctor's advice with my adopted family. They thought it was a great idea. We called my adopted sister

Lindsay and she said I was definitely welcome to come there for a while. But this would have to be kept so quiet that only my closest family members would be told. If word got out about my leaving with the girls all hell would break loose and then where would I be. I was still not convinced that I should leave my home and city, but everyone thought it was a good idea and told me it would be a good thing to get away for a while. I was pissed off that I had to leave my home and family because Carter would not let me be. I never ever thought about leaving because I never thought it was an option. Now it was an option and I had a very big decision to make. How could I take my children from their home and their family? Was this a good idea? I did not want to leave and I struggled with this decision but it was as if I was being led to leave. And of course being told by my doctor (who I trusted and looked up to) that I should leave was the main reason I thought I was doing the right thing by leaving.

My stomach was sick the day we waited for the train to leave. I envisioned Carter showing up and it filled me with fear. With a heavy heart, we left on the train. My adopted sister/best friend Mary came with me so I wouldn't be alone and then she was going to come back by herself a few days later. She was my rock during that train ride. But even on the train I was still not sure I was doing the right thing but the one thing I did know for sure was that I didn't want my girls to be exposed to a life of abuse anymore. I did what I thought was best for my girls and myself. It took a lot of courage, but eventually I decided this was a good decision to leave my city and live with Lindsay and her family until I got a place of my own. I was determined to get a place of my own and just breathe again. Surely there will be light at the end of this tunnel.

Just before we left to go to live with Lindsay, I sent my guy friend a letter and he called me. He was excited I was going away and said he would meet me at the train station and stay with us for two weeks and then go back to work where he lived then. He was living six hours away from where I was going. I was happy he would do this for me and my girls. When we got off the train we were met by him and when I saw him I could see sadness in his eyes at how I looked. I was so thin and my eyes were full of fear. But he put on a brave face and said he was glad we were there and things would be okay. That was it for me I latched right on to him and didn't let go. As I said earlier, he was to stay for two weeks and go back to his new home. I was going to look for an apartment where I was because I did not want my girls taken away from their aunt and uncle and their cousins. Eventually if things worked out between me and my friend he could move this way and try to get a job here. At least my girls would have some family around them. So I started looking in the paper right away, but I was also still in a depressed state so while my girls played with their cousins I would cry on the shoulder of my new boyfriend Adam. I am not proud of that time when I was so fixated on my new love but I was not in a good state. I needed his shoulders to cry on and I needed his strength to get me through. One thing I knew for certain was that I had no intention of leaving my adopted sisters city. I felt safe for the two weeks I was there.

Then all hell breaks loose! Lindsay got a call from her sister Mary and she told us Carter was on his way to this province because someone had told him where I was and that I was living with my adopted sister Lindsay and her family. Carter was on his way and no one was going to stop him and he was pissed that I took his children away from him. I was devastated and I was freaking out. It took everyone around me to keep me calm. The next thing I know we are on a train heading to a small city in this province six hours away but close to where my sister Rose lived which was just forty-five minutes away. It took no convincing at all to go there as I was scared to death. I could finally see my sister and I could hide myself and the girls away from Carter. He did show up at Lindsay's house and they would not tell him where I went. I believe someone from my hometown did tell him what area I headed to as he ended up in a big city close to the small city I went to. He moved to that city shortly after that episode and he was only an hour away from me. So I began the next adventure in my life and it was quite a ride.

MY THOUGHTS

Sometimes in our lives we make choices and we question those choices but as dark as the cloud was that was following me I had to have faith that I was doing the right thing for myself and my children. Running was not easy for me. The adrenaline I had just knowing that I was getting further and further away from everyone and everything I knew was devastating to me. But I had to look at the big picture and believe in my heart and soul that we would be okay. I had to trust that the man I was running with would keep us safe and that my choice to run was okay by God.

I've heard it said that "faith makes things possible…not easy."

CHAPTER 10

My daughters and I stayed with Adam and his sister Katie and family in a small town just outside another city. We stayed there for the weekend and then went into another city (just a half hour from where Adam lived). My girls and I went directly to the welfare office and had a meeting with a nice man who said he would help me find an apartment. For three days, a nice lady I had never met had paid for my girls and I to stay in a hotel and each day the social worker would take us around looking for an apartment. We found an apartment on the second day and the welfare workers helped me get used furniture and beds for the girls and me. I was so overwhelmed with thankfulness for these people who helped us. Also, I was still on medication at this time but once I was settled into this apartment I decided it was time to get off them. And so I got off the medication. It was tough but I did it. The only thing I couldn't get rid of was that dam cloud that followed me.

The apartment we lived in was in a three-story building. Once we got settled, I phoned home to my neighbors and said I was ready to get my furniture and other things shipped up to my new place. My adopted dad had a truck and he was going to drive my stuff up to his daughter Lindsay's and then I would get it from there. My neighbors hated to tell me this but Carter had come over to their house as he found out that all my stuff was there. Someone kept telling him whatever he needed to know and that is why I didn't give anyone our new address until I felt it was safe. And so he took everything and sold it. I lost things that meant a lot to me. But in the big picture, my girls and I were safe. So as angry as I was at first, I let it go because they were just material things. I was more concerned about whether or not Carter would find us. I lived in fear every day for at least a year that he would find us and hurt me.

We started off in a basement apartment. I kept to myself most of the time. I did meet a nice girl who lived down the hall and she was a single parent too. Her name was Kaitlyn. We became friends and would be each other's cheer leader. She taught me how to cook certain things and I admired her for her independence. My girls would play with her daughter and they became friends. Across the hall from us lived a young couple with two young girls. I could tell they were having problems by the arguments I could hear them having. I would see her and her two girls every now and then and she was very friendly. We were very cordial to each other but her husband was not someone I wanted to be friends with. When Adam would come to stay sometimes, he would meet him in the hall and he would invite Adam to go to his apartment for a drink. That would have been all right but he was a scary guy and I really had a bad feeling around him. I didn't trust him at all. Adam eventually told me he didn't want anything to do with him because he did some really strong drugs and talked about doing crazy things. This neighbor even talked about having a foursome and I said, "Hell, no, that is not happening." I started being very nervous around him and found myself wanting to get away from them. I asked the manager of the building if I could move up to another apartment as soon as one came up and several months later I was living on the second floor. I felt a lot better that I didn't have to listen to the arguments that were going on across the hall.

I was in a state of constant fear for the first year we were there. One night the ambulance came to our building and the young woman who lived downstairs with the two young girls and husband had an overdose. I still don't know if the police got the right story about what happened but the young lady died that night. I felt so sick to my stomach. She was leaving behind two small girls with her husband. I had to get out of that building. We kept looking for something but there was nothing in my price range. So, we had to stay there longer but at least Adam was staying with us a bit more which made me feel safer. We started going camping almost every weekend just to get away from the apartment. We would have so much fun camping with the girls and they loved sitting at the fire and having marshmallows and hotdogs. Camping was a release for all of us and we did this for many years of our relationship.

The good thing about being where we were in this city was that I got to see my sister. She would come to visit whenever she could. When she graduated from nursing school I was so proud of her. I went to her graduation and I was so happy for her. I looked up to her all the time even though I was and am taller than her. She made something of herself and she was an inspiration to me. I could always depend on her.

Another good thing while I lived in this city was that my adopted sister Lindsay's husband had a sister and family that were moving just about fifteen minutes or so from where we lived. It was Lindsay who called Daniels sister Tatiana to tell her I was living here and maybe she could be there for me. Tatiana got in touch with me and the next thing you know she and her family visits me and my family. Tatiana was the one who sold me that beautiful bedroom set. She and her husband had two children (a boy and girl) named Christopher and Mel (Mel was short for Melanie). What were the odds that she and her family would move up this way and become our family? We become and still are today the best of friends. Tat was always there for me to talk to and always came to visit and hang out. It felt good to have family around. My girls now had two cousins to visit. They all got along really well and we spent a lot of time together.

Going back to when the girls and I first came up here and we stayed with Adam's sister Katie and her husband Richard for that first weekend. They had a young son of four whose name was Scott and a baby boy named Mark who was in the hospital since he was born. The little guy was born with a heart defect and would be in the hospital about eight months. I went to see him with Katie at the hospital and he was so beautiful. It broke my heart to see him all hooked up to so much equipment and so I just looked into his big dark brown eyes. I fell in love with him the moment I saw him.

My heart went out to Katie and Richard as they were going through hell waiting for their little boy to be able to come home with them. They would go back and forth to the hospital (which was an hour away) and it took a lot out of them physically but the emotional impact was very hard on them. It was hard to watch them go through this. We spent a lot of time with them. We tried our best to be as supportive as we could. When Mark finally came home it filled their home with so much joy but it also was hard on them. Mark had to learn how to drink from a bottle as he was used to being fed by a tube. It was very hard for Katie as Mark didn't want the bottle and he was eight months old. We all helped out as much as we could. I tried feeding him the bottle once in a while and I felt so bad that he wouldn't eat for me. Even though he was eight months old it was like he was a new born as he had to learn everything new now. It took a lot of patience but Katie and Richard did very well at teaching Mark his new way of life. Eventually Mark was well on his way to being a healthy little toddler walking talking and he always had a huge smile on his face. He could brighten your day in a heartbeat when you were having a bad day. He was so inspirational to all of us. He was a true survivor and we all adored him deeply. Mark was my hero and we will talk more about Mark later in my story.

My first job in this small city was for a cleaning company. The owner was a woman and I always admired her as she was a strong woman and owned her own company. I cleaned houses with her for a year. I didn't have a car at that time so she would always pick me up. We cleaned several houses just outside the city and they were big beautiful homes. Some were small and quaint. But, no matter the size of the home I took pride in my work. The only thing that I didn't like was the cleaning of the floors on my knees. And even though I really liked the woman I worked for I decided cleaning houses was not good for my knees. I looked high and low and finally found a job at a restaurant. My mode of transportation then was the bus. It was a high-class restaurant where you wore white dress shirts and black pants or black skirts. It was owned by two brothers and sometimes it was frustrating as one would tell you one thing and the other would change it. I only stayed there for three months as it was just too high classed for my taste and the brothers were hard to work for. I was very lucky getting jobs and so my next job was at a drugstore. I liked working there. It was in the downtown mall and it was always busy. I was a cashier but also would work the floor when needed. It was a nine-to-five job Monday to Friday. I met a lot of people there and started to fit in to the city.

Shortly after I got this job, Adam proposed to me. It felt good to have a ring on my finger and to know that he was serious about us being together. And shortly after we got engaged we moved to another area of town into a townhouse and I was happy to be out of the apartment and because we had more room and the girls could have their own bedrooms. They also made a lot of friends and liked the area we were in. And remember Kaitlyn the first friend I had made at the first apartment we lived in? She was now living in these townhouses and she was the one who got me to go there and apply for a unit. I felt safe there and Adam was living with us full-time now.

I became friends with another amazing woman who lived in the townhouses where I lived. Her name was Marion and she was a great influence on me and I was thrilled to learn that she was born and raised in the same province as me. She was a very smart and talented woman and we hit it off quite well. I met her through my first friend Kaitlyn and we all hung out together for a lot of good years. We shared many stories together and looked out for each other. She was a god send to me as she was so positive and upbeat and a joy to be around. I was very lucky to have made the friends I had made. I not only had my best friend Tat who lived in the next city (only ten minutes away) but I also had Kaitlyn and Marion living just doors away from me. It made living there so much easier when you had friends.

But sadly things started to change once Adam and I were living together full-time, and not for the better. I noticed that Adam actually drank a lot by himself. He was a quiet guy normally but when he had a few in him he would open up. It wasn't too long before Adam started staying late at his job and drinking with the guys. Then he would drive home. That would just piss me off. I would have dinner ready and by the time he got to eat it would be dried up and cold. I would get so frustrated because I wanted him to get a good dinner as he worked a hard physical job (not that I cooked amazing meals, our budget was very limited). But that didn't seem to bother him. He enjoyed staying after work to drink with his coworkers and it didn't change. I was really bothered the most by the drinking and driving home. That was unacceptable. My children would see him come home like that. Whether they knew he was drinking or not I don't know. But I knew and it was really bothering me. Sometimes he would stay up all night at the table on the weekend and drink until he fell asleep. Another thing I noticed was when he was loaded he would flirt with whoever was around at the time. He chalked it up to being friendly and said I had nothing to worry about. I didn't like what was happening but it was better than being abused. Or so I thought.

Shortly after we moved into the townhouse Adam's cousin and wife (Roger and Kathy) came to our province and moved about twenty-five minutes away from us in another city. This was so good for Adam to have one of his cousins here. They became good friends and Kathy became a really good friend to me. She was a beautiful person inside and out. We laughed a lot together and we spent a fair amount of time together on the weekends. Once we got closer I trusted her completely and would open up to her about Adam's drinking. It was good to have so many wonderful women that I could talk to.

I hate to say this, but just when I think, "Okay, I have a really good guy this time and I am very lucky," and I think, "It's amazing that he accepts me even though I have two daughters," "Yes, I am pretty lucky," "He is a great guy!" "Okay he may have a drinking problem but he isn't abusive." I mean, after all, my nickname from him is "Fancy Face." Then something happens that makes you sink into a hole again and cry out, "Are you messing with me?" Yup, that's what happened! Adam got a phone call from his brother's wife (not unusual) but the conversation was one of panic. You see, Adam's brother and wife and two children lived in the same apartment building we had lived in before we moved to the townhouse. They had lived in the same town as Adam when he first moved here. Not a big deal. It was great to have his brother here. Then his brother and wife decided to move back to their home in the east coast. But you see, while Adam was sending me letters and calling me all the time (before I moved here) he had an affair with his brother's wife. Oh, yeah, it happened, and now his brother's wife was calling Adam in a panic because she had told his brother the truth about their affair and his brother was on his way up to our province to have a chat with him. And not only was his brother pissed off at Adam for the affair, but shortly after that his wife got pregnant with their second child and now Adam's brother was questioning whether or not his son was actually his! Again I said, "Are you fucking kidding me? Wow, this is a lot to swallow! What the hell do I have stamped on my forehead, 'Pick me, I'm stupid'?" Adam had no other choice than to tell me; otherwise, I was going to hear it from his brother and that would not go over well. So, Adam told me and I was devastated. I could not believe that Adam would ever put himself in this position with his own brother's wife. I had to leave the house for a while and think this through. He told me he was disgusted with himself but he had gotten drunk and slept with her a couple times. Okay, one time is a mistake, two times is asking for trouble and obviously he knew what he was doing! I didn't know what to do. I was so disappointed in him and I felt stuck with what to do. I felt bad for his brother and I was pissed off at his wife. I went to see Adam's cousin's wife Kathy and talked to her for several hours until I finally calmed down. I went back home to him and told him he would have to give me some time to adjust to this news and I would have to make a decision if I wanted to let this go and move through it or break up with him. He begged me not to break up with him but I still needed time to process this news. We may have been living in the same house but I could not look at him the same way.

His brother arrived and I thought he was going to kill Adam or at least punch him out. That didn't happen. You see, his brother loved his younger brother and knew that he had a hard childhood and there was no actual fistfight but there were a few days of giving it to Adam with words. I just let them figure it out and his brother stayed for two weeks with us and then went back home to his wife. They worked it out and stayed together which was their business and not for me to decide. It took me a while before I could warm up to Adam again but I loved him and decided to keep it in the past and move beyond it. As for his brother's wife, she still insisted that their son was not Adam's son. How they ever came to that conclusion I really don't know but I believe her.

Shortly after this happened, Adam, the girls, and I traveled out east to my brother Brad's house as he was getting married to a really great girl. I did not know her very well but I liked her the moment I met her. Her name was Christine. Their wedding was beautiful. My sister Rose and I were to sing at their wedding. Well, I was so nervous I kept moving my leg and I sang very low. Rose sang louder than I did and I felt so bad that I wasn't singing the way I should have but I was so nervous. I didn't have much self-esteem and I was very self-conscious about singing in front of people. But we got through it and it actually got taped by one of Brad's friends. When I asked my brother how it turned out a couple years later he said, "Oh, pretty good." He said this with a clown smile on his face that tells me it was pretty funny. He said that I look scared and I am singing low and my sister Rose is standing tall with her head up and proud as a peacock and singing her heart out. He said the singing was good but we looked funny. At least that is what I got from our conversation. I started laughing and pictured me and my sister up there. I never did get to see the tape but one day I will and there will be a great big smile on my face. Just the fact that my sister and I did this together for our brother and his bride, it will always be a special memory of how much the three of us loved each other.

I also remember when my sister Rose got married. She and her husband Roger got married in a small church and had the reception on a boat at a marina in a big city and it was beautiful. Rose asked my two daughters to sing at their wedding "All Things Bright and Beautiful." My girls practiced this song over and over. I was so proud of them. Now both my brother and sister were married and I couldn't be happier with the spouses they chose. I was a happy sister-in-law and proud of my siblings.

I guess seeing my siblings married stirred up some feelings in me and it was around this time I thought since I was engaged I should get my divorce. It took a lot for me to come to that decision but I knew I had to do it sooner or later. This meant I would have to see Carter after not seeing him for a couple of years. But, I was feeling stronger emotionally (mostly because I was keeping all my fears and sadness tucked way down inside). So, I started the search for a lawyer. I knew I didn't make enough money to hire one on my own so I checked with the social services and they directed me to a place for legal assistance where I could get help. This company was paid through the government and they were happy to help me out. The first lawyer I had was a male which was good but after my first meeting with him I felt he was not the guy for me (not because he was a male but because he didn't make me feel like he was on my side). I got the courage to speak up to the company and told them how I felt and they sent me to a female lawyer next. I wasn't sure if she would be any better but I went to meet with her. I was very nervous about this whole ordeal. Just the thought of having to find and face Carter was enough to make me feel ill. I was still afraid of him. I knew he had moved up my way and was only an hour away from me but I was not exactly sure where.

I am happy to say this female lawyer made me feel right at home. She told me she would do everything she could to find him and get the ball rolling. She was very empathetic to my situation and made it clear that I was to tell her the truth and we would get along just fine. She was amazing. Her secretary said to me, "Don't you worry, she will make you look like Princess Diana." This made me laugh and I knew I was in the right place. She was a spit fire in the courtroom but she was very kind and treated me with a lot of respect.

As she was searching for my husband, I waited for her to call me when she found him and was having him served with papers for my divorce. In the meantime, I had gone down to my hometown on vacation with Adam and the girls. I was so excited to see all my family and friends. I missed my family so much. We visited so many people and had a wonderful time. While I was there I also visited one of my cousins and she opened up to me about what happened to her on my wedding day. She was one of my bridesmaids in my wedding and she was also about seven months pregnant at my wedding. She finally got the courage to tell me that while she was sitting with everyone at one of the tables at our dance she was molested by Carter's father. He reached under the table and grabbed her in the crotch! I was devastated and felt so bad for her. All this time she kept it silent from me and I never ever guessed he would do that to anyone else. But I was very naïve to think that he had never grabbed anyone else besides me. Maybe this was something he did whenever he was drinking and had the chance, I don't know. But I felt sick to my stomach knowing this happened to my cousin and especially while she was pregnant. And then I remembered that one time when I was sitting with Carter and another girl in the back seat of a cab going to the same party (Carter had been drinking), she looked over at me and told me to ask my husband to stop touching her. Whenever I was looking out the window, he would reach over and touch her. I told her to tell him herself but I just didn't want to deal with it at the time. And then I thought about Carter and the night he went out to get me ice cream and didn't come back because he went to a party and forced his way in by grabbing the poor girl's breasts and pushing his way through. It was incredible how much he was like his father. I had heard rumors after I had moved away with the girls (from Mary's aunt who lived across from Carters family when they were young) that his father used to throw furniture out the window and beat his mom. How horrible for Carter and his siblings to witness this as children. And how sad it was that Carter would grow up in that abusive environment. I now saw a different side of Carter and I felt empathy for him, but I also knew that he was who he was and I could not trust him. If he was still drinking the way he used to, then there was still a problem and I had to protect my children. Not that I believed he would ever hurt them but I was concerned that if he drank he may put them in harm's way somehow.

When it came time to leave my hometown, I cried and cried but I knew I would be back again the next year so I left knowing I was coming back. There were so many memories, good and bad. But I was also afraid someone from my past who knew Carter might see me and tell him I had been there. It was hard to leave but I was making a home for myself and the girls and I was excited to get back before someone I didn't want to see had seen me. The following weekend after we got back Adam decided to go fishing a couple hours away with a couple friends and his brother-in-law. I decided to take a drive to his sister's house and visit with her (which was a good thirty-five to forty minutes away). The kids didn't want to come with me as they were playing with my neighbor/friend Kaitlyn's daughter and they were happy to stay at my neighbor's house while I was gone. It was just another beautiful day and I played my music in the car and just felt good after our visit to my family. If it wasn't for that cloud that always seemed to follow me my life was going okay.

Well, soon my day was shot to hell. I got a call from Kaitlyn not an hour later at Adam's sisters house. She sounded very upset and didn't know how to tell me that my husband was in our neighborhood and recognized my oldest daughter. He went up to her and asked her who she was and where was her mother. My neighbor proceeded to tell me that she flew out of the house and asked who the man was my daughter was talking to. My daughter said "I think it's my dad." My neighbor immediately got the girls in the house and she called the police. I had always told her if a big man ever comes to her door looking for me and my girls to immediately call the police. I was in shock when she was talking to me. All I could think of was getting back to my girls. It was like I was having an out of body experience. I knew what she was saying but I was too stunned to talk to her. My heart was beating fast and I couldn't breathe. I kept thinking Carter was going to pay me back and take my girls away. I quickly explained the situation to Katie and then I jumped in my car and drove like a maniac. I was driving so fast but I had to get to my girls. I was devastated this was happening. I made it home in less time than normal. When I got there, I saw three cop cars and two policemen talking to my husband and a friend of his that I recognized. Thank goodness it was a good, decent friend who was with him. I parked my car and flew out of it like a mad woman.

I went right up to my husband and looked him in the eye and said, "What the hell do you think you are doing? You are not taking my children!" I said a few other things and I used the *fuck* word a couple times. I wasn't very ladylike but I was a mad woman when it came to the safety of my girls. The policeman calmed me down and Carter said calmly, "You took my girls away from me and I haven't seen them for a couple of years. How could you do this to me?"

I told him he made me leave my home and he was the reason I left. I would still be there if he would have left me alone. But he made me look like the bad guy and so I shot back at him, "And apparently you slept with a friend of mine when we were still together." He just stood there and smiled.

The policeman said, "Okay, this isn't the time or place so let's decide what we are going to do here."

Carter said he was going to get a lawyer so he could see his kids. The policeman told him not to come back to my place until it was settled by the courts.

After he left with his friend who drove him there, I was scared to stay at my house. The one policeman asked me if I had a place to go for the night and I said yes back to my boyfriend's sister's house. They followed me all the way there and made sure I was safe and not followed. I felt so sick to my stomach. All I could think of was my girls and how they would have to go with Carter on outings. And then I thought of how Carter would think that I had an affair with Adam (he knew Adam was the guy from next door from our old house) and moved here with Adam. He would tell people that I was probably having an affair the whole time with Adam while Carter was married to me. I knew this wasn't true but Carter didn't. But I didn't have time to obsess about all the things that made me look bad as there was so much to think of for me to do. First thing Monday I would call my lawyer and tell her he found us. All I did was cry until Adam came home. He was shocked and got a baseball bat from his brother-in-law and put it beside our bed just in case there was any violence. He never told me about getting the baseball bat. I just found it there one day. I think I actually laughed and he said it wasn't funny. He wasn't taking any chances. I guess he was more afraid of what might happen to him if Carter decided to go after him. I wouldn't blame him. Carter was intimidating to say the least. But, I must say he was on his best behavior in front of the police which I was glad to see. The friend he was with was a brother of one of his friends back home. I always liked this guy, he was married to a nurse and they had a little boy. Carter got hooked up with him and this would be the only reason he would be able to come and see the girls as he didn't have a license. That was a blessing in disguise. But wait a minute, how the hell did he find us? Who told him where we were? I was so pissed off at not knowing who exposed our whereabouts. I still don't know to this day who told him but I do have my suspicions.

🦋 MY THOUGHTS

Am I scared now that this is really happening? Oh, shit, yes! It really doesn't matter who found who at this point. I wanted to find him anyway so whatever! But if I ever needed courage in my life this was the time to have it. I couldn't show my fear to Carter or he would be all over that. At least, that is what I thought. I really didn't know anything about him anymore. For all I knew he was not drinking anymore and living a much better life. And what I did know was that this was my opportunity to get my divorce and start fresh without any ghosts of my past haunting me. I needed to have more faith than I ever did in my life. This was a very big deal. There will be more sleepless nights and lots of knots in my stomach ahead, but I was as ready as I would ever be. Would it be easy? Not in my lifetime. Divorce is never easy.

CHAPTER 11

I called my lawyer that Monday morning and she was shocked to hear the news but she said, "Good, that saves us time." She always made me laugh because she would lighten the mood and I needed that laughter. That Wednesday there was a knock on the door. I opened it up to this tall, young man and he handed me papers and said I was served and I should get a lawyer. I smiled at him and said, "Oh, I figured this was coming. Thank you. I will give this to my lawyer right away."

He stood there for a minute and said, "Oh, you have a lawyer."

I said, "Oh, yes, I have been looking for my ex but he found me first."

He smiled and said, "Okay, thank you and have a nice day."

Meanwhile as this is all going on Adam's sister would get us to go to her house and watch her two boys sometimes so they could go out for a well needed break. As I said earlier Katie's son Mark was born with a heart defect and he needed a lot of care (which by the way was never a chore to Katie as she loved him so much and would do anything for Mark and Scott). So this one weekend we went down to their house (thirty-five minutes away) and were having a great time with all the kids. Katie and Richard had gone out and Adam and I eventually went to bed. Around one thirty that night we were awakened by some hollering and shuffling around in the kitchen.

I said to Adam, "Is that Katie and Richard arguing?"

Adam answered, "I think so!"

I said, "It sounds like they are coming in here!"

Adam said, "What the hell are they doing?"

"I don't know but it doesn't sound good!"

A few seconds later in the living room come Katie and Richard (Adam and I are on the pull-out couch in the living room). Only they are not walking into the living room, Richard is pulling Katie into the room and she is fighting him but he drags her into the living room. In the meantime, I turn on the light beside me and say, "What is going on, you two?"

Richard looks at me and says, "I don't love you!"

I say, "What the hell are you talking about?"

Richard looks at Katie and says, "See, is this what you need to hear in order to believe that I am not in love with your brother's fiancée?"

By this time Katie is swearing at Richard to let her go and he's telling her no, not until she says she believes him now! I am so confused but I get the gist of what is going on. Katie thought Richard loved me! Okay, now I am embarrassed and the whole house hold is awake now. The girls are up and the boys are crying. It was not a nice scene. Adam was pissed right off and the next thing I knew we were heading home with the girls.

Let me say this, jealousy is not a nice thing to take a hold of you. When jealousy rears its ugly head, it can be an emotional roller coaster. I know this because I too was jealous a few times in my life and it's not pretty. We did not go to see his sister and family for about two weeks as Adam was livid. But I missed them so much and I loved them dearly so we worked things out and put that night behind us. I did feel a little awkward if Richard talked to me in front of Katie but after a couple weeks we were all back to our normal selves again. Katie was having a rough time in her life and I was able to let go of any ill feelings. All was forgiven and we went on with our usual visits.

I had enough on my mind with the courts and the thought of Carter having my girls. What I really needed was support, not drama.

Well, as anybody knows, when you go through a divorce and you want full custody of your children, it will either be smooth or hell. Guess which one mine was. You guessed it—hell! To make a long story short, our lawyers went back and forth with our requests. I requested that my husband could not be drinking at all when he was with the girls and he could not have them over night. I also requested for the first couple of times he had to be within a half hour of my house (I was so afraid he would leave town with my girls). In the end, we agreed on the time and day and so it began.

It ended up that anytime he came he was driven by his friend who I really respected and trusted. His friend was not a drinker and I had met his wife and son. Was it easy? No flipping way! Letting my girls go was very hard on me. I was a wreck every time they left until they were back safe in my care. Those were some of the worst days of my life. Not knowing if Carter had a plan to take them away from me as I took them away from him. But I had no choice but to take them away from their home if I wanted some sort of peace in my life. It was that or I feared that my girls would be without a mom. I grew up without my mom from twelve years old on. I did not want that for my girls. So as hard as it was, yes, I took them away from Carter. The only thing I regretted for a long time was that they grew up without knowing a lot of their relatives. That's why it was so important for me to go down home as often as I could afford to so they could see their family.

For several months, my girls would go with Carter and his friend and family on outings to places that the girls would enjoy. He never started any trouble and was on his best behavior. I am very thankful for his friend as he was a good role model for Carter. Then came the dreaded day when Carter wanted to have the girls overnight. I fought it with all that I had in me. I will not lie, my words were something like: "No bloody way is he getting them over night. What if he drinks? I cannot let this happen to my girls." I was sick to my stomach and such a wreck when I even thought of them going with him. My lawyer calmed me down and said don't worry we will figure this out.

Meanwhile, Carter's brothers came up to visit him and they were excited to see the girls. I agreed that he could take them to a big theme park an hour away. So, they went for the day and came back a little bit late but I swallowed my anger and was just happy they were back home with me. But, what I did notice when they were getting out of the car, Carter got out with them and hollered something to me but he rarely got out of the car and never spoke to me any other time and it looked like he stumbled out of the car. I didn't hear what he said so I started toward the car and I heard his friend say, "Get back in the car and shut the door." Carter got in and so I stopped where I was and his friend just waved and they left. I thought that was strange so when I talked with the girls about their day, I asked a few more questions.

I asked my oldest daughter how her day was and to tell me all about it just like any other time she went with him. She told me she got on a lot of rides and had so much fun with her uncles and would love to go there again. I asked her, "Did you get on any rides with your dad?" She told me no because when they were at the gates to go in, they lost him.

"What do you mean, honey?"

She said they couldn't find him until it was time to go.

"Oh, that's too bad." Then I asked her how was daddy in the car. She said he kept falling asleep. I said something like, "Okay, honey, I am glad you had a good time."

Then she said, "Mommy, I didn't like his kiss good-bye, his breath stunk."

Okay, now I am pissed right off. That means to me that he was drinking. I saw red. I called my lawyer on Monday morning and tried as calmly as I could to explain what I thought happened. She said we will have to approach this in a calm manner or they will think I coerced my daughter into saying these things. I was beside myself every time I thought they may have to have overnight visits and thought of him drinking around my girls. My lawyer called me several days later and said they denied everything my daughter had said. But, when I thought about the moment when they dropped the girls off and how Carter got out of the car and then back in and his friend drove away rather abruptly, I knew I wasn't imagining things and I believed my daughter. My lawyer told me they were getting a social worker involved and she would be visiting Carter in his environment and his friend's environment. Then she would come and visit me. My lawyer advised me to be as calm as I could and show the social worker that I was not out to get Carter and that I just wanted my girls to be safe.

So, the social worker visited Carter and his friend and family first. Then it was my turn. Wow, I don't know how I held it together. I could tell the minute she walked in that she was not impressed with me. She met me, my girls, and my fiancée. At this point I called him my fiancée as boyfriend sounded silly to me. I wish I could say it was a good visit but it was far from that.

She sat down and basically let me know everything that Carter said about me, and she was not friendly about it at all. You see, when she went to visit Carter he was at his friend's house. She walked into a beautiful apartment where she met his friend, his wife, and their young son. They were such a nice couple that I totally understood how she would think highly of them even on one visit. Then she saw Carter's apartment and it was very small but clean. But he had to share the bathroom with other tenants and the bathroom was outside in the hallway. That was not the best news, but the hardest part of the whole visit was the way she spoke to me. She told me that according to Carter, that one day he came home from work and I had taken the kids and moved here with another man. I saw red when she said this and I almost lost it.

I coolly said to her, "No, that is not true. I was legally separated from him for two months before I ever even left my old city and I never had an affair on him, ever! As a matter of fact, I had to leave my city because Carter kept threatening me."

She didn't respond and went on to tell me he also said I was a street girl, I had a temper, and I was an alcoholic.

"What the hell!" That is what I wanted to say but that would've made me look bad. So, instead I just said to her very coolly, "Well, I can assure you that none of what he is saying is true." My fiancée just sat there and never said a word. Both of us were floored, mostly because of the way she described what Carter said about me. She was not friendly and she definitely should not have been involved with any decision on this situation. It was very clear to me that she had already made up her mind. After she left, I called my lawyer just balling my eyes out. My lawyer tried her best to calm me down but I was too distraught to calm down. I hung up the phone, made sure the girls were settled and I told them I was going to lie down for a bit. I went into my bedroom and cried and cried and cried.

Almost two weeks later my lawyer called me to come in for an appointment. I went in to hear the results of the social worker's findings. The social worker was very impressed with Carter's friend and family and felt they were a good, decent family for my girls to be around. I agreed. She was not impressed with Carter's apartment as she felt the girls should not have to use a bathroom that other strangers were using. I agreed. She said that my girls seemed happy and well treated with their mom and fiancée. I agreed. And then she said she believed it was a good idea if Carter wanted overnight visits that the girls would have to stay with his friend's family. I half agreed. I was so happy that he would not get overnight visits at his place, but I was unsure if going to his friend's house was a good idea either. I was still scared that something would happen to them. But my lawyer reminded me that this was best case scenario. He didn't get them overnight by himself. I eventually warmed up to the idea but I had a hard time letting my girls stay away from me as it was. I had to accept that this was going to happen and I had to put my girls in God's hands and pray they would be safe. We had a date for the court to discuss the divorce and the custody of the girls on top of the social worker visit. My wonderful sister and my best friend Tat came with me to the court. I needed support. We waited for a while and finally Carter's lawyer said to the judge that he hadn't seen or heard from his client in two weeks. I was so afraid I was not getting my divorce but I just sat there as calm as I could (my heart was beating fast and I was sweating). My lawyer got up and said it wasn't fair to her client to have to wait on this. Could we please continue without her husband? She said a few more things and there was no objection from my husband's lawyer so we did continue. I had to go on the stand and swear on the bible to tell the truth and nothing but the truth so help me God. The judge asked me several questions and I answered them with the truth and then sat down. The judge sat there and looked over the file and we all waited while he spoke with the two lawyers. I was a very lucky girl that day. The judge said several things but all I heard was that I was granted my divorce and I had full custody of my girls. If Carter wanted to have anything to do with the girls again, he would have to go back to court. He was not to have any visits or any contact with the girls until such time. I was overjoyed with emotion and happiness. I started crying again only this time my tears were full of joy. I had full custody of my girls! As a bonus, I got my divorce but in the big picture I got my girls. They would be safe and I was elated! I hugged my lawyer several times and she laughed at me. I couldn't thank her enough. I gave her a big basket that I had decorated nicely and it was filled with so many nice things. I was in heaven and I thanked God that it was over. Maybe now I can actually get some peace and move on with my life. When I think of that day how it started out as gloom and doom and then it turned into something wonderful and positive it still makes me smile and fills my heart with love and thankfulness.

I would like to say here that the times in this book when I use the word *fuck*, it is because that was a word that released my anger at the time (and it still does). I did not like that word but it felt good to say it sometimes. To be honest with you that word is only used when

I am very angry. I do not like hearing the word being used as a casual word in a conversation and especially from other women. I am not a Saint but I do have respect for myself and others around me. The one word that I do say more than I should is *shit*. But what are you going to do.

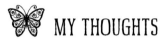

MY THOUGHTS

I am ecstatic to say the least. My girls, my precious girls are safe. The end result outweighed all that I endured. I am happy. Thank you, God.

I believe in forgiveness and I believe people can change. My prayer for Carter would be that he has worked through his own stuff and has come to a place where he has forgiven himself for things he did in the past. Let us not forget that Carter is a child of God and is loved by God. We all deserve a good life but we have to stop blaming others and take responsibility to make changes in our own lives. We need to have faith in ourselves and faith in God. I know for myself I have to let my faith be stronger than my fear. It is not easy but it is definitely possible.

CHAPTER 12

Several months after my divorce and Carter had dropped from the face of the earth (there was a rumor he was in jail), I decided it was time to tell Charlie about her biological father. By the time Charlie was two, she hardly saw Jack. He only showed up when it suited him and he was then married and having another child. He stayed away once too often and I told him that was it. He was not to be a part time dad and break her heart every time he said he was coming and didn't show up. I went through that as a young girl and it is devastating on the self-esteem. That was it, I gave him chance after chance and finally told him not to bother coming around any-more. He was having problems in his marriage and got involved with another woman and it just went on and on. I was not putting Charlie through this anymore. It was a hard decision but I thought at the time it was best for her. She was five years old when we moved to this city and she hadn't seen her biological father in several years and she really thought Carter was her dad. I let her believe this because she was almost two when Carter came into her life and he treated her like his very own. But now I had to tell her while she was still young enough yet old enough to understand. So I planned it all out. I had my neighbor watch Ava as Adam was working.

I made a little picnic basket with things that Charlie liked and grabbed a blanket and off we went to the park across the rail road tracks. We played at the park on the swings and teeter totter for a while and we laughed and played until it was time to eat our picnic. When we were done with our picnic, we put our garbage away and lay on the blanket and looked up at the sky. While we lay there looking at the clouds I thought of how I would start this off. And slowly and with so much love I told her a love story about two young people who fell in love. I made sure my story was done in a very positive and kind way and told her the story was about me and her dad. I cannot remember the exact words I said but I felt very happy and relieved with the way I handled telling her and the way she received it. She then asked me many questions about Jack and I told her the best I could and I never once put him down. He was her biological father and I respected him. He gave me a beautiful daughter and I was very blessed with her. When we were done and she didn't have any more questions, we played again in the park and then we went home holding each other's hand.

And now here I am with my divorce behind me and custody of my girls. Charlie now knew about her biological dad. It was a big relief for me to have finally shared that secret with her. I felt that for once in my life I actually got what I wanted and needed. I was over the moon with joy. That being said I still had another issue happening close to me and that was the drinking and driving I was dealing with from Adam. I tried desperately to stop him from driving when drunk. He would say he wouldn't do it and then do it anyway. He would not think of the consequences. He just did it. We started to argue more and more about the drinking. He didn't think it was a problem. (Just a side note: during the seven years we were together, he got caught drinking and driving three times and lost his license on the third time for a year.)

Needless to say, Adam didn't stop drinking and driving any time soon. This really scared me because I would sit at home worried sick and full of fear and panic that he had killed himself or someone else in a car accident. I laid awake many nights praying for him to come home safe. I probably stayed in the relationship so long because he didn't abuse me and he really was good to me. But I found myself pouring a lot of alcohol down the sink. I would pretend I was drinking it so he would have less to drink. It got to the point I hated alcohol. I could see no good in drinking, not even socially. For me, the alcohol caused the problems. Adam would pass out on the kitchen table or the couch. I was always waking him up and dragging him to bed. It was no problem for him to drink by himself at the table and pass out. I was constantly on edge and that made me very cranky with the girls. Here we go again, I thought. What do I do now, leave another relationship?

So I talked to Marion and she heard about a program called Al-Anon. She talked me into going and she went with me for support. She was there through it all with Adam and I will never forget her kindness. She got me started in Al-Anon and then let me go on my own. I wasn't sure about this program at first because they mentioned something called a higher power. They also said the Lord's Prayer at the end of every meeting which I was familiar with but I didn't want to be in any church group. But, the middle of the meeting caught my interest. They would break off into little groups and talk about certain questions and topics that someone had prepared for that night's meeting. The questions were not really focused on the alcoholic but on each individual person. At first I thought, "Oh, no, wait a minute, I'm not the one with the problem, he is!" I wasn't sure if I was in the right place, but something about the calmness, the laughter and the non-judging people made me keep coming back every week. And most important, this was an anonymous program and whatever you said there stayed there. It was an unbelievable bond of trust.

In the meantime, I put my girls into dance lessons for jazz and ballet. Tat's children were involved with a dance group and I thought it would be good for the girls to have something to look forward to and they loved music. So, I enrolled them in the dance classes and they enjoyed it very much. Charlie stayed in the dance classes for four years and Ava was in the classes for three years. I loved watching the girls dance and Tat and I were very proud of our children. I didn't make a lot of money but I was determined to keep them in dance for as long as I could. So the last year of dance I paid for the classes by working in the dance studio as a receptionist at night. This was a great way to keep them in for another year.

During this time, we moved three doors over from our three-bedroom townhouse into a bigger two-bedroom townhouse and it was a great move. We decided we would build a bedroom in the basement for my eldest daughter but the girls would share the one bedroom for a while using bunk beds. I continued going to Al-Anon and learned a lot about myself and about alcoholism. I decided I was not going to act like I was my boyfriend's mother anymore and let him make his own choices and if he fell on his face then so be it. I had to get him to start taking responsibility for his choices and not covering up for him. This may sound mean but it wasn't cut and dry, it was done in baby steps and a lot of love. As I grew in the Al-Anon program, through many hours of reading Al-Anon literature, I eventually got a sponsor. A sponsor is someone you would call when you were having a rough time and they would help you to calm down and focus on yourself rather than the alcoholic. I got my first sponsor who was older than me, like a mother figure. She was a wonderful sponsor and she helped me through many nights of despair. She eventually moved away and although I was very sad, I knew I had the support of the members who would be there for me. Eventually I got myself another sponsor who became a very good friend and someone I admire and love to this day. She was there for me many times when I would call her upset. She helped me get through some very rough times. It's amazing how much help there is in just listening to someone in distress. Giving of your time to offer your ear to someone in need is a real blessing to the person on the end of the telephone line. Giving of your time and meeting someone at a coffee shop is a selfless task. And giving someone a hug or a smile with a few words of encouragement may be all someone needs on that dismal day. My sponsor gave me all this and more and that is why she will always have a special place in my heart.

As I continued going to Al-Anon, I met some wonderful people from all walks of life. There was a huge mix of people, such as doctor's wives, writer's wives, artists, construction workers, waitresses, hairdressers, lawyers, business people, counselors, teachers, and those who were jobless. They were both men and women. They were all different but had one thing in common and that was how each of them was affected by someone who was an alcoholic. These people all came together and put aside what they did for a living, put aside their status in the public eye, and helped each other deal with their different situations. Those rooms were full of compassion, courage, and strength.

Meanwhile I worked at the drugstore downtown for two years, and as much as I loved it I felt like I should be doing more for myself. I decided I would like to go back to school and get my diploma. I was so excited to do this, I was so proud of myself. I worked really hard and made straight As. But during this time when I was going to school I didn't have as much time to spend with Adam as I was so into doing well in my subjects. I would study during the week and on the weekends I would have reports to do so I was really busy. This was a five-month program Monday to Friday. Five months of my life to do something important for myself. And during those five months, Adam drank more and said I wasn't the same as I was the first several years we were together. I argued the point that I have been very good to him and always made sure I had given him so much attention and the girls. This was a short time for me to get my diploma. Why couldn't he be happy for me? My girls understood that their mom was working hard to get her diploma and try to get a good job. But he didn't see it that way. As a matter of fact, on my graduation day, my best friends Tat and her husband Kevin were the ones who celebrated my achievement by dropping by with a cake and a handmade black robe and cap. They took my picture and made me feel so special. I don't remember where Adam was but I was truly hurt that he didn't make an effort to be with me and celebrate this very important time in my life. And as a matter of fact, it seemed he was always gone when the girls had something special they wanted us to go to. The girls would have a big performance at the end of the year with their dance routines for all the parents and family to go and see. It was a huge production and meant a lot to the girls to have us there. It was absolutely no problem for me to go but Adam only went once. I had to always make up excuses for the other three years of performances. It hurt me that he didn't want to participate in any of their activities, whether in dance or school. When I thought about all the ways that he wasn't there for the girls or me anymore it made me realize I was just fooling myself. I finally realized that Adam (because of his childhood) needed a mother figure to take care of him and I also realized that he was jealous and selfish when it came to the girls.

So it was shortly after this that I suggested it would be a good idea for him to move out and get his own place. I was learning how to stand on my own two feet for a change and it felt good. He did get his own place and we broke up due to the alcohol. I decided I had enough and the only way we would get back together was if he went to AA. My heart was breaking and I still loved him but I needed him to stop the drinking and move on from his past. (He had past issues to deal with but that is his story).

You know, before I went to Al-Anon, I truly thought when I looked into someone else's window (from a distance) that they probably had a wonderful stress free life and a beautiful home inside, with little drinking. I thought many other people, especially those who had top jobs, definitely had a much better life than me. Until I went to Al-Anon, I was so blind to what really went on behind closed doors. Let me tell you, it doesn't matter whether you come from money, have a top job, have a beautiful home, wear a suit every day or live life luxuriously, alcoholism doesn't just hit the person you see living on the street.

It is so much easier for many people to put down the person they see bumming for money for a drink, but don't fool yourself, alcoholism can hit anybody! I know from experience of going to Al-Anon, people are just that, people. Nobody is exempt from becoming an alcoholic. Not everyone is an alcoholic, don't misunderstand what I am trying to say, but I am saying if you think someone who is a doctor, or a lawyer or a top business man can't possibly have a drinking problem, guess again. We are human and as humans we all have our problems. I fortunately, with everything I went through as a child, am not an alcoholic. And I am very thankful that I am not. Trust me, I have other issues.

But in order for me to forgive the alcoholics in my life for pain and misery I felt they had caused me, I decided to go to open AA meetings. Man, was I in for a surprise. I did not expect to see people laughing and hugging. I did not expect to see the respect for each other I saw. I really don't know what I expected, but the first night I was there I left quite angry. My thoughts went something like this: "How dare they laugh and have fun, how can they stand up there and make jokes, how can they not be angry with themselves for the people they have hurt, I am not impressed with this meeting, I won't be coming back here."

I asked the wife of one of the speakers how she could smile and be so calm about the things her husband was saying and she told me to give the open meetings a chance. "Keep coming back," she said. "This didn't happen overnight, it took a lot of hard work, forgiveness and understanding about the disease of alcoholism before I could get to this point."

And so, I decided to come back the following week and then I continued to come back for about six months. And then one night I found myself laughing with the speaker, and feelings of compassion and understanding enveloped me. It was then that I realized I had finally come to a point where I could forgive the alcoholics in my life. It was then that I decided that I needed to forgive them if I was ever to be free of the pain and anger I had hung onto for so long. When I left the AA meeting that night I knew I was headed in the right direction and I actually felt excited about forgiving the alcoholics in my life. It took a lot of work but I finally did come to a place where I accepted that alcoholism was a disease and I could eventually forgive those who hurt me. It would take time to forgive but I was on my way. The more I learned about alcoholism the more I could go forward. I could now think about the alcoholics in my life with new eyes. I knew that eventually through the Al-Anon program, maybe I could forgive my dad, my uncle, Carter, and Adam. Maybe with all this knowledge I could be free of the pain I felt they caused me. After all, just because I am not an alcoholic does not mean I am a perfect human being. I did things and said things that were hurtful to others and I was no angel.

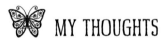 ## MY THOUGHTS

Where do I begin to thank the Al-Anon program that saved my life many times? This program was the best thing I ever did for myself. This program filled me with so many positive ways to think about things. The Al-Anon program is a twelve-step program and the steps are amazing to say the least. There are many slogans that you could say to yourself over and over and then over and over again. Here are a few slogans I still use to this day: One day at a time. Live and let live. Let go and let God. How important is it? Came to believe. Easy does it. Keep it simple. Just for today. Think.

Al-Anon has a wonderful prayer called the Serenity Prayer. It goes like this:

> *God, grant me the serenity to accept the things I cannot change, courage to change the things I can, and wisdom to know the difference.*

I remember saying this prayer over and over in my times of panic and helplessness. I would let the words sink into my brain and these words helped me over and over to let go of the things I had no power over. I absorbed as much as I could to help me to realize I was powerless over anyone's drinking and most of all I was not to blame. Also, at the time I was in Al-Anon I purchased one of the programs book called *One Day at a Time in Al-Anon*, and eventually I purchased a second book called *Each Day a New Beginning*. These books were heaven sent. I read these small daily meditation books constantly. I had to learn to change the way I thought about things and every day I would read them to put good positive thoughts into my head. I was not brought up with all this wonderful positive information and it felt good to know I was not alone. These two amazing books will always be a part of my life. There is so much more literature to be read from the Al-Anon program and I read a lot but these are my go to books.

I have said this many times over the years and I will say it again, Al-Anon saved my life in so many ways. I was so lost and full of fear and sadness because the people I loved over the years would not give up the alcohol. I learned through this program that I didn't cause the drinking and I could not cure it. It was out of my hands. This was a disease and I had to let the alcoholic take control of his or her life. The only person that had control was the alcoholic themselves. No amount of arguing or threatening or crying would make the alcoholic quit. I had to learn to let go and let them fend for themselves. It was not an easy thing to do but I had to do it if I wanted my sanity back (as much as that was). I had to trust that God was with me and I would put the alcoholic in God's hands. It was not easy, but in the end, it relieved me of thinking I was the reason they drank.

I truly recommend to anyone who is living with or has someone in their life whose drinking is out of control to go to Al-Anon, and if it is dangerous for you to go then go in secret. It is nobody's business where you go, and the great thing about Al-Anon is that it is an anonymous program. What is said there is kept there and you don't have to say anything at all for as long as you want until you feel comfortable going there. It is a great place to go because you will meet others who are living with a similar story and you realize you are not alone. This is a place where you learn so much about yourself and who you are and what you need. All people are welcome to these meetings and all people don't have to be alone anymore. Al-Anon was a blessing and a gift to me and I hope you will give yourself this gift too.

CHAPTER 13

Okay, now, just because I was finally getting the fact that alcoholism was a disease and thinking about forgiving the alcoholics in my life that I felt let me down, it did not mean this was going to be easy. You can't just say, "Okay, now that I know you have a disease, I forgive you for all that you did to me." It doesn't work that way. You still have to relive all that they did to you and work through it and there is no time limit on how long it will take you to get to that freeing place of forgiveness. Where do I begin? I couldn't do this on my own. I was thinking of my past and the sad times I went through and I was having trouble opening up all of those feelings again. But lucky for me during my early days at Al-Anon I also met another special person and she became a very dear friend. I was so blessed to have her in my life. Her name brings a smile to my face. We spent many wonderful times together. But in the meantime, she was very beneficial in bringing me back to church. And one day, when I was really down and needed guidance, I called this person who I had met through the Al-Anon program. I needed to talk but she was headed for church. She asked me if I wanted to go along. I asked her what kind of a church was it, she said United. I wasn't comfortable going to a church I didn't know, but I really needed to talk to her and if that meant going to church, then that's where I was going.

So, off to this United Church we went. I was in for a surprise for as I entered the church I started to cry and the minister came over to me and hugged me. Her name was Sarah and she told me to call her if I needed to talk. It turned out she was also a family counselor. I immediately felt welcomed in this little united church on top of a hill. And I decided I would like to go again and also give this lady minister a call. I was doing so well in Al-Anon but I was still weighed down by my past and this dam cloud that hovered and haunted me. I knew it was time to get outside help.

This is when I came back to church and when I started counseling. I needed to get on my feet. There were many issues I had to address. Little did I know it would take a good year or so before I felt like I was actually letting go of some of my past nightmares. My counselor Sarah was very beneficial in helping me to address some major childhood traumas. As for going back to church, this united church was the place for me. I was impressed with the atmosphere and their way of thinking. The people I met at this church seemed very sincere and friendly. The minister (Sarah) was talking about faith and problems in today's society. I found out that they were an inclusive church, meaning all were welcome. And the one thing that I really liked was the fact that all were welcome to come up and participate in communion. All were welcome to God's table. I didn't feel judged there at all. They talked more about forgiveness and God's love for us. And after several weeks of going every Sunday I felt like I had come home. I knew I was in for a rough ride but I felt safe there.

So, I started the hard and torturous journey into my past. I remember after a couple of sessions when Sarah said I had a lot of anger toward my father, I told her she was crazy because I loved my father and he had to do what he had to do. Yeah, right. She didn't buy it for one minute. She said when I was talking about my father my chin was very stern and she could see the anger written all over my face. I couldn't hide it. I was angry at her at first. How dare she tell me how I felt about my father? My dad was a good man. Yes, he may have been a good man, but he still hurt me. And then one day after a few more sessions I realized I really was angry at my father. I had been angry at him for many years but I had shoved it way down for fear of how I would react if it ever came out. And it came out. Oh, did it come out.

When I first started dealing with the anger it scared me. I would punch the crap out of a pillow. I would cry and have temper tantrums. Mind you I would always wait until my children were out of the house at school or at a friend's house before I would blow up. I was a mess inside. I had all these emotions that were starting to come out and I didn't know if I was coming or going. I tried so hard to keep strong for my girls and I would talk to my friends and for once in my life I just kept talking and talking about how hurt and angry I was. Once I got through most of the anger I started to feel depressed. That was harder to deal with as it was such a dark place. I started to think that maybe this was that cloud that always followed me, the one that I refused to deal with for fear of where it would lead me. I had two girls to take care of. How could I take care of them if I fell apart? But I did fall apart and put on a show in front of them so they wouldn't have to see their mother fall to pieces. Then, I started writing letters to my father but I never sent them. I wrote many angry words and I couldn't believe how angry I was. My counselor would help me to voice my feelings of anger and hurt. It was really hard to deal with because I couldn't just drop by my dad's house and say, "Hi, Dad, I have a bone to pick with you!" My dad lived in the east coast and I lived in another province. I couldn't just pick up the phone either and blast him. So, I decided to make a trip down to see him. My good friend Marion was going down to see her family and said I could travel with her. She had a good-sized van and so I packed up a suitcase and my girls and I went to see my dad.

I was nervous the whole way to the east coast. I felt very sick to my stomach and I felt out of sorts. I wasn't sure if I was doing the right thing. How could I confront my father, this was many years later and what if I hurt him and what if he got mad at me and what if he stopped loving me. I was a wreck! I respected my father very much and was taught at a very young age to respect your elders and you never showed your anger. Showing your anger, fear or sadness was a sign of weakness. And boy was I feeling weak then.

So, as much as I was feeling all the signs of fear to talk to my dad, I still went through with it. I had come a long way to confront him and I wasn't backing out now. If he stopped loving me then that was a chance I had to take because I was so tired of feeling angry and hurt inside. Now that it was finally coming out of me, I wanted to deal with it and let it go. My amazing brother Brad had graciously let me have my conversation with our dad at his house. He picked up my father, step mom, and our two little brothers from dad's second marriage. Then my brother took all of their family out for a drive and let me talk to my dad. My father didn't know how to respond to me when I asked him why he gave his children up. Why didn't he stop drinking and come and get us? Why didn't he come and see us? Why didn't he call me? Why didn't he come and pick me up when I was waiting for him at the end of the driveway? Didn't he love me? Didn't he miss me? Was he mad at me? I told him I thought he didn't love me, I thought he abandoned me and I thought what he did was very wrong. I told him he should have come to see me and he should have called me and he should have showed up at the end of the driveway to pick me up. I told him he hurt me very much and asked him how could he give up his children?

My father looked at me and with a very sad face he told me he thought we were better off without him. He told me he had many, many regrets, but there was nothing he could do to change what he did many years ago. He told me that he loved me very much and it broke his heart over the years when he thought of how he didn't show up when he said he would. He said if he could go back and change the things he did he would but he couldn't. He said he did the best he could just to hold on to life after mom's death. As I looked at my father I could see the regret and strain of life in his face. He never got over the death of my mother. A huge part of him died when she passed away. He was never the same. She was the rock that held our family together and my dad did not know how to keep us together. He gave up and turned to alcohol and the alcohol dulled his pain. I had always known that my father had a drinking problem, but after going to Al-Anon and open AA meetings, I was able to understand the effects of alcoholism.

Here I was finally confronting my father and it didn't matter what his answers were, I just needed him to say something so I could have some closure. We talked for several hours and then we wrapped it up. I got up and went to him and gave him a big hug and thanked him for being honest with me. I told him I loved him and I always would. When he left, I felt so very sad inside but I knew it would take some time to heal. Time was the only thing left now that would bring me to forgive my dad for abandoning me. I remember it was about six months or so later, and I just felt really happy one day. I felt like a burden had been lifted off my shoulders. I realized that I felt peace when I thought about my father and I knew I had forgiven him. Forgiveness is a funny thing. It's one of those unspoken miracles.

And during those six months I worked on a lot more letters. Letters of anger toward Jack and then when I didn't have any more to say to Jack I started writing very angry letters to Carter and I found myself spilling out everything I ever wanted to say to my exes. I would punch pillows and kick buckets and pound nails into old boards just to get all the anger out of the pit of my stomach and my head. My counselor worked through all of this with me and helped me to come to a place where I didn't have anything left to say to Jack and Carter. Mind you I concentrated on one person at a time. When I was done with Jack I moved onto Carter and I had so many, many letters that I put in a bag and hid until it was time to destroy them. I felt so free after writing weeks after weeks of letters and letting all of my anger and sadness out. I was finally able to forgive them and to forgive myself for my part in our relationships.

And then, boom! Just when you think things are finally going your way and you may be finished counseling, you are knocked in the head again with another memory. I believe because the death of my mother was so traumatic I must have shoved these memories way down until it was safe for them to come out. It started out as a normal day like any other, my two girls were outside with their friends and I was looking out our big picture window enjoying a cup of tea. Then out of nowhere I started to feel my heart race and my palms were sweaty. I started to feel like I was being swallowed up and then came to a huge realization that I was remembering something from my childhood.

I can still hear the sound of horror in my voice as I screamed out loud, "No! This can't be true, it can't be true!" My hands were shaking as I reached for the phone. I started to panic as I waited to hear a voice on the other end of the line. Please be there, please pick up, I need to know the truth. Thoughts were spiraling in my head and I knew it was true. I just needed to know how old I was when it started and how did it stop. The voice on the other end said hello and I'm sure I said hello, but I don't remember. I felt sick to my stomach and couldn't believe what I was saying. "My uncle molested me!" The person on the phone talked to me and calmed me down and I got the information I needed and after the conversation ended I broke down.

I was molested by my uncle from the age of four or five (not quite sure which year it started) for several years until the age of eight or nine. It stopped because someone had the courage to tell my parents about this very sick and hurtful deed. I was not told that my parents knew what was happening and I was never asked by my parents if my uncle was touching me inappropriately. It was all hushed. I had no idea that my uncle was not allowed in our home anymore and he could not babysit us anymore. I only knew that we never saw him like we used to. I remembered it would happen when my uncle would babysit for my mom and dad. My parents trusted my uncle with their life, who wouldn't trust their own brother. (It is a very sad fact today we know that the perpetrator is usually someone you know and trust and that includes our own parents).

Now the memories were coming back and I couldn't stop them or deny them. Here I was between the age of four and five (not that any age at all is appropriate), but that is usually the age the molester preys on his victims as that age puts their trust in the adult figure. He was my uncle, I trusted him, who wouldn't. He was very good to me, giving me candy and playing games with me. He babysat me since I was a toddler. He was a good babysitter in every other way. For the first couple years, I was so young I can only remember that he always wanted me to sit on his knee. So, I guess he played it like a game, but I was always told it was our little secret and it was okay, I wouldn't get in trouble. He did this for several years, always bribing me with candy or other things and somehow making me think it was normal. So this is what I was taught when I put my trust in someone.

It had been a while since our uncle had babysat us children and like I said earlier I was never told by my parents that my uncle was banned from our house and I was never asked about anything concerning my uncle. And then this one time I remember when we went to visit my grandmother, my uncle (who was still single at the time) lived there and he asked me if I wanted to go for a ride on his motorcycle down to the light house and look for whales. Everyone was in the house and he said it was okay that my parents would let me go. So I didn't ask my parents, I just hopped on the bike. I was very excited to go as I wanted to ride on his bike and go look for whales. The next thing I know we are leaving the lighthouse and he asks me if I wanted to sit on the front and I could steer the bike, of course a ten-year-old is going to jump at that offer, so I did. My uncle started to touch me and I started to cry and said I wanted to go home. Somehow I was able to realize what he was doing was wrong. I felt sick to my stomach and scared. I didn't ever want to be alone with him again. He took me back to my grandmother's house and when we drove into the yard, my parents seemed very upset. I got in trouble for not asking my parents if I could go. I just wanted to hide until it was time for us to leave my grandmothers.

And now I was letting these feelings out after all these years of hiding this from myself. I needed help right away. I felt like my world was closing in on me and I needed to be strong as I had my two girls to think about. After I finally let those painful disgusting memories out I went back to my wonderful minister/counselor that I had already been seeing about the anger I felt about my father. She helped me to confront my uncle by writing him several letters of the anger I felt toward him for violating me as an innocent child. The letters were never sent but it still felt very good to write down all the things I wanted to say to him. We had a session that involved me putting my uncle in a chair in front of me and confronting him. There was a lot of anger coming out of my mouth. I will share those comments with you shortly.

I continued to write many more letters until one day I stopped writing. I didn't have anything left to say. After many sessions with Sarah I was able to get out all the filthy and disgusting memories I had of my uncle molesting me. The good thing was I didn't feel like it was my fault anymore, I started to love myself for the first time in years. I had truly let go of the feelings that haunted me for so long, I was free of that nagging cloud that followed me (or so I thought).

 MY THOUGHTS

Let's talk about what I learned. I learned that I was taken advantage of at a very young age and I never at any point gave any consent. I learned that my uncle was sick and needed help. I learned that it was definitely not my fault. I learned that my parents did the best they could at the time with what they were taught. You didn't call the police on members of your family. You didn't talk about it at all. It was a skeleton to be kept in a closet. My parents did not talk to me about this, ever. I had to make up my own conclusions and live with a lot of confusion. I thank God for what I know today through the help of other people. I know that I am not unworthy of being loved. I was an innocent child of God who was harmed by a sick individual.

After great counseling sessions, I was able to picture my uncle sitting in a chair and I screamed at him for what he did to me. I said the things I couldn't say as a child. I said things like: "How dare you do that to me!" "I trusted you to take care of me." "You are a sick man, you need help!" "How can you look in the mirror and know what you have done to me?" "You took advantage of me and lied to me." "I hate what you did to me!" "You took from me what should have been a beautiful intimate moment between me and my first love." "You disgust me!" "I was an innocent child, I hate you!" I know I said a whole lot more but I think you get the picture. As I said earlier I also wrote many letters to my uncle but I also wrote this one letter and I addressed it to my uncle but I didn't have an address for him. I didn't know much about him or where he lived. I never mailed it and that was okay. I eventually burned all of the letters. This was the beginning of a letting go process that enabled me to finally let go of the pain and anger I felt.

Not right away, but eventually, I was able to look in the mirror and not be disgusted with myself or blame myself for what my uncle did to me. I finally learned and believed that it was not my fault and I was a victim. Eventually, I was able to feel good knowing I had the courage to face this part of my childhood that haunted me and left me scarred in many areas of my later years. I was given a second chance to think of my innocence as exactly that. I was innocent and I reclaimed my innocence by voicing to another human being and to God the wrong that was done to me. I was a victim at the time but I refuse to be a victim today.

It doesn't seem fair sometimes that we who have suffered this abuse have to be the one to work through it, but we are not doing it for the asshole that did this to us, we are doing it for us to be free of the feelings we lived with for many years. He does not have that hold on me anymore. I live free from any guilt or shame as I know I have worked through this and I am a beloved child of God.

Was this an easy thing to remember and get past? My answer is no, not at all! And even though it isn't about winning I did win in the end. I took my life back. I looked that monster in the face sitting in the chair, I faced him with my letters, I faced him through the countless sessions I had with my counselor and I faced what he did to me with God and eventually I did face him at my father's funeral.

When my father passed away, I traveled down to my father's funeral. I saw my uncle at the funeral parlor. His wife walked over and introduced herself and my uncle kept his head down. I reached out my hand and shook his hand (very lightly and quickly, I still didn't want to touch him) and thanked him for donating his plot for my father's resting place next to his mother. I told him it was a very nice thing to do. He sheepishly looked at me but did not look into my eyes. I could see the guilt he still carried or maybe I saw the coward he was, I don't know. It was so strange to me that I was not angry and I didn't really feel anything. I truly knew then that I was well on my way to forgiving my uncle for what he had done to me. It was a bitter sweet meeting, and one that I will never forget. The bitter part was seeing him and the sweet part was I was no longer his victim. I heard a saying once that goes like this: forgiveness is a funny thing; it warms the heart and cools the sting. But, I have to make one thing clear—I forgave him for me, not for him. He no longer had any control over me, I was in control. Will I ever forget what he did to me? My answer is no, never. His judgment day will come and my spirit is free.

Before I wrote this last part of my story, I was very naïve to think that I was the only innocent victim that my uncle molested. It was brought to my attention after I wrote this section of my book that my uncle did in fact molest other children. When I found this out I was devastated! I truly thought after he was caught that he never molested anyone ever again. Unfortunately, that wasn't the case! It deeply saddens me and pisses me off that my uncle molested other children. This news was horrendous for me to hear. My uncle was a monster and a pedophile. I cried and cried for these innocent children, boys and girls. I do not know how many, I only know that it sickened me and my thought was "What the fuck do I do with this information? How do I process something like this when I forgave him for what he did to me? It is not my place to speak up for those who were molested because that is their story and some victims just want to forget it ever happened but I can honor them by writing my thoughts on this horrible act in my story."

Well, first of all, my uncle is dead. I have no remorse for his death. He should have been charged a long time ago when he did it to me and who knows who else at that time. This happened to me in 1962 to 1963 and ended in 1967. There were a lot of families back then who had skeletons in their closet and that is where they kept them. Thank God we do not tolerate this kind of behavior today. Thank God we know it is for everyone's best interest to speak up and have the molester charged for the despicable crime he or she has committed. I find it hard to even say this man is my uncle and as a matter of fact I would like to say that he is not my uncle. He does not even deserve a fake name in my story. He should have been held accountable for his crimes against innocent children. But now he is gone. He has been gone for about fourteen years. My only hope is that these children who are now adults like me have worked through this most hurtful crime against them and that they have a full and rich life despite him. We can be sure of one thing and that is that he will be judged for his actions and rightly so.

My heart and love go out to all who suffered at the hands of my relative. May God hold you in the palms of his hands and comfort you and let you know how beautiful you are and how much you are loved.

CHAPTER 14

During this time of going to my minister/counselor Sarah, I was still trying to get over Adam. I became very independent and for six months he would call me and ask me if we could get back together and I would ask him if he was in AA yet and he would say no. He would always say he could quit on his own. Okay, well, I've heard that before and I know how that ends. So, I never gave in. I kept praying to God every day, "Please, God, guide him to AA." I had heard about the power of prayer and thought it wouldn't hurt at all to ask God to help me.

I tried my best to let go of Adam. I knew that the chances of him going to AA were slim if he didn't want to quit. I was working through my matters of the heart one day when Adam called and said that Katie's son Mark was going into the hospital for his major heart surgery. We knew this day was coming as the doctor told Katie several years before that when Mark was five years old they would have to do the major surgery that he needed on his heart. Adam wanted me to go down to the hospital with him the next day but I was too emotional to go with him. I was so afraid for little Mark. I just had an awful feeling and I couldn't describe it but I felt sick to my stomach just thinking of him in the hospital. So I told Adam to call me as soon as the surgery was done to let me know that Mark was okay. I loved that little boy so much, and Katie had asked Adam and me to be Mark's godparents when he was just eight months old. Even though Adam and I were apart I still was a part of Mark's life and he meant the world to me. I would always be his godmother.

So the next day Adam called me from the hospital and said they were doing the surgery and it would take several hours but everything was going well. Adam was so happy that things were going well and I told him to give my love to Katie and Richard and let them know I was thinking of them. He said he would and before he hung up he told me he still loved me and he wished I was there with him. He said it was hard for him to be there without me to support him. I told him it wasn't fair for him to use Mark's surgery to make me feel guilty. He hung up saying he would call me as soon as Mark was out of surgery. Several hours went by and I was feeling very anxious for Adam to call. Finally, he called and nothing prepared me for what I was about to hear. I fell to the floor with the phone to my ear. Adam was crying hard and I knew something terrible had happened. I told him to take his time and when he was ready to talk, I was there to listen. Eventually, through sobs of a broken heart, he told me that Mark was on life support and that he was brain dead. He told me that the heart surgery went perfect but somehow when they were at the very end, some air had gotten into the blood stream through the tube (a horrible mistake on someone's part) and now he was brain dead. They were going to have to take him off of life support and let him go. He told me through many more sobs that his sister Katie and Richard were in with Mark holding him in a rocking chair beside the bed and sobbing their hearts out.

By this time, I am crying hard and saying, "No, no, no. This can't be happening! You said he was okay, you said the surgery was successful and everything was going well. No, please no!" We hung up devastated. I knew I had to tell the girls. They loved Mark like he was their little brother. They had been in his life for five years and I knew they would be devastated. I gently told them what happened and we all cried together. Once we all were calm I called my friend Tatiana and told her the news. We were all devastated by Mark's death.

Adam and I had talked a few more times out of a common thread that bound us together, the fact that we were Mark's godparents. My friend Tat and her husband Kevin picked me up and we all went to the funeral together. They walked close beside me and gave me the support I needed. I was a mess to say the least but I was nothing compared to Katie and Richard and their son Scott. I sat down with my friends and just cried. Adam noticed me and came over and asked me if I wanted to see Mark up at the coffin. I couldn't breathe and I felt so weak I said no at first. Then I knew I had to see him one last time so a few minutes later I said yes. Adam put his arm around me and walked me up to the coffin. I looked at Mark and my heart broke. How could this happen to such an amazing little boy who worked so hard to get to where he was? I started to cry and Adam walked me back to my seat. He stayed there with me until the funeral was over. We all went to Katie's house after everything was done. As I walked into Katie's house all I could hear was the cry of a brokenhearted mother. It was so unbearable and heart breaking I could feel myself falling to the floor. Tat grabbed me and held me up and took me in to have a seat. Adam came over and talked to us and put his arm around me to comfort me as he could see I was not doing well. Finally, Katie came out of her bedroom and I went to her and held her as she cried for the longest time. It was so heart breaking to witness the death of a child so young and to witness the loss and torture that the parents were going through. I will never forget the cries of Katie mourning the loss of her beautiful boy Mark. Nor will I ever forget how much Mark was loved by so many people who were fortunate enough to know him. He was my hero.

Well, if there was ever a time to get back together, you would think that this would have been a good time for Adam and I to work through our differences and make it work. At least that is what one of my friends told me at Katie's house after the funeral. This was an old friend and neighbor who I lived across from when I lived out east, the same neighbor who kept my furniture and who became a very good friend. Adam was her nephew and she really wanted us to get back together. My response to her was, "I am devastated by Mark's death but I will not get back with Adam for that reason. If, and I mean if, we get back together it will be because he came to his senses and accepted the fact that he has a drinking problem and needs to seek help." She completely understood but I could tell she was hoping we would get back together through this tragedy or I may lose him. I took my chances.

Well, guess what? The prayers I said worked. One day out of the blue Adam calls me and says he had decided he needed to go to AA. He asked me if we could get back together right away and he asked me to go with him to the open meetings to support him and I was shocked. God had answered my prayers. He was going to go to AA. Wow, this was awesome! I said yes of course after all this was my prayer for six months. Obviously, this was my sign from God, I was elated with joy. Now life was going to be perfect and Adam would get help and would change and we can be happy.

So, he went to AA, just like he said. He got himself a sponsor (the sponsor was young like Adam and was only in AA a short time) and we went to open AA meetings. We started dating again but I told him he still needed to live where he was as I needed to be 100 percent sure this was going to work. So for a couple of month's things seemed to be good. But sometimes all good things must come to an end so they say (whoever they are). And it did. He called me one night and said he had started drinking a little bit and said that he wasn't coming over to see me that night as he knew I didn't like him drinking. I decided to play this a different way so I told him not to worry, I would come to his place and we would talk things out. He kept acting strange and finally I said listen I am coming over. I didn't take no for an answer. The girls were both at a sleep over so I went over to pick him up and bring him back to my house. On my way over to his place, I quickly said a prayer to God asking for him to be with me as I felt that something was up. I said something to the effect of letting God open my eyes to what I need to see. Something was wrong and I couldn't put my finger on it. Things were going good, why did I feel nervous all of a sudden?

When I got to his place (a small house he rented with another guy), there were several guys and girls there. Adam greeted me at the door and then suggested we go upstairs to get his stuff. I asked him who was downstairs and he said they were all friends of the guy he lived with. I felt like something was going on. He said he was happy I came and he loved me so much. He was also happy that I was letting him come to my house with a six pack. I was like, "Okay, well, let's get you packed and let's go."

We went downstairs and while he was getting a six-pack out of the fridge one of the girls asked me who I was and what was my relationship to Adam. I thought that was a strange question but I answered her. I told her who I was and that he was my boyfriend. Then she asked me how long I had been with him. I told her about seven years with a six-month breakup, why? Meanwhile, when we were talking, the whole place went quiet and Adam was nowhere to be seen. I asked her why again. She said, "Well, your boyfriend has been seeing my best friend for the last two years."

I turned around and looked down the hallway and Adam was just standing there and I screamed at him, "You fucking bastard!" I was beyond shocked. The girl standing beside the girl that told me was the one who was seeing him. They started to go out the door and I ran after her and said, "Please talk to me about this. I don't understand what is happening here." Adam came running out after us and I ignored him and she spoke to me. She said it was true that she had been seeing him for two years.

He was so angry that they told me that he looked her in the face and said, "I don't love you, I love her," pointing at me.

I was so confused and hurt. It was like being in a soap opera. I asked her a few more questions and we started to walk away from everyone toward the driveway and Adam broke a beer bottle to get us to stop. I hollered at him and said, "Well, now that's really going to change things and make things better, isn't it?"

Then he said to me, "The only reason I was with her is because you weren't there for me."

"What? What about the first five years of our relationship when I was there for you. I have been trying to better myself by going back to school, going to counseling, and taking care of my girls. How can you be so selfish?" Wow, I thought I had heard everything, but the sad thing was he thought it was true, I was not there for him and I was the selfish one.

I told him it was over and there was nothing he could ever do now to make me want to be with him. I could never ever trust him again. I was broken hearted and drove home with tears streaming down my face. I went home and couldn't get myself together so I went to my neighbor Marion's and stayed with her the night and cried and cried. My heart ached so much I couldn't breathe. And then I remembered I had prayed to God before I went over there to open my eyes to what I need to see and realized I got my answer. Yes, I got my answer and it was not what I expected in a million years.

Of all the people in the world he was the one guy I trusted to never cheat on me. And then I started putting things together that I found odd at times during the last two years. And then I realized the six months we were not together he was with her but he kept calling me to take him back. During those six months I prayed every day for God to get him to go to AA. Well, my friend Marion said to me that she always heard it said "to watch what you wish for and in my case watch what you pray for." Needless to say, I was devastated. But, I will say that I was very impressed with the friend of the girl who was with my boyfriend for two years. It takes a lot of courage to tell someone you don't know that her loved one is cheating on her. I know she didn't do it for me and that she did it for her friend but she did me a favor with her honesty. Otherwise, this soap opera could have been going on much longer and that wouldn't have been fair to either of us girls.

In the meantime, he tried for weeks to get me back. I kept telling him the same thing over and over that I could never trust him again, ever. I mean, come on, while he was calling me he was still seeing her. I may be slow sometimes but I am not stupid. And what clinched it for me was the day I saw them both sitting together on the veranda of the house he rented when I drove by and just a few nights before this he had called me and begged me to take him back. I was so angry when I saw him with her that I turned my car around and drove into his drive way. I wanted things settled once and for all. I got out of the car and when I got to the veranda his girlfriend had gone into the house. I asked him where she was and he said he was there alone. I went into the house and found her in the kitchen. I asked her what she was doing there and she said she and Adam were together. I asked her to come with me for a minute to talk to Adam.

She followed me to the veranda and sat down. The only question I asked him was, "Do you love her?"

He sat there for about a minute and finally said, "I love how she treats me."

I repeated what he said. "You love how she treats you?" Okay, I don't know about you, but if a guy said that to me and didn't say, "Yes, I love her," I would be furious and out of that relationship. But it was too late for her. I could tell she was in love. I just shook my head and walked away. I got into my car and knew it was over for me.

He came to my car window and said, "It's you I love, I will always love you."

I started my car, looked at him, and said, "Good-bye, Adam."

I knew now that it was over for me and I sold the wedding dress I had bought shortly after we had gotten engaged and I hawked the engagement ring he bought for me. I wanted nothing to do with him and nothing to remind me of him. One day when I was visiting my friend Marion my daughter came over with a huge glass vase filled with red roses and a white teddy bear. The card on it read something like, "I will always love you, Fancy Face." I started to cry because I missed him, but I knew that I could never be with him again.

Then he called several months later and said he was going away out west to deal with some of his past issues. I told him that was a good idea and I wished him all the best. My heart was finally starting to heal and even though I knew I could never trust him again I did want him to be free of his past and forgive those who hurt him. It was his journey to take and I knew it would be the best thing for him. The day before he left he came to see me and it was a surprise to open the door and see him standing there. He told me he couldn't leave without seeing me one last time and he hugged me. I hugged him back but when he tried to kiss me I pushed him away and then I told him to take good care of himself and have a safe trip. While he was out there my daughter had called him for a favor. He couldn't help her out at the time but he did want to talk to me. I spoke with him because I wanted to know how it was going for him and he told me things were going good and he was glad he went out there. I was happy for him but then he told me we should still be together and that we should never have broken up because he still loved me. I was shocked that he was still saying that to me because I knew in my heart and mind he was probably calling the other girl he had the affair with on me and telling her he loved her too. What a soap opera! I had enough and told him not to call me anymore unless it had to do with something important about his family. I told him I had moved on and was never going to take him back.

You know, even though we never got married, it still felt like a divorce to me. It felt like my heart was never going to totally heal so I reached out to my friends for support and one of my friends suggested a support group. I didn't find a support group but I did find a ten-week course on a book that helped people who were going through a divorce to let go and get through all the emotional feelings that are attached to getting a divorce. It ended up that all of us that did the ten-week course became close and we did support each other through the whole book. It was a really good course and it came to me at the right time in my life. I must say here that no matter what a person is dealing with we are very lucky and blessed to have so many programs out there that can help us deal with and overcome anything. Knowing that we are not alone and that our story can help someone else was a real eye opener for me. Sometimes I would be so consumed by my heartbreak that I could not see what was happening all around me. This group of people that I got to know and who I listened to while they shared their heartbreak was a gift to me. It takes a lot of courage for anyone to talk about their personal story and it leaves you wide open for criticism. But when we are all their together with a similar story and the same outcome we identify with that person and we do not judge or criticize because we are going through all the same emotions. I highly recommend for anyone going through a divorce to reach out to someone you trust and who you can share your most intimate story with or reach out and go to a support group with people who may not know you but will be there for you anyway because you are there for them. But whatever you choose to do try not to do it alone. You are important and your voice needs to be heard and you are loved dearly.

CHAPTER 15

It took me a good year before I was able to trust myself to go out with anybody again. I did go out with two guys after about a year but they ended in disaster. The first guy I dated was very nice but he decided we were better friends as he just had too many issues to work through himself. We had met through some mutual friends. At first I was really upset and felt disappointed but it wasn't too long before I realized he was right. We both had issues to deal with and it wasn't fair to either of us to bring these issues into the relationship. So, we stopped dating and I respected him for making that move.

The second guy I dated you could call a rebound. I have to admit although I knew I was better off without the first guy I did jump too fast into the next relationship. I jumped in with both feet and knew right from the beginning it wouldn't work, but I did not want to be alone and so I put my blinders on to the things I didn't like and ran headfirst into the relationship. We dated for several months and I think we both knew we were not on the same path, but instead of breaking up like we should have I did not want to be alone. But one night we had an argument and the next thing I know he had taken off into another city with my daughter Charlie's good friend Meagan. To make a long story short, they became an item. He came to my door and told me it was over between us and I was better off without him as we were too different and he could never be what I wanted him to be. I was really upset but not so much because of the break up but more because he was with my daughter's good friend Meagan. She was young and she was always with my daughter and we were very close. It felt like I was stabbed in the back, and the worst thing was that my dear friend Marion and I lost our friendship over it. You see Meagan was my good friend's niece. I was so hurt and angry that I wrote Meagan a long hateful letter about the guy she was now with. I regretted that letter because it was written with so much anger and he did not deserve the things I said. But at the time I was worried that Meagan was making a mistake. I tried to explain to Marion my side of the story but somehow things got really messed up between us and she had to stick with her family. And to be honest, I totally understood where she was coming from. But because of one man, I had lost two very good friends (Marion and Kaitlyn) who I adored and loved so much and I lost a relationship with Meagan. And my daughter and Meagan were not close anymore. It was just a sad thing that should never have happened. I wish I would have handled this situation differently. We were all hurt and lost years of great friendships within minutes.

When I look back at that time in my life, I realize I was still in such need of therapy. That damn dark cloud was always there and I had no idea that what was still inside of me would never go away until I dealt with it. I guess I still wasn't ready for a relationship and just didn't know how to be myself anymore. That's when I decided that I had enough of men. I decided I was going to be by myself and concentrate on me and my girls. The men I always ended up with hurt me and my self-esteem would take a beating. I wasn't perfect in the relationships now either. I realized I had trust issues and had to work on myself and my issues before I could get involved with anyone again or I was going to crack. And at this time in my life my girls were teenagers and they didn't deserve to be put on the back burner because I was lonely.

The one good thing in my life was that I still kept going to Al-Anon. The group was a lifesaver to me. They helped me through my sorrow and anger and I will always have nothing but good things to say about the Al-Anon family groups. I started speaking at some of the Al-Anon functions they had and found that I enjoyed being a speaker. They really helped me to open up and become more involved. I would take my girls to the Al-Ateen groups they had as I wanted my girls to know about the effects of alcohol. And you know it was just as well that I was alone now because my children were getting older and the teenage years were a bit tough. I asked my oldest daughter if I could share a story with you that I feel is important for all teenagers to hear. It's not a nice story but it could save someone's life so I will share it with you.

It started off like any other day in our home. Both of my girls were having a sleep over that night and their cousin was here from Ottawa. My oldest daughter Charlie was in having a bath and getting herself ready to go to the show with her cousin MacKenzie. I was having a cup of tea and having a nice conversation with my niece. All was pretty normal and the day was a beautiful day. As my niece and I were talking we got on the subject of alcohol. It was not a planned conversation we were just talking and that's where our talk led us. For some reason, I felt it necessary to tell my niece a story about my cousin's friend who died from alcohol poisoning. It was a sad story that ended in my cousin's friend dying. My cousin worked at a bar and became friends with most of her customers as they were regulars. To make a long story short this one guy friend had left the bar and went into the back parking lot and went to sleep in his truck. Unfortunately, the next morning, when someone saw the truck still there, they went over to check the vehicle and found this guy sleeping lying down on his back in the truck. When the person tried to wake up the guy they realized he may be dead. They saw puke on his face and it was very disturbing. Of course, they called the ambulance and it was too late, the young man had died of alcohol poisoning. They figured he lay down to sleep on his back and when he passed out he choked on his throw up. How horrifying this was for many of the customers who frequented this bar. It was a really sad and tough time for all who knew him and my cousin had a hard time with this also. I told this story to my niece and I told her that because she was at the age where kids experiment with alcohol I wanted her to promise me that if any of her friends were ever loaded and passed out in front of her to make sure they were not left alone on their back and that they were okay. And also if they thought the person may be in danger to call the ambulance. I drilled into her head how important it was never to get out of control with drinking and that it was very dangerous if too much was consumed. So, she promised me and then we talked about something else. By that time my daughter Charlie had her bath and was dressed and ready to go out. They were going to the movies the late show and I said I would pick them up. They just had to call me when it was over. So, I watched some TV while my younger daughter Ava hung out with her other cousins. All was well.

All was well, that is, until three hours later my niece came charging through the door calling my name in desperation. "Auntie, come quick. There is something wrong with Charlie!" I flew out of my chair and ran to the door. When I looked out the door I saw two guys carrying my daughter up the walk way toward our house. My first reaction was "What the fuck, that little bitch." I am not happy to say that I said this but I have to be honest. My words were spoken in anger and all I thought of was she lied to me. She was drunk. I told the boys to put her in the bathroom so I could sober her up and at least get the puke off her shirt and wash her up. But as they brought her in and I got a closer look I realized with great alarm and panic that she had wet herself and was out cold. I thanked the boys and they left. When I knelt down to my daughter my niece quickly told me what happened. She said they had gone to a party instead of the show because they ran into some of Charlie's friends. There were several of them who were drinking shots of something strong. I assumed it was probably rye because she said she was drinking it with coke and she was drinking slowly especially after the talk we had just had. She said that Charlie was being dared to drink a lot of shots.

She would pinch her nose because she didn't like the smell and then drink it down. My niece said she kept drinking shots one after the other and all of a sudden she just dropped to her knees and passed out on the floor. My niece asked a couple of the guys to help bring her outside to get some fresh air and maybe it would sober her up. They took her outside and my niece went back inside to get some water for my daughter. When she came outside with the water she noticed Charlie was on her back. She screamed at the boys to get her off her back and ran to Charlie and tried to get her to wake up. She then realized that Charlie was completely out and she was starting to throw up but her mouth wasn't opening all the way and she noticed that she had wet her pants. Without any more hesitation, my niece said she needed someone to drive them home to her aunt's house as she was concerned her cousin was in trouble with her life. Two other guys just pulled up to the party and were good friends of my daughters and saw her condition and said they would drive her home. So, that is where my nightmare began.

I thanked my niece profusely for bringing her home and assured her that my daughter would be okay but I had no idea if that would be true. I tried to wake Charlie up but she lay there so limp and her color was not good. I screamed for my younger daughter Ava to go and get our neighbor Marion. When Marion saw Charlie, she said we needed to try and see if we could get her mouth open. I tried to get my fingers to open her mouth so we could get the throw up out of her mouth as by this time we were afraid her breathing and pulse were almost nothing. I could barely get my fingers in her mouth as her mouth was locked up and I could only get a little of the throw up out. I started to panic and said, "Oh my Lord, she is dying." I started to shake and felt like I was going to pass out. I said we better call the ambulance and my friend said we didn't have time to wait. We needed to get her to the hospital right away.

I said, "What about the lights? We have to stop."

She said, "Fuck the lights, let's go."

We quickly loaded Charlie into the car and I told Ava everything would be okay and I would be back shortly Mackenzie would watch her and her cousin until I got back.

My friend drove fast and steady and did not stop for any lights. By this time, I am a basket case. I am so full of anxiety and panic but I start praying in my head asking God to please help her. I say this over and over. We get to the hospital and they take one look at her and rush her to an emergency room. I want to go with her but I have to explain what happened and give the lady all of my daughter's information. I am not doing well with this and I am cranky at the lovely lady taking the information and I say I just want to be with my daughter. Please can I not do this later? She assures me that I am not allowed to go in right now because the doctor and nurses need to help her. What I heard in my head was the doctors and nurses are trying to save her life, which was more to the truth of it. I am just beside myself, I am beyond reason and my friend tries her very best to keep me calm and trust that the doctors will save her.

What felt like forever was a couple hours and then a doctor comes out and talks to me about my daughter. He tells me she had alcohol poisoning and they pumped her stomach to get the poison out of her. He said now it is a waiting game, she is okay for now but has not woken up yet and at this point he didn't know if she had any brain damage. He said she drank triple times over her body weight and we just had to wait for her to come to. I was devastated but I was allowed to go in and see her now.

Do you remember when I told you at the beginning of my book when I saw my mother in the coffin and I lost my breath and I ran into my father's coat? Well, the feelings were similar when I saw my daughter lying in the hospital bed. I lost my breath and my heart was beating out of my chest. Only I didn't run away. Instead, I went right to her bedside and touched her still hand. She was hooked up to several contraptions and her mouth was hooked up to a tube where green bile was making its way out of her and into a bag or some sort of contraption. I couldn't stop crying as I looked down at her pale face and didn't know if my little girl was still there in her mind. Eventually, a very sweet nurse came over to me and she had tears running down her face. She said her daughter was the same age and watching me look at my daughter really hit her that this can happen to anyone's child. She just couldn't wait to get off her shift and go and be with her daughter. She was very kind to me and said listen it may be awhile, maybe several more hours before she wakes up why don't you go home and we will call you immediately when she wakes up. She said she would call me personally. I didn't want to leave. I hesitated for a long time and then my friend said, "Come on, honey, let's go. She is in good hands. We will come back as soon as the nurse calls us." I agreed as I thought I should check on my youngest daughter and my nieces, but it was very, very hard for me to leave.

When I returned home I thanked my friend and told her I would call her when I got the call. She hugged me and assured me everything would be okay. I went into the house like a zombie. I was so distraught and the adrenaline in my body would not settle down. I checked on Ava and my nieces. They were fine but very concerned about the situation. I assured them she was okay and will be home the next day. They were all in bed when I got home but now they could go to sleep. I went into the living room and there was a bench in front of my big living room window. I kneeled down beside the bench, put my hands together and prayed like I never prayed before. I begged and begged and begged God to save her and to let her be okay. I cried and cried. I did not sleep at all that night. How could anyone sleep when their child was in the hospital and you didn't know whether they would be okay when they woke up? I started to put myself down for leaving the hospital and said I should be there. Several hours had gone by and still no word. It was now close to five in the morning I was starting to panic again. What if the nurse left before my daughter woke up and the new nurse doesn't get my number? "I need to be there, how could I leave? God, please help me. This is too much to bear. Please, please, God, let her be okay." The prayers just kept going and going. I could not stop praying and

I would not stop praying. I decided if I hadn't heard word from them soon I was going to the hospital because I needed to be there. About twenty minutes later, around six that morning the nurse called me and said my daughter had woken up and she was okay. I got down on my knees and thanked God and praised his holy name and felt the biggest relief to hear that my daughter was going to be okay. I didn't want to wake up my friend Marion to take me back up to the hospital as she had two young children to get up to that morning. So I called my friend Tat and told her what happened and asked her to come and take me to the hospital. She was at my house in a matter of minutes and she was pissed at me, which I don't blame her. She was my closest friend and I should have called her when this was all happening but I was so freaked out that I just wanted to get Charlie to the hospital and then time just slipped away. She forgave me but told me that the next time her daughter Mel was here at my house and wanted to call her mother to let her. Apparently, when this was all happening, my niece was so upset and wanted to call her mom and I said, "No, keep the lines free," and nobody was allowed to call anybody. Then later I totally forgot that I told Mel not to call her mom and I felt so bad because she was afraid and I just left them all there while I went to the hospital. I just wasn't thinking properly.

So, Tat and I went to the hospital. When I walked in to see Charlie the tubes were out and she just had a breathing apparatus on her face and an IV in her arm. When she saw me, she started to cry and lifted the mask and said she was sorry and asked me what happened. The doctor was a very smart man because before I could answer her question he said something like, "I hope you realize that what happened to you could have taken your life. You are one very lucky girl to be alive." He didn't pull any punches. He wanted her to realize the actual danger she put herself in. I was glad he took the time to tell her this. She started to cry when she realized she could have died. She couldn't remember anything. I told her we would talk about it later and for her to rest for now. She had panicked when she first woke up because she woke up in a hospital bed hooked up to things that were unfamiliar to her. The nurse assured her I was on my way and she would be okay.

Needless to say, I was happy and thankful she would be okay and after a half hour of visiting with her I went outside with Tat to talk to the doctor. The doctor was very optimistic that she was okay and the worst that would happen to her now would be a terrible pounding headache and a very bad hangover. I thanked him several times and he was just happy Charlie's story turned out okay. He told me not all patients who have alcohol poisoning live to share their story. I asked him what was the next step if there was one and when could she go home. He smiled at me and said, "Well, I would like to make a suggestion that might seem mean but it is up to you." I was not sure what he was going to suggest but I was open to hear him out. He told me he could keep my daughter there for the whole day and keep her on the IV and make her hangover somewhat bearable by doing this. "Or, you can take her home and let her suffer for a couple days with a pounding headache and hangover."

I smiled at him and said, "I see where you are going with this and I appreciate your suggestions. My biggest fear is that if I take her home what if she is still not okay, what if something happens?"

The doctor assured me she was out of the woods and she would be just fine. He felt she needed to see that drinking the way she did was not smart and he wanted her to remember the hangover and pounding headache as a reminder of what happened to her. I thought about it and agreed with him. She would stay another hour and then we could take her home.

Well, it was quite the ride home! We had to have all the windows down because she was not feeling very good and thought she was going to be sick several times on the way home. Tat and I didn't say too much but did not have a lot of sympathy for her once we knew she was okay and the symptoms she was having now would be gone in a day or so. She still seemed a bit out of it. She was actually funny but this wasn't a funny situation. She lay on the couch and I gave her some Tylenol. She slept most of the day and when she was awake she complained of feeling sick to her stomach and her head pounding. I thought to myself that I would rather see her sick to her stomach and complaining than not to see her at all. The next day when I used some hairspray on my hair she said the hairspray reminded her of alcohol and it made her sick just smelling it. She had a rough few days and then she was grounded and wasn't allowed out of my sight for a week. She didn't argue with me for she knew better and her birthday was just a week or so away. My daughter was just shy of fifteen years old when that horrific episode happened.

There were other things going on in my life at this time with Charlie that were very tough times but we managed to get through those times. Those tough times are Charlie's story and it is not my place to share them but it is my place to say that no matter what she did I never stopped loving her. I stuck by her through it all and never abandoned her. But some of her actions did end up having me to make a big decision about high school. My good friend Tat offered to let Charlie stay at her house and go to the Catholic high school for grade 10 and as hard as it was for me to make this decision we decided it was the best thing for her. She was to spend time with her sister and me on the weekends. Charlie did not want to go at first but I wanted her to finish high school and she was not doing well at the high school she was in as she had a problem with peer pressure. With a heavy heart, I made her go to her aunt Tat's house which was only twelve minutes away. I was very thankful to Tat and Kevin to open up their home to Charlie. They didn't hesitate to take her in for the school year at all. They were always willing to help our family in any way they could. It was so great to have them in our lives. We were very blessed. Now they had three children to take care of and I appreciated their kindness so much. I know without a doubt I was meant to have Tat and Kevin in my life. Sometimes I think they knew me better than I knew myself during those years. And Charlie actually did well at the high school and she passed grade 10. But after being home with me for the summer, she wanted to finish her high school back at her old school and she missed living with Ava and me. So, because I missed her too I let her come home to finish high school with us. I was very happy to have her home again. Even when she was at her Aunt Tat's house and I saw her all the time I still wanted her home with me. I guess I felt I needed her to be home because she was my responsibility and I needed to feel like I was a good mom.

Eventually, Charlie met a young man at her high school and they became a couple. His name was Jacob. He came into Charlie's life when she was just about sixteen and a half years old. He went to the same high school as Charlie and seemed like a nice young man. I was concerned that he was older than her but he treated her good so I treated him with respect and trust. Needless to say, Jacob and I became very close and he became like a son to me and he looked out for our family, especially Ava. She was like his little sister.

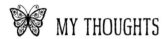 ## MY THOUGHTS

Wow, where do I begin? I think that this story would make any parent feel the same sort of feelings I was feeling. Yes, I could have been very angry at my daughter when she finally woke up in the hospital but that was not how I wanted to handle it. I was so thankful that she woke up and was still my little girl. I knew that the hospital was not the time or place to have a discussion about the alcohol she had consumed. When she woke up she was truly sorry and was full of fear of not being able to remember what happened. I could tell by the look on her face when the doctor said she was lucky to be alive that she was serious about being sorry.

I waited a couple of days when she was home after she was hangover free to talk to her about the situation and how we all felt. I know she didn't want to have this conversation but it had to be dealt with. We talked for a long time and shared each other's thoughts on the situation. I told her I was so surprised that she would do this when she knew what alcohol could do. After all I had her going to Al-Ateen and she learned what alcoholism was. But, there was something I didn't think of, these groups are for family and friends who love a loved one who has a drinking problem and is an alcoholic and to teach us how to cope with that and understand alcoholism. These groups were not exactly about teaching how to stay away from alcohol yourself or how to drink sensibly. I should have given my daughter the same story I gave my niece. But, I can't totally blame myself. First off, she was a teenager, trying to find herself. Secondly, she was with her friends and the last thing she would think about was the Al-Ateen meetings she attended sometimes. And thirdly, life happens. I can analyze this to death and still I won't really have the answer to why this happened to her. It happened and I am thankful she didn't die. That may sound strong about her dying but it is reality, she could have died, end of story.

Now, I have a question that I would like to put out there: "Why did my niece and I have a conversation out of the blue about the alcohol poisoning that my cousin's friend died of?" I have thought about that for a long time. Some people may say it was a coincidence and that is okay. But I say it was something beyond my comprehension that put that thought in my head so my daughter's story would end happily and not the way my cousin's friend's story turned out. I believe with all my heart that it was God or an angel of God who put that thought in my head. I don't know how it works but I do know that I had no idea why I brought up that story to my niece. If I hadn't of brought up that story my niece may have just waited thinking my daughter would soon wake up and then it may have been too late for my daughter.

So, how do we keep our children from making a similar mistake that my daughter made? I am not an expert but in my opinion the best way to help our children is to talk to them. Even if they say, "Mom (or Dad), I already know this stuff you don't need to tell me about it. We do need to talk about what can happen." I would rather have my children upset with me for a few minutes of talking to them than not having the conversation and them finding out for themselves. Our children need to know that alcohol can be deadly.

Yes, a few drinks at a certain age is fine, but succumbing to a dare to drink straight liquor and keep going is not fine, especially at a young age. I just think that every child should know that there are dangers that come with drinking and if they are going to drink with their friends then be aware of their surroundings. Always have a buddy that watches out for you and you for them when you go out drinking. Never let someone you don't know make you a drink. Say that's okay, I can make it or let your best friend make it for you while you watch him. But never think, "Oh, it's okay, nothing will happen." Too many of us think nothing can happen to us and then we become a victim or another statistic. Be a good friend, when you see that your friend may be way over the limit it would be a good time to suggest let's go get a coffee or start drinking water. It may sound silly and not hip but when we are talking about your life it is not silly. I am not saying that we shouldn't drink at all. I am saying there comes a time in our life when it's time to drink sensibly or not at all.

Do I think that having a conversation with our children will keep them from drinking too much? I would like to think so, but let's be honest, would I have listened? I really don't know. What I do know is that it may help some children to be more aware of how much they drink. And it may not help children at all because there is always that sense of adventure in all of us. But wouldn't you feel better knowing you did have a conversation with your children about the dangers of alcohol and that may stop them in the future from going too far. I think it is worth it.

Seeing my daughter in the state she was in when the young boys brought her home to me was a nightmare. It is a nightmare that I will always hate and I still to this day have problems when I see people, young and old, going too far with drinking. It is never too late to tell a story about alcohol poisoning. Share this story and know that it may save a life.

CHAPTER 16

During the last couple of years when my relationship with Adam was on the rocks and then we had broken up and then there was a long period before I dated again, I got a job at the university in my city. It was a great job and paid well and it was with the Parking Administration. My job was to get parking passes made up and charged out to all the students and faculty. It was a very busy job and I really liked it. The only downfall about this job was that it was always a contract position. So, the first year I worked full time hours for eight months, the next year I worked another eight months, and the last year I worked six months. I loved this job but I felt like I needed to still look for other jobs when I was on hiatus. The months I wasn't working I made little on unemployment and I realized as much as I loved the University job I needed to look for a permanent full time job. I started looking every day and put out applications everywhere. Nothing was biting but I was determined to get a job.

Charlie and Jacob were still together and that made me happy. Charlie got her first job at a fast food restaurant and she was a hard worker. She took pride in her job and did very well. I was proud of her. Then Charlie came to me one day and started to cry and said she was pregnant. She was eighteen and I wasn't happy with this but I accepted it. What was I to do? It was a little late for a scolding and she was excited about having this baby. As I said earlier I was always there for my girls as best I could be and would never abandon them especially in their time of need. But I must say the one thing I regretted when this was all going on that my youngest daughter Ava should have had more attention. I tried my very best to spend time with Ava but I feel I may have let her down sometimes. Those are years I can never get back. Ava did not give me any problems and it was such a relief for me but I regret being more hard on Ava. I was very strict with her. She was my baby and I was so afraid something would happen to her so I didn't let her do other things her friends were doing. My girls were everything to me but I also made mistakes. I wasn't a perfect mom but I did the best I could with what I knew. If I could go back, I would change a few things, but I can't go back. The one thing I did do was give them so much love and I let them know how much I loved them and how proud I was of them. I taught them good morals and values and let them know they could do anything they wanted in life but they had to work hard for it. And I am happy to say that they both turned out wonderful. Charlie and Ava are both amazing daughters, mom's and wives. They have both worked very hard in their career choices and are doing extremely well in their fields. I am so blessed and very proud of both of my daughters.

Moving on to where I left off, I was looking for a job. During this time, I got a call from Ava's friend's dad. I had no idea who this man was except that his daughter went to school with Ava and she had been to my house for Ava's birthday party. He was wondering if I was interested in going out for coffee. Well, this was not a good time for me and the last thing I wanted was to go out for coffee with any man. So, in my politest voice, I said, "Thank you for calling, but I am not interested in going out for coffee with any man. I just got out of a bad relationship and I am not interested. I am sure you are a nice man but no thank you." That was the end of that. I knew that I was done with men. I did not want anything to do with any man. All I wanted was to be there for my girls and go to Al-Anon and church. I was very hateful and angry toward men. It didn't matter to me what kind of men all men were now off limits to me. I was not going to put myself out there anymore. No way, no how, uh-uh, not happening!

So in the meantime a month goes by from that phone call and I get another phone call from Ava's friend's mother. Her name is Kerrie and I know her from dropping Ava off at her house to hang out with her daughter.

She says to me, "I hear my friend Michael called you to ask you out for coffee."

"Yes, he did, and I said no." She told me she knew him very well and that he was a really great guy. I tell her, "Well, I am sure he is a great guy but I am sick of all guys, whether they are great or not."

She laughed at me and told me I just had to give him a try and I wouldn't regret it. I kept arguing with her that I was quite happy on my own and I was done with men and that was the end of it. She would not give up. I was on the phone with her for a long time and she had me laughing. She said, "Well, would you at least come to my house for a game of cards and I could invite him and his girls and it will just be a get-to-know-you kind of thing with no pressure?" She exhausted me and I finally gave in. I told her not to expect me to date him but I would meet him. I already knew his daughter Bree and I thought she was a sweet girl but I had no intention what so ever getting involved with another man.

So, that Saturday night I went to Kerrie's house to play cards with Ava and Charlie and be checked out by this great guy she told me about. I got through the night and was so glad when it was over because I felt like I was on display. Yes, he seemed like a nice guy and he was tall with nice blue eyes, a handsome face and nice arms. But I was not interested. Why can't people see that I am a very angry person right now and the last thing I need in my life is another man? Come on, people, leave me alone. But there you have it, my only hope was that he wouldn't like me and not call me again.

It hadn't even been twenty-four hours later when I got the call I did not want to get. Yes, Michael called me the very next day and asked me out to dinner. I wanted desperately to say no but now I felt that I would offend his sweet daughter Bree if I didn't go out with her dad. I was not a happy camper. But I said yes.

He picked me up and we went out to dinner. We made small talk and I couldn't wait for the dinner to be over. He genuinely was a nice man but my head and heart were not in it. I was damaged and I knew that no one would be able to repair me. I had accepted that at my age of thirty-nine I was too old for this. I was so sick of all the niceties and then came the real truth of how relationships go for me. I had to look out for myself and I was not backing down. Then Michael called me a few days later and asked me out to dinner again. I told myself I had to be honest with this guy and so I planned to talk to him at dinner and tell him what I felt about dating. And so the poor guy had no idea what he was in for when we went out for dinner the second time. I started off telling him that I thought he was a nice guy but if he wanted anything more than friendship that I was not interested. I told him I had a few bad relationships and I was done with men. The only thing I wanted from him was his friendship and if he wanted to be my friend then we could continue to see each other. I was brutally honest about my intentions and I wasn't giving him an inch. He agreed that he would like to continue seeing me and become friends. This made me suspicious but I accepted his answer and we did in fact become friends.

He wanted to come to my house but I never let him in my house ever. I put up a wall and it was a high wall and nobody was going to break that wall unless I wanted it broken. Let's just say I was told by my friends, especially Tatiana that I was a bitch to him. I would always say, "He knows that I am only seeing him as a friend, he agreed to it and that's just the way it is." Wow, I really was a bitch. I had never been that way to anyone and he took it. He would call me every several days and see if I wanted to go to the show or go for a long walk along the river. We would go out for dinner or lunch sometimes depending on the day. We talked about everything and got to know more and more about each other. During this time, I was still dealing with the loss of my friendship with my good friend

Marion. It was so hard for me to live next door to her knowing she was so upset with me for my part in our friendship dissolving. I was heartbroken to lose her as my friend and not only did I lose her but I lost another dear friend. There were things said between us that were misinterpreted and it just became a mess. I am happy to say that eventually all was forgiven. And though my friends moved away I am blessed to still have them as friends for life.

But in the meantime, I got the news that the townhouse I lived in was going up in rent. It was going up another two hundred dollars a month. I was so upset because I loved my townhouse but there was no way I could afford this. I had been there for nine years. I had also written a beautiful letter (several months before) and read it to the mayor of our city at an open meeting asking that the tenants of these townhouses who have lived there for years be allowed to buy them. The owners of these townhouses wanted to be able to sell the townhouses to us but had to get approval from the city. Several of us tenants all went to the meeting and spoke up on behalf of the owners to allow this to happen. I was even on TV, which I found to be so funny. About a year later, the townhouses were up for sale and the tenants were allowed to buy the townhouses and use the money they had spent already as a down payment. It was a great deal for those who were still there.

But some of us had to leave before this deal came through. I had to move fast and get a place to live for me and my girls. I was in a state of panic as I was a single mom and was on unemployment until the university called again. It was down to several weeks left of finding a place to live. Then someone told me about these town homes that were not far from where I lived that were rented to low income families. I could try there. I called and talked to a nice lady who felt bad but wasn't sure if I could get in until the next month. I started crying and told her I had nowhere to go and that I would be out on the street with my two girls. She said she would call me back in a couple days and let me know if there was any way to get me in sooner. She knew there was one of the townhouses available but did not know if it was already taken and the lady who took care of the rental was not available until the following Monday. I was on pins and needles as the following Monday meant I had two weeks left to find a place. I dragged my butt everywhere and called everywhere but I did not have any luck.

I knew that my good friend Tat would take us in but I did not want to be a burden. And where would I put all my furniture? And I still needed to find a job. I just wanted my own place again. I had raised my girls in this one home for nine years and I was so proud of not having to crash at other people's homes again. I had enough of that in the early years when Charlie was just a baby and then a toddler. So, on that Monday, the nice lady called me back and told me that I could have the townhouse and to come down right away and we could get all the paper work done. I was ecstatic to say the least. I thanked God right away and just before I moved into the townhouse I even got a job offer. I was elated with joy. Something good was happening for me and I was so thankful.

Michael asked me if he could help me move and I told him no. I told him that would be too personal for me. He owned a big truck and I didn't care. I had to do this on my own and if he helped me then it meant he would get closer and I couldn't have that now, could I? So my best friend Tat and her husband rented a truck and came to help me move. They were always there for me through thick and thin. My brother Brad and my sister-in-law Christine just happened to be coming up to visit from the east coast at the same time I was moving and they were there when I moved into the new townhouse. I was so happy to have them there and have all the help that I needed. I just wished that I could have had more quality time with them as they came a long way to see us. But, they were just happy to be with us and happy to help out. By this time in my life I had been down east to see my brother and sister-in-law and their family a couple of times and I adored my brother and his family. This was one of many happy times we got to spend with each other and get to know each other better since we were kids.

CHAPTER 17

I would miss my old townhouse and my dear friends but I knew I had to move on with my life and start fresh. Now I was in my new townhouse with my girls and I was starting a new job. I was scared and unsettled but I knew I had to go forward. My life would be different now which was okay, but I still had that black cloud that still followed me. I would just shove those dark feelings down again and get on with the next step in my life. I finally asked Michael if he would come over to my new place and help me put up wall paper. He came just like I knew he would. Now, wallpaper is not one of my favorite things to put up and this was a wallpaper border which was worse. But we got through it and I started to look at Michael a little differently and then would just shake it off. No way, not going there!

But he must have noticed that I was being nicer to him and allowing him to come over more often because one night he decides when he is at the bottom of my staircase to ask me if he could give me a kiss goodnight. My reaction was one I am not proud of as I said, "Oh, for goodness' sake, I guess so." Well, would you really want to kiss someone after they gave you that answer? I know I wouldn't but he came back up the stairs and gave me the quickest kiss on the lips ever. I wasn't sure if it happened or not. The poor guy, I felt like a heel the next few days. And then something came across me and I admired him for putting up with me for this long and I knew I had to give this poor guy a chance.

So, we got together one night and I told him I was going to give him a chance and be his girlfriend. After all, anyone who stuck around for three months and put up with the shit I put him through deserved a medal, and so our friend relationship turned into something more. We were really just into our relationship about six months and then my brother called and said our dad was dying of lung cancer and the doctors were not sure how much time he had. I was devastated to hear this news as it had been a while since I had spoken to my dad. Not because of anything wrong between us just that I was so consumed with the things happening in my life. Shortly after this call my sister called and asked me if I wanted to go down home with her to spend a week at my aunt Maggie's house and visit our dad. She was flying down and I just didn't have the money to do that but I really wanted to go with her and see our dad. And wouldn't you know it Michael came to my rescue and made it possible for me to go down and spend a week with my dad. He also offered to take care of Ava at his house while I was gone. Charlie was okay as she had Jacob to take care of her. So, off to the east coast I went. We stayed at my aunt Maggie's and our dad's brother Elton would pick us up just about every day and take us to the hospital.

As I stood in the doorway of my dad's hospital room, I started to panic at what I saw. My dad was so thin and frail and his skin had an eerie yellow tone. He had the look of fear on his face as if he had seen something scary. I looked at him for a moment and saw a man who was so ill that he already looked like death to me. I didn't know how I was going to be able to walk in to his room and talk to him like nothing was wrong but I knew I had to. My sister is a nurse and she instinctively walked right into his room and starting talking to him. I made my legs move to get to the bottom of my dad's hospital bed. I looked right at him and said, "Hello, Dad." He didn't know who we were. It broke my heart. My dad didn't know me. I wanted to run out and cry somewhere but I knew I had to be strong. My brother sat beside our dad on a chair and told him who we were.

"Dad, it's your daughters. They flew here to see you."

He looked at us for the longest time and still had no idea whom we were. Then my sister said we should sing "Tiny Bubbles" to my father and maybe it would jog his memory. I didn't want to because I was being a brat. I was so full of emotion I couldn't focus on the task at hand.

Then she said to me again, "Come on, sis. Let's sing for Dad."

I said okay and we started singing "Tiny Bubbles."

When we were almost done, my dad looked at my brother and said, "That's my girls singing."

My brother smiled and said, "Yes, Dad, that's your girls singing."

I was so happy that for a few minutes our dad knew who we were. You see, the cancer was now in his brain and he was having a hard time placing people. He hadn't seen us in a long time so we probably looked really different to him. He would put the blanket up to his neck and look at me and say, "Did you see that bad ice storm that was a bad ice storm?"

I would say, "Yes, Dad, it was a bad ice storm." Before he went into the hospital there was a bad ice storm from Ottawa right across Quebec and through the eastern provinces. It was horrible as it had taken down so many trees and power lines across the provinces. After we talked about the storm my dad kept saying he was cold. I went to see if we could get him extra blankets but there were none available. My heart was breaking. All this man wanted was a blanket. There was nothing left to him, he was skin and bones and he was cold.

When we went back to the hospital the next day we took our dad down the hall to get his hair cut and we had a good laugh together as a family. I remember as if it was yesterday, the four of us, my dad in the wheelchair, my brother pushing the wheelchair, my sister pushing the IV pump, and me just walking along with them. It was the first time we had all been together as a family in ages. It was bittersweet.

When we went back to my aunt Maggie's that night I stayed upstairs and cried and cried. And then I wrote a letter to God begging him to take my father to heaven with him where he could have some dignity and peace because he was so lost and dying. I wrote several pages just asking God to free him of this torture. He was in pain and he just looked like a lost little boy to me. I was so torn apart inside to see my dad like this. My two brothers from my dad's second marriage were having a rough time in their lives at this time. I did not see them at the hospital while I was there. I only knew that I felt very bad for them. I knew that their life growing up was not a happy one either and losing our dad would be hard on both of them. By the time I went down for dinner with my aunt Maggie and uncle John and my sister, I was feeling much better but the one thing that still nagged at me was the fact that my dad was cold. I couldn't get that image out of my head. The man just wanted an extra blanket. I mentioned this to my aunt and she said she would look for an extra blanket. In the meantime, Uncle Albert came to see us and took us to a secondhand store to find some sort of blanket and pajamas for our dad. By the time we got back to see our dad we had a blanket and it was an old wool blanket that my aunt Maggie gave me. I was so happy that my dad had a warm blanket for his bed. It was the only thing I could do for him and it filled my heart with so much love. I just wanted my dad to be warm, that's all I wanted because that's all he asked for. I loved my dad and when my sister and I left him the last day we were there someone took pictures of the four of us. That picture was the last picture of our dad and his first three children. I kissed him on the forehead and hugged him and then told him I loved him. I whispered, "Good-bye, Dad," as I walked out of that hospital room knowing that was the last time I would see him alive. My sister and I left later on the plane and my uncle John drove us to the airport. He had tears in his eyes as he said good-bye to us as he knew we were heartbroken.

When we arrived at the airport, Michael was waiting for me. I was so happy to see him. When we got in his truck and we were sitting there he passed me a gift bag and said he bought me something he thought I would like. I opened the package and it was a book with the title *Chicken Soup for the Woman's Soul*. I was so full of love that day for him. He couldn't have gotten me a better present at that moment and time. I read the book and loved every story that was in it. It was around this time that I knew I was falling for Michael and it scared me but I welcomed the warm fuzzy feelings I was having for him.

Three weeks later we got the call that my father passed away. I had told my family when I came home from seeing him several weeks before that I was not going down to the funeral. But when we got the news, I told Michael I had changed my mind and I had to be there to say my last good-bye. Michael said I should go or I may regret it. I wanted to go and be there with my family and so Michael drove me to my sisters and I went down with her and her husband. Michael watched Ava for me. Actually, by this time, Ava is in her mid-teens so she just needed someone to be with her at night.

When I arrived back from the funeral I was so depressed and cried a lot at night. But three weeks after my dad was buried my granddaughter was born. Jacob and Charlie had a beautiful baby girl and I was smothered with joy and happiness. My daughter Charlie actually wanted me in the room when her child was born. I was there for her as she gave birth and it was amazing to see my granddaughter born. Her birth took the sting out of the death of my father. Charlie and my granddaughter Jordan lived with me and Ava for the first eight months of her little life. She was spoiled with so much love and taken care of with so much love. Jacob at this time lived with his parents but he was over all the time with Charlie and their baby girl. Jordan was such a cuddly baby and we used to just lie on my couch together and cuddle. I didn't know that a grandchild could bring a parent so much joy and love until Jordan came into my life. She was the apple of my eye and I adored her. My very first grandchild, and I couldn't be happier than I was when she was in my arms.

Michael and I had gotten much closer and he told me he loved me. I couldn't tell him how I felt at first. But as the time went on and I knew I could trust him I let myself fall in love with him. It was my turn to tell him and so this one day when we were walking by the river hand in hand I stopped by this bench and said let's sit here for a while. We talked about silly things but eventually I told him I had something to tell him. The poor guy looked concerned at first and then I put my hand on his arm and told him that I was falling in love with him. He leaned over and held me close and said, "I love you too." He was smiling from ear to ear. I looked at him and told him I was scared but he assured me that we were meant to be and we would be happy. From that day on I never looked back and I trusted him to love me and be faithful to me.

Eventually, Michael asked me if I would buy a house with him so we could live together and be a family. I was so scared because this was a really big step for me and I was petrified that something would ruin it and I would be alone again. I still had a dark cloud following me and I wasn't sure what to do. And besides all that I had a cat and he had a big dog! My friends Tatiana and Kevin thought it was a good idea. I had never owned a house before and this was so over-whelming for me but Michael convinced me that everything would work out so I said yes and we went searching for our house. Charlie and Jacob were to move in together and take over the townhouse that we were living in so I was happy they would have a nice place to live. In the meantime, Ava was pretty excited about a new house and that made me feel better because it wasn't just about me, I had Ava to think about. My girls and I had been living on our own for a long time and now we would be living with a man.

We looked at a few houses and then one day when Michael and Ava were driving to our townhouse they spotted a house up on a hill for sale. They drove up to the house and liked the look of it on the outside and couldn't wait to get home and tell me. I went to look at it with them and I fell in love with the house. It needed some changes and my spin on it but it had everything we needed and a huge yard for our animals. We made an offer and the house was ours. Just like that, we were house owners. I was so nervous at first but Michael assured me it was just like renting, only we would own this house one day so I eventually relaxed into that way of thinking and enjoyed making the house our own. I would like to say that we all fit together like a fine-toothed comb but that was not the case at first. Like I said earlier, I had a cat and he had a dog. They did not get along for the first six months and that could be stressful sometimes. But after six months or so they warmed up to each other and became somewhat friendly. Michael and I had been on our own for a long time too and we had to get used to each other's way of living. Ava and I had to get used to Michael's way of saying things. Ava was a lot like me and we would take things to heart. But, in the big picture we all came to know each other better and worked through the things we had to work through and moved on to the next chapter in our lives.

"I have something to tell you, honey."

That was how Michael started this conversation. So because he called me honey I figured what he was about to tell me was going to be bad. But I said, "What's that, honey?" with a smile on my face.

And here is what he tells me as slowly and as carefully as he can: "Okay, I have to confess something to you. I saw you long before I first saw you at our friend Kerrie's house. Remember how we first met at her house and we played cards and the next day I called and asked you out?"

"I remember."

"Well, one day I was at a store called VV looking at books to buy. And while I was there I saw this slim, pretty-faced woman who looked a lot like Bree's friend Ava from school."

"Aha."

"Well, I thought this woman looked so much like Ava that I thought somehow I have got to get to know if that is Ava's mother. So, I waited for this woman to leave VV and I watched her get into her car and leave. And then I followed her."

"You what?"

"Let me explain. I had to follow you because I had to know who you were because Bree had said a long time ago that she had the perfect woman for me and I told her that I was not going out with one of her friend's mom. She told me it was Ava's mom and I told her no I am not interested."

"So what are you telling me, Michael?"

"I am saying I followed you home to see where you lived and then I drove home and called Bree and asked her what kind of vehicle you drove and where you lived. And she told me what I needed to know and I was correct that you were Ava's mom. Bree asked me why I wanted to know about Ava's mom but I just told her never mind, thank you."

"Michael! Do you know what this means? You stalked me!"

"No, no, honey, I didn't stalk you!"

"Oh, yeah, then what would you call it?"

"Well, I wouldn't call it stalking!"

"Really, Michael? I can't believe you stalked me! Of all the crazy things to do to someone, that is not acceptable! This is really creepy! What the hell I am supposed to think?"

"Honey, it's okay, it all worked out. The moment I saw you in VV I knew you were the woman I was going to marry, have you ever heard of love at first sight?"

I was speechless for a few minutes. He told me in a few months I would laugh at this. He asked me to see his point of view. Bree's friend Ava had a single mom. He saw this woman who looked identical to Ava and he thought I was good looking. He also said if it worked out that I was Ava's mom that he would be very lucky and happy. I asked him if that is how he usually met his woman. He laughed at me and said no of course not. He said he was desperate and thought he may never see me again and had to take desperate measures to find out who I was. He made it very clear to me that this was the first and only time he ever followed anyone home. He said the resemblance of Ava and I was so strong that he had to be sure.

So, after I somewhat accepted the confession he told me, I decided he would pay and pay dearly. So what better way to get him back then to tell our four girls the creepy story. Hahahahahaha. Yes, that is exactly what I did and he had no choice but to sit there when I told them. They were shocked and couldn't believe their dad had done this. I was enjoying the way the girls were cross examining him and making fun of him. That's the day that they started calling him "the stalker." And I didn't stop there, I told the story to our good friends Tat and Kevin and a few others who had the biggest laugh over the whole situation. I must admit that I eventually had a great laugh about the way Michael handled things and I totally understood why he didn't tell me at the beginning of our relationship as I was pretty rough on him. Not to mention there would have been no relationship with anyone telling me they followed me home. But, I shouldn't be surprised by this as it could only happen to me.

 MY THOUGHTS

Stalking—don't even think about it, ever!

CHAPTER 18

Ava came running into our bedroom around one thirty at night. I woke up first and asked her what was wrong as she had the phone in her hands. She told me that Michael's ex-wife was on the phone and she sounded panicked. I woke Michael up and he took the phone. The next thing I knew he hung up the phone and said we had to get up to the hospital and that his oldest daughter Ella had been in a bad car accident. I started to panic but I knew I had to keep calm for his sake. I threw on some clothes and I drove us up to the hospital as fast as I could. We parked the car and ran to the hospital doors. Once inside we saw his ex-wife and her husband and went to them immediately. They explained to us what had happened and we both were relieved that she was going to be okay. Both of us felt sick to our stomach but we stayed there until we were able to see her. We just sat there feeling helpless and we hardly spoke a word. Then we got news that we could see her. The doctors said she had a concussion and would have to stay in the hospital for a few days to make sure everything was good. We went in to see her one at a time and told her we loved her and we were happy she was going to be okay. We didn't stay with her long as the nurses said she needed to rest.

Later when we went home, we didn't say much to each other at first as we were both in shock that this had happened. I had gone up to bed for a nap (and a cry) and Michael stayed downstairs for a while. When he didn't come up for a long time I went down the stairs to see where he was. I found him sitting on the couch crying. It was the first time I had ever seen him cry. My heart was breaking to see him like this. I knew what it was like to watch your daughter lay helpless in a hospital bed and it is devastating. I went to him and hugged him and talked to him for a bit and then he told me to go back to bed and that he would be all right. I didn't want to leave him but I knew he needed to be alone and so I went to bed.

The next day before we went up to the hospital we were told she was moved to a different hospital. We panicked at first and for a few moments thought she must have gotten worse through the night but that wasn't the case. They had more room for her at the other hospital and so they moved her. We visited with her for a while and then let her get some rest. She was in good spirits and told us she would be fine. A few days later she was released from the hospital but had to rest at home for the week. She had a head trauma and they wanted to make sure she didn't overdo it. She did have to go through several big tests on her head to make sure she was okay as she was getting bad headaches but all the tests said she was good. I thanked God that she was going to be okay. My minister from my church at that time went to visit her in the hospital and Ella was very appreciative. She actually came to my church a few times after she felt better to be out. I was so proud of her and so happy she was okay. I know she is my step daughter but to me she means so much more than that. I love Ella and Bree as if they were my own and I would die for them in a heartbeat. That may sound extreme but it's not when it comes to any of my children or grandchildren. Love is love and my love is forever.

To me there is nothing more devastating than having your child go through something that hurts them. We have no control over someone else's life, only our own, and even then, nobody has control over life's tragic moments. We can't put our children in a plastic bubble. We can't be with them 24/7. For me, the best thing I can do for our children is to put them in God's hands and pray for their safety and if something terrible happens I ask God to be with them and carry them through whatever that tragedy may be. I know I cannot go through anything tragic by myself, I would be a basket case, I am not strong enough by myself but I can get through it eventually with God's help and my faith. I can't imagine going through any tragedy without the help of God by my side as I would fall to pieces. I trust that God would pick up all of my broken pieces and put me back together again, whether it was through my family and friends or strangers, I know God would help me if I asked him to. He always seems to put the right people with me at the right times and I hear the messages I need to hear. I am so blessed to have God in my life.

Several months after Ella's accident, Michael and I got engaged. His plan was to ask me to marry him on this park bench down by the river where I first told him I was falling in love with him. But apparently, I put the brakes on that idea when I surprised him with a weekend getaway at Niagara Falls for his birthday present. He wanted to ask me on the twelfth of February because the twelfth day was the day we met. I booked our weekend for the twelfth and thirteenth. So, unbeknownst to me I squashed his surprise with my surprise.

The story goes something like this: I was getting packed for our three days away in Niagara. I was so excited. As I was getting packed I noticed Michael had left his dresser drawer open and there was a little square box sitting in plain sight that I hadn't seen before. What would you do, ladies? Yup, that's what I did. I looked in the box and there was nothing in it but I could tell it was a jewelry box of some sort. All of a sudden I clutched my chest and smiled from ear to ear. I said to myself, "Oh, my lord, is he going to propose to me? Did he buy me an engagement ring?" I started to get so excited but I had to calm down so he wouldn't wonder why I was bouncing around like a fool. I closed the box and closed the drawer.

We arrived at our hotel and put away our belongings and then Michael said he was going to get some ice. I was glad he was gone as now I had a chance to see if there was anything hidden inside his clothes that resembled a jewelry box. I know this is bad and I felt guilty for a few seconds and then just went for it. I felt around in his clothes and couldn't find anything at first and then just like I guessed there was a box hidden inside one of his socks. I didn't take it out as I knew I didn't have time and I didn't want to see the ring until he opened it before me. So, I quickly put things back and jumped on the bed and lay there innocently when he came through the door. He didn't notice a thing and it was priceless.

I could tell that Michael was nervous. I told him we should head over for dinner and then hit the casino for some fun. He kept stalling and then said well I thought we could relax for a half hour or so and just enjoy the room. I knew then that he was going to ask me and it took all I had inside of me not to ruin his surprise. I had to act as if I knew nothing and let me tell you it was hard. I was so happy inside and yet I had to be calm. It took him the full half hour to finally ask me to marry him. He had a hoodie on and inside the pocket of the hoodie was the ring. We were talking about nothing really and then he started talking about how long we had been together (two and a half years) and how he loved me and my girls.

He was very kind and said some really nice personal things about me. Then he got down on one knee and took the box out of his hoodie and opened it and said, "I love you very much. Will you marry me?"

I let go of my held-in feelings and said, "Yes!"

We hugged and kissed and I was so happy I jumped around like a fool and kept looking at my ring, which I loved. I called Ava and Charlie and told them the good news. We told Bree and Ella once we got home. I never told him my little secret until several months later.

And not only did he propose to me once but twice. Yes, I said twice. He told me about his original plan and I told him he could still do it as I thought it was so sweet. I didn't think he would but a couple months later he did. We went to the bench by the river and he got down on his knees again and he asked me to marry him. I was very impressed that he did it a second time and I still said yes!

So Michael decides we have six months to prepare for a wedding. I wanted to wait a year but he didn't want to wait so I had some fast preparations to take care of. We looked for a place to get married and nothing felt right to me until one day we went to this beautiful place about a half hour from our house. It was breath taking and as soon as I saw it I started to cry because it reminded me of the old movies that my dad and I would watch that had the old plantation homes in them. This grand estate was built in 1898 and has quite a history to it. The grand building was way in off the road on a beautiful country lane way surrounded by beautiful trees on either side, and when you came around one corner of the lane way there it was standing in all its glory. It was a majestic manor boasting four large columns in the front of the main building. I was taken back to my child hood right away and I fell in love with the building the moment I saw it.

We went inside and it was everything I thought it would be. Everything about it spoke to me of history and happiness. In the back of the main building was a beautiful apple orchard and to the side of the orchard was a breath taking huge room with tall windows all around the elegant room so you could see the orchard. I pictured myself coming down the path from the room into the orchard where we could get married in amidst the apple trees. I couldn't imagine getting married anywhere else but I knew it would be expensive so I had to calm down and contain my excitement. Michael knew that I loved it as he watched me take in all the beauty around the estate. We spoke to someone about the prices of having a wedding there and the meal and while we were standing talking with the young woman Michael saw a famous female actor out by the pool area. That was crazy. I didn't realize that a lot of important and famous people stayed here not only because it is beautiful but because of the privacy of the place. And the week before we got married there was another huge named male actor that stayed there while in town for a movie.

Once we got the prices, we thanked the lady very much and told her we would be in touch. When we got inside our vehicle we sat there for a few minutes and took a deep breath. Michael asked me what I thought and I told him I absolutely loved it and told him how it reminded me of my dad and me watching old movies together when there were old plantation homes in some of the movies we watched. I told him it would be amazing to be married there but I also knew it was expensive and I didn't want to spend that much money on the wedding. This was our second wedding and I wanted to keep it as simple as possible. We talked it over and we talked about how we could keep it simple in other ways and how it would only be a small wedding with about fifty people.

We sat there for about twenty minutes and then he looked at me and said, "We are getting married here. This makes you happy and I want us to be married in the place you love."

"Are you sure? It is expensive and we can still look for another place."

He was adamant. "No. This is the place. It feels right and I don't want to look anymore."

Needless to say, I was thrilled beyond words. And we cut corners in every other way for the wedding. I didn't go for the big expensive flowers, I went for simple white and yellow daisies. I didn't go for the beautiful long gown. Instead I went for a beautiful three-piece, off-white outfit that looked elegant. I didn't go and get my hair done or my makeup done, instead I did my own hair and makeup. You get the picture, we kept it simple.

Our four daughters stood up for us. Charlie and Ella were the best men and Ava and Bree were the bridesmaids. I walked down the path to the man I would marry and our four daughters were standing there beside him. The song "Destiny" was playing in the background and the words surrounded me with joy. My heart was full of love and I was humbled beyond words. This was our day. We stood there amongst our family and friends and said our vows. Everyone was given a small bottle of bubbles to blow when our minister announced we were husband and wife. We walked arm in arm up the small hill through the apple orchard to the beautiful reception area as husband and wife as the song your love is the "Greatest Gift of All" by

Michelle Wright played. And when the photographer took pictures of us and our girls, the song "Feels Like Home" was playing in the background and it brought tears to my eyes. Michael and I were smiling from ear to ear. We did it. We got married for the second time but it felt like the first time for us. Everything about our wedding was perfect. There were bubbles everywhere. Our son-in-law Jacob had put together a CD of love songs to give out to our guests. It was one of the happiest days of my life that day under the apple trees with the sun shining down on us and I knew that God and my family in heaven were watching me from above.

 ## MY THOUGHTS

Most of us all have vivid visions of how we would like to see our wedding day. Some of us don't have a vision at all. When I got married the first time it was a very sad time for me. As I said earlier I had strong feelings that I was making a big mistake because there was such turmoil in my relationship with Carter and I wanted to call the wedding off. Marriage was not a good idea for us. There was too much to be worked out before we should have even considered marriage. Maybe back then it was that nagging feeling I had of having two children with two different fathers and not being married that made people look down on me. It was a number of things going on in my head, being down on myself and then feeling defeated. Whatever made me get married the first time was different from the reasons I was getting married the second time. Michael was a good man for me. He was more relaxed and less stressed than I was. He was a straight shooter as he said what he thought and didn't lie to me. He was a hard worker and didn't have a problem with alcohol or drugs. He never abused me in any way shape or form. I loved him with all my heart when I walked down the pathway to marry him. I cried tears of joy when I said my vows and I never felt for one moment that I shouldn't get married. My second wedding day was totally opposite of my first. I married Michael for better or worse, for richer or poorer, in sickness and in health, till death do us part.

All of that being said, was Michael perfect? Of course not, but neither was I, but we loved each other, flaws and all. That is the beauty of marrying the right person we love each other and work through the things that we don't like. Communication is key, baby. You have to let each other know when one of you are upset and listen to each other's thoughts of what is upsetting your spouse. Life is too short to waste time on petty things. Pick your battles. If it's about something trivial and you can live with it then move through it. If it's something you truly do not like and are having a problem with it then speak up and face it together. Give each other the respect you each deserve. Let's face it we all have our own opinions and thoughts on things around us. We are not always going to be on the same page. Honesty, respect, communication and love are the key tools to a good marriage and if you don't have these four ingredients then please step away from the altar.

CHAPTER 19

Michael and I had gone to a ski resort for our short long weekend honeymoon. We made some really good memories there. We had the honeymoon suite which was way too big for us but it was a nice experience. We went horseback riding which was funny to say the least. I insisted I needed a helmet and the only helmet available was an old hockey helmet. Michael laughed at me the whole ride. We went on a long hike to get to the top of a hill to see the surrounding area's which was breath taking. And we just had those days to absorb the fact that we were married. Then three months later we went on our second honeymoon with our good friends Tat and Kevin to Nassau, Bahamas. They were celebrating their twenty-fifth wedding anniversary. It was my first time seeing beautiful aqua color water and it was simply amazing. We had a great time and I wish I was more relaxed but I had this nagging feeling and I found myself panicking and feeling anxious about things I couldn't control. I didn't tell Michael right away that I was feeling this way as I didn't want to ruin our honeymoon. But I had brought my Al-Anon book of daily meditations with me and was reading them nonstop. I needed a lot of positive reinforcement at this time because I was nervous for some reason about being away from home and so I felt calmer after I would read something positive. I would tell myself to enjoy the moment as I may never be here again. We took a boat taxi over to the Atlantis resort and I found myself feeling overwhelmed in the boat. When we walked through Atlantis and checked out all the amazing décor and ambience of the place I was still feeling nervous inside but I couldn't shake it. I was worried about the drive back in the boat and it kept me from focusing on the beauty of Atlantis. When we were outside I was okay, but when we were inside with all the people I felt more anxious. Eventually I decided I needed to focus on what was here for me to enjoy and I did my best to enjoy myself. Michael, Tat, and Kevin wanted to go parasailing and I was not having anything to do with that. And so because I was too afraid to do it, I stood on the beach and watched them go parasailing. They had the time of their lives and just loved it. I couldn't join their conversation as I had chosen to stay behind while they jumped at the chance to parasail. I regretted not joining them but it was too late. It was done and I missed out on it. When we came home, I was happy to be home but I was upset with myself for not totally being there with Michael. I couldn't put my finger on it but I just shoved those feelings down and moved forward.

Life was going pretty good when I didn't think of that black cloud of darkness that haunted me every day now. For some reason, the feelings of darkness were starting to feel stronger and closer to taking me under. I fought the feelings and continued my daily life as best I could. I was working my full-time job now for a couple of years and it could be stressful but I was happy there and enjoyed the people I worked with.

Then out of the blue on a Saturday morning I was on the phone talking to Lindsay in Ottawa and there was a beep on the phone. I told her to hold on. I went to the other line and said hello, and who was it but Adam! I told him to hold on as I thought, "Oh, no, something must be wrong in his family." I told Lindsay I would talk to her later and told her who was on the phone. She told me to just tell him I was married and it would keep him from making a fool of himself. So I went to the other line and said right away, "Is there something wrong? Are Katie and Richard okay?"

He said, "Oh, they are fine."

"Then why are you calling me?"

He sounded insulted by my question and said, "I just wanted to call you."

I stopped him in his tracks and said, "I got married several months ago."

He didn't say anything for a few seconds and then said something like, "Oh, I was just calling to see how you and the girls were."

Somehow I didn't believe that. It was early in the morning on a Saturday and he sounded like he was drinking or just woke up from a bender. He was calling from his nephew's house and I knew that he got married the year before to the girl he had the affair with so why was he calling me from his nephew's house. It really didn't matter to me, I was just furious that he had the nerve to call me when he was now married and talk to me about their personal stuff. I ended the conversation because I was not impressed with the content of the conversation and told him that I prefer he didn't call me and that I was going to let my husband know about the call and maybe he should tell his wife. I did not want to start my marriage off with secrets. And that was the last time I ever heard from him. When I got off the phone I told Michael who it was and why he called and that I told him I was happily married. Michael just laughed and took it with a grain of salt. If he was upset with the call, he never let on and I never made a big deal of it. We just went on with our day like the call never happened. But I must say, I was angry about the call for a few weeks because I knew he wouldn't tell his new wife and I don't like dirty little secrets. And the part that really bothered me was he was giving me a poor me story about how his wife didn't trust him and how he had a problem with not being able to say anything about her children. Wow, did that ever sound familiar only now I was on the other side of the fence. I was the one he was calling about her and before he was calling her about me and my girls. I just couldn't believe it and I just shook my head. He didn't learn a darn thing about having an affair and being with two women. One woman would listen to his complaints about the other woman and he still stayed with both of them. He had his cake and he ate it too! What he didn't realize was that I had no intention of listening to his woes about his marriage! I finally just let it go and said I could be a real witch and just call his wife myself and tell her to tell Adam to stop calling me. But what would that accomplish? I did not want to be that person, and so I needed to forgive Adam and ask God to help me not be angry with Adam. And you know, I got the best deal with my honest and trustworthy Michael. Lucky me! That being said, I really do hope that Adam quit drinking and became a good husband and father. I don't hate Adam I was just very disappointed with the call but I really do wish him well wherever his life takes him. Alcoholism ruins so many families and relationships. I do hope he found AA again and really gave it a try. I could never ever trust him if he still drank. But that is his story and I am blessed not to be an alcoholic, besides I had other issues to deal with. I hope he faced his demons and is happy like I am. God bless him.

Michael and I kept up with our daily routines and had a lot of family dinners and went away on the weekends once in a while. Whenever we went away I found myself always feeling anxious and I would talk to myself and assure myself I was okay. I started buying more self-help books but they were just temporary fixes.

We were married now for about a year and I went to my doctor as I was having a lot of stomach issues. My doctor decided I should have a colonoscopy and as much as I did not want to have one I knew it was a good idea as my dear mom had died from bowel cancer. But cancer was the last thing on my mind when I woke up from the colonoscopy. You see while I was somewhat incoherent and having my test done there was a devastating attack on our neighbors in the United States. The date was September 11, 2001. When I woke up from my test my husband was beside me and he told me he had some horrible news to tell me. He looked very serious and I just laid there quietly waiting for his news. He told me that everyone in the waiting room were watching the news on the television that was set up for patients and it was showing a horrific attack in New York City on the Twin Towers. What?

The first words out of my mouth were, "Oh my goodness, Michael, our nephew works across from the Towers!"

Michael said, "I know, honey. I will call my sister as soon as we get home!"

When we got home, Michael called his sister right away and he inquired about our nephew. She told Michael that her son called them the minute he saw what was happening (which was a plane crashing into one of the Twin Towers) and the staff was told to leave their building right away and then he was yelling that he had to get out of the building and he hung up on her. She was so worried about her son which was totally understandable. Michael told her to call him when she knew that her son was safe. We didn't hear from her until four and a half hours later. She said that her son got out of the building safely but there was so much disaster and things flying everywhere that he just ran and ran to the ferry that goes to Stanton Island where he lived. Four hours later he called his parents and he told his parents that it was so devastating and horrible to witness. We were glad to hear that he was okay but we were so upset about the people who were not that lucky and who perished because of a senseless and violent act against the innocent American people.

We kept watching the news for weeks about the attack on the United States and it was so heartbreaking, to say the least. My heart blesses all of those who lost loved ones through this senseless act of violence and my heart and mind give thanks to all those who were heroes in being there for their brothers and sisters of human kind alike. You will never be forgotten.

Just four days after this devastating news of the 9/11 attacks on the Twin Towers, we were blessed with the arrival of our second granddaughter. She was beautiful. It was a nice distraction. Now Charlie and Jacob had been blessed with another healthy baby. Jade was adorable with big round cheeks that you just smothered with kisses. I loved feeding her the bottle and holding her little fingers.

She brought so much joy into my heart and I couldn't imagine life without my Jade or Jordan. They were a big part of me and I was so smitten with both of them. Jordan now had a little sister to play with. It was so cute to see Jordan hold Jade in her little arms on the couch. She was a proud sister and a good big sister to Jade. Our two granddaughters were our pride and joy. Charlie and Jacob eventually moved into a bigger place and they both worked hard at their jobs and raising their family. During this time, Ava and Bree were at university and working hard on their studies. Ella was also at University and living with several friends where she met her boyfriend Scott. All of our girls were busy with school and work. We were so proud of all of our girls as they were making their way in the world and doing it on their own. All four girls were smart and definitely not lazy as they all worked hard to make their dreams come true. Michael and I were very fortunate to have such amazing hard working daughters and couldn't be more proud of all of them.

CHAPTER 20

Though the four girls were all getting older and doing their own things, we always made time for family dinners. We spent a lot of time with our family and always did our best to be there for them whenever they needed us. Michael was outnumbered by females though. That is why it surprised me so much when I came home one night and he said he had to talk to me. I had no idea what I was in for but he proceeded to tell me first of all not to ever leave him alone again with a stranger and that we were going to have an exchange student from Colombia live with us for a year. What?

Okay, so let me start from the beginning. My good friend Tat worked at a company called YFU, which stood for Youth for Understanding. This was an exchange student program that was a great program for young people to have a chance to live with another family in another country and learn their culture and the host family got to learn about their student's culture. We were asked by Tat to have a young fifteen-year-old girl stay with us for the weekend as she was heading to London where her exchange family would host her for a year. I had no problem with this at all. She came to our house on the Friday and on the Saturday I was out for a bit. I was only gone for maybe two hours from home, just two hours and my husband was to entertain this young lady. Apparently when I was gone she cried to Michael that she was very afraid of going to London because she was concerned she wouldn't like her host family. She just kept crying and Michael had to console her and when she wouldn't stop crying he said she could stay with us for the year if she wanted to. Yup, that's what he said.

And she said yes.

Well, I was surprised to say the least! "Michael, what did you do?" We had three bedrooms, one for us, one for Ava, and one for our two daughters who came on the weekends. And not to mention that we didn't discuss this with our girls. I couldn't get mad at my big-hearted husband because I may have done the same thing but I think I would have asked the girls first. Needless to say, we had to make arrangements for Marcela to stay with us. Once all the arrangements were made (which by the way surprised my good friend Tat, who laughed at us), we now had five daughters to love.

While Marcela was with us we learned many things about Colombia and of course many things about her. She was very strict with herself when it came to homework, probably a little too much as this didn't count for her with her schooling back home. But, she wanted to make good marks at our Canadian high school and that is exactly what she did. The only problem we had with that was she would get carried away with the one computer available and Ava needed to do her homework too (which counted for her) which became a problem quite frequently. I felt bad for Ava but I didn't want to make Marcela feel bad so far from home. It was a battle some days and I honestly wished I had two computers. But that is the way things happen when you are a family. Sisters are there for each other when push comes to shove but there are also stresses that factor in to being sisters. Marcela was the only girl in her family and our family already had four girls. But other than several very tense moments about the computer most of her time with us went smoothly. I could have left this part about the computer out of my story but I wanted to be honest and let others know that it is always an adjustment for any family hosting a student. But if you can get through the awkward moments then you can have an amazing experience with young people from other countries.

Marcela got to see part of our country while living with us and she also went to the YFU outings. She tried new foods in Canada and introduced us to new foods from her country. We took her down to Niagara Falls and to London and to Ottawa. She was thrilled in Ottawa because she was really interested in politics. Over the course of the year, I believe she had a very good time as she also went places with the whole YFU exchange students. The one thing we taught her in her time with us was to take time to relax. Take time for yourself and do something fun and spontaneous. Don't be so hard on yourself because in the big picture you deserve to have some free time. We all need time to play. And I believe when she left she took those words with her and actually changed in ways that she hadn't before. She was a good first and last exchange student. I told Tat I couldn't do it again because I found it too hard to say good-bye. I came to love Marcela like a daughter and for me it was hard to see her leave. My heart did not like saying good-bye and so we never took another student in again. And of course my big-hearted husband wasn't allowed to even think of being left alone with any of the exchange students. But I must say, because of Tat, we came to know many of the exchange students from all over the world. She hosted many students and they became a big part of our life. It was a very interesting and educating time in our lives and it gave me more people to love. I highly recommend taking in an exchange student as it broadens your horizon on people outside of our country. I will always think of Marcela as a very beautiful, smart spirit who brought more joy and love into my life.

Michael and I had been married now just a year and a half and we both did not see what was coming for us. You know the line in most wedding vows that says "in sickness and in health." Well, I took ill. Not the kind of illness one has from obvious parts in their body. But the illness that people are still afraid of and don't know how to deal with, the sickness of the mind.

I was driving to an appointment to a city just twenty-five minutes away from my house. I took the back roads to this appointment as I loved the country drive and I always felt calm with this drive. This was an evening appointment and it was for my back. I had trouble with my lower back and my coworker suggested this doctor. I was going to this doctor for several weeks now and I really liked him. He was a very nice man and I always felt calm when I left. As I was driving my car that night I started to feel a bit strange. To be honest I felt like I was losing my mind. My heart started racing a mile a minute and my hands were sweating, I started to hyper ventilate and I honestly thought I was going to have a heart attack. The adrenalin in my body would not stop pumping. I found myself racing to get to the doctor's office as I was just about ten minutes away when this was happening. I knew he had a calming effect on me so I thought it was better to see him than drive back home in this state. Maybe he could figure out what was going on.

I arrived at his office in a panic and he could tell by my face that something was wrong. He got me to sit down and gave me a drink of water. I explained to him how I was feeling physically and how mentally I felt like I was going to die. I had the look of terror in my eyes and he was quite concerned for me. He got me to lie down and when I calmed down he worked on my back. Then he got me to do some breathing exercises and that helped me to relax a bit more. He didn't want me to leave right away as he knew I had to drive home in the dark but I assured him that I felt much better. As I drove away from his office the whole thing started again. I felt so light headed and was so afraid I would pass out. I felt so hot inside and the sweat was dripping off me so I rolled the window down and let the cool air help me to breathe better. I was so full of fear and I had no idea what was going on. I started praying and started crying and soon I was feeling better. I didn't want to go right home because I didn't want Michael to see what was happening to me and what would I tell Michael. So, I drove to the house of a girl I knew from my church that I could get to pray with me. Her name was Bridgette. We had known each other for a while now and I trusted her not to judge me. Bridgette and I are still very good friends today. But as I sat outside in my car across from her house, I felt that I should be sharing this with Michael. I drove home and went in to our house as calm as I could. I told Michael that something wasn't right with me and I couldn't explain it but I was feeling really fearful that something was terribly wrong. He hugged me and assured me that everything was okay that maybe I just got nervous driving there in the dark and by tomorrow I would feel fine, but neither one of us saw what was coming.

I didn't sleep too well that night as I was so scared and I truly thought I was losing my mind. My thoughts were all over the place and I couldn't focus on anything. I got up and got ready for work and felt so out of it when I was driving I thought, "What the hell is happening to me?" When I arrived at work I looked pale according to my coworkers as if I had seen a ghost. I had the look of complete terror on my face. I tried to concentrate on my work but everything around me was closing in on me. At noon, I finally told my boss that I wasn't feeling well and had to go home. I raced home and once I got inside I fell apart.

Now the next part of this story is tough because I really lost a few days here and there as I was so full of fear and so scared that I can't remember everything. Poor Michael didn't know what the hell was going on. He just knew that something was terribly wrong with me. That is where the depression came in. And for anyone who is reading this and has ever had a full out knock you down depression you know how debilitating and devastating a depression can be. This was a full-blown depression that hit me like a ton of bricks on both sides of my face and a double fisted punch to the stomach. I was down and I was out of commission. Where the heck did this come from? Wasn't my life good and safe now? I was happy except for some weird feelings of anxiety that I was having every now and then. Why was I in this sad heavy weight depression? Well, I had to do something and I had to do it fast. We had a mortgage to pay and we had kids to take care of and what about my husband. He didn't sign up for this. What the hell, what is happening to me? Somebody help me please I am helpless and I feel like I am being swallowed up inside. Where are you, God? You are supposed to take care of me, why are you letting this happen? Where are you? Do you not hear me? I am crying out to you but you are not here. What did I do? Is this my punishment? How can this be happening to me? I am a good person. God, please, I am begging you to help me. I am drowning in this and I cannot get out without your help. Please, God, help me, help me…

CHAPTER 21

The hole I was in was dark and fearful. I knew this was the black cloud that had been following me all my life. I knew it was taking over my whole being. I was falling away from reality. It was taking every bit of light I had and was stamping it out with all of its power and I was losing the battle. I thought I had worked through every possible heart ache and bad thing that ever happened to me. I had done a year of deep therapy letting go of all the anger and hurt I had buried for so long with the minister of my church several years ago. Why was this happening now? After all of the things I worked through was I truly meant to go out like this? Why was it that every time I found a piece of happiness it was short-lived? I couldn't answer any of my questions by myself, I couldn't hear God through all the darkness so I fell apart and my husband watched me slowly slip away.

My friends Tat and Kevin came to see us one day to tell us that Kevin had found out he had cancer in a mole in his back that had to be removed. Michael had to be there for them without me. I couldn't function. I couldn't be with them as I was not in a good state of mind. They never told me what was happening as they were concerned for my wellbeing. Kevin was like a brother to me and I would have been in a worse mess knowing what he was going through. I never knew about it until a year or so later when Tat had mentioned Kevin's cancer (I was truly upset that I was not able to be there for Tat). In the meantime, Michael took care of everything, the house, the bills, the groceries, the laundry and especially our girls. I felt like I was letting my whole family down when I was in this state. I was so depressed I can't even tell you what my girls went through. I know what Michael went through because he was with me all the time when he wasn't working. I was in my own world and I did not and could not relate to anything else around me. The whole house could fall apart and I would not have known.

As I felt the darkness slithering all around me, I knew my only chance was to call the one person I knew that could help me work through this horrible nightmare. Remember Sarah and remember she had been the minister who I first met at the United Church? Remember she was also the counselor who helped me get through my past issues with my dad and my relative who molested me and my ex-husband Carter and my ex-fiancé Adam? I worked through so much emotional crap that I thought I was clear and free of any more darkness. But no, just when I think I am safe and happy and let my guard down, pow, right in the face come the most gut-wrenching sadness and the fear of falling apart and never coming out of the depression. So, I called my counselor Sarah, whom I also call my dear friend. She was now running her own company and it was based on Mediation. She was helping married couples and families to work through their problems with her as a mediator. At first I thought, "Oh, no, she won't be able to help me as she has moved on to something else." But that wasn't the case. She was more than willing to help me through my depression. I was very thankful that she would be there for me yet again. When I went to see her I had someone drive me and wait for me. When she saw me, I don't think she was prepared for what she saw. I am only speaking of what I think she saw but I believe she saw a woman on the verge of a major breakdown who needed some major help. I will never forget the look on her face when she saw me. She quickly hid her expression and got down to the matter at hand. The first thing she wanted me to do was to go to my doctor and explain the situation and for me to think about getting on some medication to keep me calm and able to focus on the therapy I would receive from her. I was not happy when she suggested for me to get on medication. I hadn't been on any medication for many, many years and I did not like taking medication. She assured me that the medication today was much better than what they had to give people years ago. So, that was the first thing I had to do and when I had been on it for a week or so then we could begin our sessions of finding out what was the cause of this depression.

Reluctantly I went to my doctor and Michael came with me. I went in by myself and I cried and cried to my doctor. I told her that the last thing I wanted to do was to medicate myself. She was very compassionate and told me all I had to do was try it for three weeks to see if there was a difference in the feelings I was having that were consuming my every moment. She said there was a new medication called Celexa that was working excellent on her patients and it wasn't addictive and she said I could start out on a very low dosage. She also told me that this drug would help me produce more serotonin in my brain and it would help me tremendously with my depression. She also told me that if I had high blood pressure that I would have to take high blood pressure pills so why was it so hard for me to treat my brain. If any other part of my body was in trouble she would treat me for that but my brain is in trouble and needs more serotonin. She was with me for about forty-five minutes and said she wanted me to come to see her every two weeks for a while so she could monitor me and make sure I was doing okay on the medication. I finally agreed and left her office feeling so afraid but hopeful that this medication was the right thing for me to take while I was going to therapy. I must say that during all this time I was praying to God to put the right things in my life and the right people to help me through this depression. I kept telling myself that even though I was feeling horrible and did not know what was going to happen to me I had to believe and have faith that God was here with me.

Taking the pill on the first day and the first week was so hard for me. I was so paranoid that I made myself feel sick to my stomach for the first week. I told myself that I had to give the medication a chance and so I did. I liked my doctor and I trusted her and she was right, my brain was in trouble and I needed more serotonin. After the first week, I started to tell myself over and over that this was just temporary and it will help me to sleep and get back on track. I wasn't eating very much, just enough to stay alive and I was starting to not want to leave the house. I couldn't drive anymore. I was so afraid I would have those overwhelming feelings I had when I last drove to my back doctor. So, every time I went to therapy it was with someone who could drive me whether it was Michael, a friend, or one of my daughters. I refused to drive and be alone. I had a tough time leaving my house to go to my therapist but I knew I had to keep going. At first I would cry and cry and I couldn't stop crying. I asked Sarah why this was happening now when I was safe and happy. She told me that is exactly why it was happening now because I was safe and happy. I was with a husband who would see me through this and be there for me. He would make sure he was there through the bad parts with me and then the good parts. She said it was the right time for this to happen and I believed her. She was right. But the other part of me said but why did this have to happen at all. Her answer was that it was always there following me my whole life and sooner or later it had to happen.

After several sessions with Sarah together we made progress. I found out that I never grieved the loss of being separated from my brother and sister. I remember that when I acknowledged this truth I just cried and cried and cried. I let myself grieve the loss of my brother and sister's absence in my daily life. I grieved that I never had the chance to be with them at Christmas Eve and Easter morning and every other holiday. I grieved not being able to get up every morning with them and go to bed at night with them. I grieved that we were separated at such a delicate time in our lives. I grieved for myself, fending for myself, fighting for my place in this world. All

I did was grieve for my loss over and over until I was ready to talk about it.

Sarah suggested that I get a drawing book and draw how I felt as that little girl saying good-bye to my brother and sister. I told her I was not the best at drawing anything but I would try to draw the best I could. After each session we had together, I was to draw something significant. The first page she asked me to draw a tree with bare limbs and caterpillars on the ground around the tree and there was nothing happy on this page. That was me. I was absolutely bare in so many ways and now I was baring it all to Sarah. After that at each session I drew four more trees so in total I now had five trees. They all were the same tree but with different things added at each session. We talked about fear and sadness and anger. Those were the three things that I was feeling every single day. Eventually all these caterpillars made it up the tree and were hidden inside the cocoons. This was me again, hiding in my house, in my safe place where no one would see me as this broken down scared little girl.

Now during these sessions there was a lot more going on, but I was in a depression and there are things that I don't remember. I just know that I was so thankful that Sarah was helping me to survive at a very fragile time in my life. I was also very thankful for my doctor as I would see her every two weeks and she would just sit and listen to my story and give me encouragement to keep moving through this. She would tell me I was doing well and not to give up. She would also remind me that it was okay to help my brain with the small dosage I was on and I would leave her office feeling hopeful things would get better for me. And so Sarah and I finally get to a place in my drawing book where I am leaving my aunt Maggie's house and going to live with my uncle Albert. On this page, I draw one of the most heartbreaking scenes in my life. I draw a picture of my uncle Albert sitting in his car waiting for me. I am standing close to the car and I am carrying a small suitcase. There are tears streaming down my face and I have a caption over my head that says, "Why can't I stay? I'll be good you won't even know I'm here. I'll do anything you say!

Please don't make me leave my brother and sister! I'm sorry I wasn't good enough! Please keep me! I don't want to go to my uncle Albert's. Please!" On this same page is a house with my aunt Maggie standing in the doorway with tears running down her face and standing away from her are my brother and sister holding their hands out to me and tears running down their faces. And the last thing I drew on this page between myself and my siblings was a broken heart lying on the ground.

I cried and cried after drawing this picture. I knew as much as I was hurting I had to let go of that painful day and move beyond it. So, that is what I did. I worked through that very sad day with Sarah and moved through the depression because I finally had some hope that once I worked through this depression I would get to the other side which was to smile again and live again with new eyes and a healed heart and I would finally be out of the darkness and into the light. So the next session we talked about the fact that I was not alone after all when I left my aunt Maggie's house. We talked about my faith and how God would not have let me be alone during that painful time. We talked about the fact that there were angels watching over me when I was in the car going to my uncle's house and most of all Jesus was with me all the way. Though I could not see any of this at the time Sarah helped me to see that I was not alone at all. She asked me to draw again the picture of me driving in the car with my uncle and what could I add to this picture to make me see this differently. So I drew a picture of the car with me in the back seat looking sad and my uncle Albert driving. Above us were two angels watching over us and over to the far right of the picture is a cloud and the sun is peaking out a little from the cloud. When I drew this picture, I had a different view of that day. I couldn't change the fact that I was unbelievably torn up inside but I now thought about God sending me two angels to watch over me. It made me feel hope and it helped me to see some light. It made me feel loved by God and his son Jesus. I saw things in a whole new way which gave me a chance to see that I was important and I wasn't totally abandoned.

On our next session, I was to write a letter to God on how I felt now knowing he was with me on that day. Here is word for word what I wrote:

Dear loving and Most Gracious God,

I write these words to you with love. I know as an adult you were with me on that depressing day when I had to leave my brother and sister, as a twelve-year-old I did not feel you were with me as the pain, anger, and fear were so strong. I had a broken heart and I felt so alone abandoned and unwanted. I guess a part of me might have wanted to die, but I know somewhere deep in my heart you were with me every step of the way. I feel you cried for me and kept watch over me. I feel you protected me. I really wasn't alone. Jesus was there carrying me, walking in front of me and beside me. I thank you, Jesus. You went with me when I got in the car you were with me the whole time, loving me, protecting me, trying to get my attention. My whole life I was never alone, you cried with me and you carried me again and again, just as you are carrying me now. My heart I give to you for mending. I love you and I thank you.

It was right around this time that I was to go back to work. It had been three months already and my benefits had run out. I talked to my boss and told him I wasn't ready to come back full time but if he agreed to me working three mornings a week to start while I was still in counseling then I would really appreciate it. He agreed and the only other issue was the fact that I was not driving. As a matter of fact, during the first three months of counseling, I didn't go any-where, even with Michael. I couldn't get into the vehicle. I would go out the door very slowly like I was walking to my doom and once I got to the vehicle I would turn around and go back into the house. This was very hard on Michael. We both couldn't figure out why I would start to panic just thinking about going away from the house. I even stopped going to church which was really frustrating for me. I received cards and letters in the mail from my church family letting me know that they were praying for me and they missed my smiling face. But I refused to go anywhere except to counseling and even that was a very nerve wracking adventure. So, if I had to go back to work I had to figure out how I was going to get there. We came up with a solution finally. One of my coworkers lived just three minutes by car away from me. So I asked her if I gave her gas money each week would she pick me up three times a week. She agreed no problem at all. I was so thankful to her for doing this for me. She was so kind to me and we became very close. When I would start to panic, she would just talk gently to me and tell me everything was okay. So, the beginning of going back to work was a huge challenge for me but I did my very best to make myself go to get back out there with people again. There were the odd days that I did not want to go and Michael would come home and I would be in my pajamas and stressed out. Every day was a battle for me to go to work and I knew it was hard for Michael to see me like that.

Then one day when I didn't get out of bed for work he came in the room and he said to me, "I think you should get your butt up and go to work. Once you are there you will be fine!"

I was angry at him because he hurt my feelings but that was what I needed to hear at the time. I got up and got dressed and went to work and from that day on I didn't miss any more days. I went to work three mornings a week and then that turned into three days a week and that was a big deal for me. I continued my therapy and continued going to see my doctor every couple weeks and we would just sit and talk for a half hour. Slowly I started to see more hope and more light come into my life.

One of the last pictures I draw in my book of therapy was a very happy page. Sarah and I had worked through all the anger, sadness, and fear of that rough time in my life. Now I got to draw something beautiful. We talked about the tree I had drawn with the caterpillars and I had named the caterpillar's anger, sadness and fear. And since I had worked through these feelings I was able to draw the trees again but this time they were full trees with big green limbs. I drew a big sun shining to the left and a big puffy white cloud to the right. In the middle I drew a big blue heron flying in the blue sky and a blue bird sitting on the big full tree limb. Below each tree are flowers. Guess what are floating above the flowers? That's right—big, beautiful butterflies. Those caterpillars of anger, sadness, and fear had now blossomed into beautiful, colorful butterflies. I loved this picture that I drew from my heart. I knew I was well on my way to recovery from my depression. I could see the light now. I could feel the warmth of the sun and soon I would be free of that big dark cloud that had followed me all my life.

On April 5, 2002, I had one more thing to do to make it official that I had let go of all the baggage and sadness, anger and fear of being alone. My friend Jane from church (who was a retired minister) suggested for me to celebrate my recovery from my depression. You see, during my months of therapy, I was also doing homework at home. Every day I was writing page after page after page of all the anger I had toward certain people in my life who I had felt had let me down. I was writing page after page of the pain and sadness I felt from the separation of my siblings. I was also writing page after page about so many angry moments in my life and let me tell you there was a lot of cursing involved in these pages. I swear I had enough pages to make an actual book and enough swear words to last a few lifetimes.

The idea from my dear friend Jane was to invite my wonderful husband and my closest friends and of course my amazing therapist Sarah and we would celebrate my freedom of the depression just the few of us together at my church and we would burn all the pages of anger, sadness, and fear that I accumulated over all the months of therapy. So this is what we did. We all got together and said a few prayers. I shared my drawing book with my husband and my dear friends and then we proceeded outside to burn my pages as a sign that I was letting go of this for good. Not that I would forget any of my past but I would move on from all of my anger.

Okay, I must say here that if you ever decide to have a ritual of burning up all the pages you worked so hard to write, make sure it is not on a cold, windy night. We were outside the church and Jane had brought this pot for me to use to burn my pages in. Unfortunately, it was just a small pot. You should have seen her face when I hauled out this big bag of pages that would take hours to burn. Needless to say, it was cold and windy so I only burned half of what I brought to the celebration. We decided we were all freezing our butts off and as much as it was a great idea we needed to stop and finish up our celebration with some hot tea. So, I took the rest of my pages home and when the time was right I burned every last page in my backyard barbecue. Not everyone has to do this, but I am a very visual person and doing this just closed up that chapter in my life and I felt like I had moved a mountain. And to make everything even better, when the evening was just about done, my therapist/friend Sarah passed me a gift wrapped in tissue paper. It was a beautiful glass window butterfly catcher. My heart was so filled with joy and love when I saw the butterfly. What a way to end the evening and start the next day feeling like that caterpillar had finally pushed her way through all the tough stuff to get out of the dark cocoon and into the light to become the beautiful butterfly that she was always meant to be!

MY THOUGHTS

I have decided to put my thoughts in the next chapter. Depression is not something to me that you can write a few lines about so please bear with me and see my thoughts in the next chapter.

CHAPTER 22

I looked up the definition of depression on the net and this is what I found through Wikipedia:

> *Depression is a state of low mood and aversion to activity that can affect a person's thoughts, behavior, feelings and sense of wellbeing. People with a depressed mood can feel sad, anxious, empty, hopeless, helpless, worthless, guilty, irritable, angry, ashamed or restless. They may lose interest in activities that were once pleasurable, experience loss of appetite or overeating, have problems concentrating, remembering details or making decisions, experience relationship difficulties and may contemplate, attempt or commit suicide. Insomnia, excessive sleeping, fatigue, aches, pains, digestive problems or reduced energy may also be present.*

The medical definition of depression from just one source says: Depression is a disorder that is characterized by long-lasting mental suffering preventing one from enjoying life and inflicting a perpetual state of sadness and feelings of worthlessness upon a person. It is an illness that inflicts the mind and medically disables someone from living up to his or her healthiest emotional capacity. My source for this definition was from www.answers.com.

Unless you have ever experienced depression, I do not believe you can truly know what it is like. I believe that people can read about depression and learn about it and know how to treat it but if you have never been to the pits of hell then you can never truly know how it feels. Describing depression is not hard, living with it is hard. I may describe depression differently from someone else. I would guess it depends on how low you get and how fast you get out of it. I would describe depression in several categories such as: mild, moderate severe and life threatening. But no matter what level we are at we are still in need of some sort of help. I believe just getting medication and not getting the therapy or counseling may not be enough to get rid of our depression. Now remember this is only my opinion it does not mean I am right. I just know for myself that if I had only taken medication and did not work through the months and months of anger, sadness and fear I would still be carrying those feelings with me. I believe unless we get to the bottom of what is causing our depression then it will just keep returning. I had a few depressions in my lifetime so far and the worst one was the last one.

So how would I describe depression? First of all, just speaking from my experience, I would describe depression as a dark debilitating horror. From the minute it grabs you, the life you were currently living doesn't exist anymore. I would also describe it like being alive in a coffin and you can't see any way out and the darkness and the overwhelming feelings of helplessness crawl all over your body. Your body becomes very heavy and you feel like you are carrying a very heavy weight on your shoulders. You move slower, you feel small and helpless. You crawl into your skin and hide. You feel afraid of just about everything around you. You cannot handle any noise, you need it to be quiet so you can try to hear your thoughts, but your thoughts are what drive you to another level of helplessness. These feelings are over whelming to say the least. They won't let you sleep and they won't let you alone. It is a constant state of fear and sadness and helplessness. When you aren't fearful then you are crying and sobbing until you cannot cry anymore. Then you go into the fear and you lay awake wanting and begging God to take it away from you.

How did I get through the depression? I cried out to God and he heard my prayers. Even though I wanted the depression to be over right away and it wasn't, I still prayed. What did I have to lose, right? I believed in God so why would I not cry out to him in my hour of need? But that was just the beginning for me. I was lucky to have my husband standing beside me no matter what was going on with me. That was very important with my recovery because we need to know that we are loved and that someone is waiting for us to get better and come back to them. For me it was my husband that showed me he wasn't leaving me, he was going to still be there while I went through the depression and when I came out of the depression. I was not going to be abandoned again. Somehow along the way I knew if I fell apart he would still be there for me. I also knew that my children were safe now. I did not have that worry of Carter coming and taking them from me. I knew they would be okay while I was not in a position to be there for them. And most of all, I knew that if I didn't go through this (as much as I hated it) I would never live my life free of that dark cloud. Then I had to try to figure out what my best course of action should be. I knew from before that I needed to voice what was bothering me even though at first I had no clue what that was. So, as debilitating as it was for me and I couldn't just jump up and get things done, I just reached out for the phone and made the call to Sarah. I don't remember what I said but I made that first step and that was the beginning for me to take whatever steps I needed to get back to my family and free me from that darkness that followed me all these years.

Was it a hard road? Oh, yes, yes, and yes! There were days I took one step forward and three steps back. There were days that the sadness was so thick around me and choking me that I never thought I would stop crying or stop feeling so intensely sad. But I just kept getting through one day at a time and sometimes literally one hour at a time. I would read my Al-Anon literature over and over trying to let it sink deep into my brain all the wonderful positive readings that I knew by heart. I latched onto anything that was positive and I would not watch anything on TV unless it was a comedy. I stayed away from any topic that was depressing. I had enough going on in my own mind that I did not need any news of negativity. My life line was God answering my prayers by putting the right people in my life at this very fragile time. I had my strong loving husband, my beautiful four girls, my family and amazing friends. I also had my church family praying for me and I had Sarah. She was an amazing therapist! She walked me through every aching part of my depression. She opened my eyes to the light that was waiting for me at the end of my depression. I was blessed to have all of these amazing people or my story could have had a bad ending.

Unfortunately, it is a fact that even though some people have a good group of people trying to help the one who suffers from deep depression, they still take their life and commit suicide. They are so tired of living in the pits of hell that they see no other way out and so they do the only thing that will end this deep depression. They are tired of feeling like a burden to those they love and they feel such hopelessness and such despair that they feel they are better off dead. What a horrifying thought! What a sad thing it is to watch someone who has lost a loved one through suicide. It is so heart breaking to witness what it does to a family. All of the unanswered questions and sometimes the family blame themselves. They think they should have done more for the person in the deep depression. There's a lot of "I should have done this or I should have done that." It is such a devastating blow to the family left behind and I would not wish this on anybody. I personally know of two amazing people who lost their beautiful loved ones through suicide and it is beyond heart wrenching to see this happen to the family.

My hope is that if there is anyone you know suffering from depression, don't take it lightly. They may need your help so please reach out to them and give them some direction as they need hope.

They need to know that they are not alone and they are loved dearly. If the person opens up to you make sure you listen. This doesn't mean that you can save them but it does mean that they will have hope and feel like they have a chance to get through their depression. And if someone is reading this right now and believes they are in a depression please seek help from professionals and get in to see a therapist, and if you are not comfortable with the first one you get, search for another one because the right person will come along. You are not alone, you are loved. There is a way out and the fight to get out is worth it. There truly is a light at the end of this tunnel and it is beyond anything you can imagine. It is not an easy road but it is the best road you can take. When you get out of a depression it is the most rewarding feeling because you see life differently. You can tell yourself that depression is not the thing that is going to take you out of this world and then punch it in the face. Step through that wall of fear and darkness and just keep going forward and when you have days when you go two steps or even six steps back just remember the ten steps you took forward. On the days that you are not in therapy, read as much positive happy articles or books that you can. Always have something uplifting to look at. Surround yourself with positive people. Stay away from negative people and negative stories. Watch only the good stuff on TV. The most important thing I did for myself was to get down on my knees and pray. As I said earlier, God was my life line and he put all the right people in my life. God will carry us through but we have to do the foot work. And another important piece of advice: "Please do not give up on yourself. You are too precious and God loves you."

CHAPTER 23

Thank you, thank you, God! I am free from my depression. I am ready to be with my family and get out there and live life again, only this time there will be no dark cloud following me. I am ecstatic, to say the least. I was such a lost girl and now I am finding my way.

One of the first things I did to get back out there again was to go to my next-door neighbor and ask her if she did fitness out of her house and she did. I would see women going into her house twice a week in the evening and they were always dressed like they were doing fitness of some sort and they were always laughing and carrying on. I wanted this laughter and companionship with other women. I called up Tat and asked her if she would consider coming to my neighbor's house and doing fitness with me. She lived ten minutes away but she agreed to do it for me. She wanted me to get back out there too and I was really happy when she said she would do it with me. So, I went to my neighbor's house and asked her if she would consider having two more women join her group. She was more than happy to have us join and I was so excited because I was going to be a part of a women's group and of course the fitness was a bonus. Twice a week I would go there with Tat and we would laugh and enjoy the new women in our lives and my neighbor whose name was Karen was such a joy to be around. She was a very upbeat woman, always talking about positive and enlightening subjects. I eventually learned that she went to church and believes in God and that gave us something in common. She became a good influence on me especially at this time in my life.

"Oh, no, wait a minute. What's going on now? Excuse my language, but what the fuck?" I am having those weird feelings again of sweating, nervousness, and fear. It's not the same as my depression but some of the feelings are familiar from the night that I drove home from my kinesiology for my back problem. I feel kind of frozen with fear in my tracks as I am going to work. I am now trying to follow my friend to work. I just have to drive to her house by myself (which is just a couple streets away) and then follow her to work. She used to drive me but now I want to follow her to work and eventually drive myself to work. That is my new goal, to be able to drive to places again by myself. She has been so good about this.

But this morning I am feeling anxious about driving by myself. I still get in the car and drive to her house but when I see her I start to cry and I tell her I am having trouble and I feel afraid to drive by myself. She assures me that she will be right in front of me and if I need to stop all I have to do is beep my horn or flash my lights. We finally drive to work and I make it. Through most of the day I feel embarrassed and down on myself because I used to be able to drive anywhere with no problem. I couldn't understand these feelings I was having again but I knew I wasn't still in a depression because I didn't feel that heavy weight on my shoulders anymore. So what the hell was going on now?

For a few months, I was still not wanting to drive anywhere by myself. I did drive to work but I got used to it and I was still following my coworker. On the days that she missed work, I would call work and they would send someone to get me and I would hitch a ride home with another coworker who lived just down the street from me (a two-minute walk). He and his family became my friends. I did this all the time for months and months. And during that time,

I was praying to God again to open my eyes to what was going on with me.

Then one evening I got a call from my adopted sister Lindsay and I could tell she was upset. She eventually told me that her husband Daniel had been sick for the last couple of months and they were going back and forth to the doctor to find out what was going on with him. None of the antibiotics or other drugs they had prescribed for him was working. I knew this had been going on because Tat was his sister and she would keep me updated when she would hear from Daniel or Lindsay. But this call was different and I knew something was up. Lindsay told me that Daniel had a very rare kind of cancer and it didn't look very good for him. She also told me that they were not going to be negative and that they were going to beat it. I was happy to hear her words of encouragement and I knew I couldn't show her my fear or sadness so I did my best to act strong for her. The clinical word for Daniel's cancer was extranodal NK T-cell (nasal type) non-Hodgkin lymphoma and it was terminal. He was diagnosed on March 6, 2003.

When I got off the phone with Lindsay, I shared the news with Michael. He was shocked and really concerned for Daniel. I went downstairs into our family room and started yelling and throwing pillows and hitting pillows and then blurted out words such as, "No, not cancer. Why is this happening to Daniel? He is such a good man and he doesn't deserve this terrible news! For fuck's sake, not cancer! I hate cancer, I hate cancer! This can't be happening!" I went on like this for a good hour and then came upstairs and went to Michael's arms and cried. He comforted me and told me that cancer can be beaten and Daniel will beat this. My heart was breaking for my sister Lindsay and her family. I prayed to God that night that Daniel would beat this cancer and asked God to be with him every step of the way and then I cried myself to sleep. The next day was one of many days that I thought about Lindsay and Daniel and I just kept putting them in God's hands. I was going through my own problem of trying to get my head in a good place but I felt selfish being afraid of what was happening to me when this horrible cancer was attacking Daniel and his family. I knew the best I could do for Daniel, Lindsay, and their family was to pray for them and believe that Daniel would beat this. I kept in touch with them as much as I could and our conversations were sometimes uplifting and sometimes stressful. I was excited to go down and visit them with Tat and Kevin when Daniel was doing much better. Kevin had shaved his head to look like Daniel and they were pretty cute with their new hairstyles.

But it was a long road for Daniel and Lindsay and his family in Ottawa. When something like this happens, everyone deals with it in their own way. It is devastating to hear such heartbreaking news. Daniel and Lindsay's families were shocked to say the least. Daniel's family did the best they could to help out where needed. Things were very tough and not going good for Daniel and the doctors finally decided to give him a Stem Cell transplant and hope for the best. But before they could do this transplant Daniel had to get through another upsetting hurdle. Only this hurdle just about took his life. My sister Lindsay was so stressed and felt so alone when the doctor came to tell her what was happening and told her she had a huge decision to make. The line to Daniel's pic was infected badly, so badly that it could cost him his life. This was a life and death situation now and Daniel's life was in Lindsay's hands. Lindsay made the decision after talking to both doctors and teams. It was touch and go but her decision eventually turned out okay and on September 22, 2003, Daniel was given the stem cell transplant. There were touch and go moments again but eventually the stem cell transplant gave Daniel a new start and literally a new blood line. This type of cancer is deadly, and Daniel and Lindsay went through hell together. I don't think any of us really knew the struggles and trials they went through at that time. They were lucky to have a family member drive Lindsay to the hospital as she didn't drive due to bad eyes. She was thankful for this, but I know I felt bad that I wasn't there for them as much as I could have been. It is hard when your family lives far away and unfortunately except for me Lindsay's family lived too far away to be there with her. But then something wonderful happened, and Lindsay's mom and dad were able to come up and be with them for several weeks. I was so happy to hear her parents (my adopted parents) were with them. I believe their visit really gave Lindsay and Daniel a boost of encouragement and hope and they needed positive people around them. Lindsay's parents are amazing and would give you the shirt off their backs if you needed them.

I can see why Daniel and Lindsay's marriage is so strong and why they are there for each other. It seems like most of the time it was the two of them fighting this cancer together. Daniel is a hero and a survivor. He now had a new lease on life and he was going to enjoy it the best he could. It was not an easy road back but it was a road he had to take in order to get to the other side of freedom of the cancer that tried to take his life. Lindsay went through her own personal hell watching Daniel go through this. She would cry her eyes out when she got the opportunity in the shower and otherwise would put on a brave face. There were a few things I wasn't told when Lindsay and Daniel were going through this as they didn't want to worry me as I was still very fragile from my depression and the new symptoms of panic. So, my version of what happened to Daniel and Lindsay is a very short version. They went through many, many months of hell that turned into a couple of years of getting stronger. He didn't just beat cancer and was healthy right away he still had to get healthy again after all the treatments he underwent and all the setbacks. But we were so amazed at Daniel and Lindsay's positive outlook and I know that the prayers to God and the faith they had in each other is what got them through many, many months and years of hardship. And I am very happy to say that on September 22, 2016, Daniel turned thirteen years old from the day he had the stem cell transplant. We are so proud of Daniel and his loving wife and we look forward to seeing him around for many more years to come. As much as I hate cancer I have come to realize and believe that cancer can be beaten. Daniel was the first person I ever knew to beat cancer and he holds a special place in my heart and always will. I love Lindsay and

Daniel very much and they were a big inspiration to me and many others for all they stood up to together.

And so in the midst of this terrible thing happening to Daniel and his family, I started looking on the net to see if I could find something to describe my feelings of fear. I found a few sites that talked about panic and anxiety. The symptoms were exactly what I was feeling. I was self-diagnosing myself but I couldn't deny the fact that I was feeling every symptom they talked about. Could this be what I had? Was I prone to panic and anxiety even though I made it through my depression? I needed to search into this more. I kept praying to God over and over to help me find what I needed to know.

One night I was talking to my adopted sister Brandy who lived in Prince Edward Island and told her how I was feeling and she sent me a tape on anxiety and panic. I tried to listen to it but it scared me. I didn't want to be that person who suffered from anxiety and the word agoraphobic scared me. So for another month of not wanting to go out of the house except for work and not driving anywhere, I kept looking for other answers. I finally found another site on the net that shared other people's stories about their living with panic and anxiety. I read all the ones that were on the website and I knew without a doubt that I was experiencing exactly what they were experiencing. I couldn't deny it anymore that I was one of those people who suffer from panic and anxiety. But the good news was that this website had a program that I could try and I could learn how to live with and cope with and possibly get rid of anxiety. And here is the funny part. Remember a couple months before this I received the tape from my adopted sister Brandy? Well, do you also remember when I prayed for God to help me and open my eyes to what was happening with me? Yup, I believe God heard my prayer and that is why Brandy sent me that tape on anxiety and panic a couple months before. I went to the tape and this time I listened to most of it and realized that I indeed was living with panic and anxiety. Not only did I acknowledge that I was dealing with panic and anxiety, but when I looked at the bottom of this tape, I found the words: "Midwest

Center for Stress and Anxiety, 800-944-0440." You will see why this was important when I continue in the next paragraph. Let's just say I really do have a hard time hearing God but in the end the light bulb usually goes off and I say, "Oh, yeah, now I get it."

So, okay, now I figured out what was wrong with me and when I went to my doctor and told her what I felt was going on with me she talked with me and came to the same conclusion. She thought it was still a good idea for me to stay on the low dosage of medication (Celexa) that I was on while trying to work through all this anxiety. The panic and anxiety got worse, much worse. I could barely go anywhere without wanting to get home. My husband didn't know what was going on and wasn't sure if this was just all in my head. Well, in the big picture he was right, it was in my head but it needed to get out of my head. I was scaring myself to death and I knew that I had to do something because I wasn't out there living life, I was just surviving again and I was so pissed off because I had come through a major depression and felt like this was so unfair. How come this was happening to me now? Well, once I got over the poor-me feelings, I realized that I needed to do something or go somewhere to get help again.

I really liked what I was reading on the net about this one program but I still wasn't sure what to do. The program cost money and I couldn't justify spending all that money and what if it didn't work. Well on the flip side of that what if it did work? Then my friend Tat called me and said she heard that there was going to be a workshop at the Holiday Inn in my city in a couple weeks about panic and anxiety and she thought maybe I should go. We found out that the workshop was from the same program I had been looking at on the net this whole time and I still wasn't sure about it. And then another light bulb went off. I ran to get the tape Brandy had sent me and there it was in big bold letters the name of the place to contact, and guess what? The name on the tape was the same name on the program I found on the net and it was also the foundation of the workshop that my friend had found. The name was Midwest Center for Stress and

Anxiety! Wow! It just seemed like God was saying to me that this was my answer and not to second guess it anymore and just go to the workshop. What would it hurt to check it out? So, I mentioned it to my husband and he said we could check it out. I mentioned it to my neighbor/friend Karen and she wanted to go with us for moral support. So off I went that night with my group of supporters, my husband, my best friend Tat, and my newfound friend Karen.

I am feeling so nervous and anxious when I walk into the room at the Holiday Inn. My palms are sweating and I feel overwhelmed with all the people in the room. The place was packed with people of all ages and status. The good news was I wasn't alone, I had Michael and my friends but I also had all these people who were here for the same reason, to find answers on what this was, what it meant and how do we stop it. Even though I was still nervous and anxious I felt like I was in the right place. The workshop was well done. There was a young man (maybe thirty to thirty-five years of age) who shared his story of his history with anxiety and panic and how it kept him from living a full and somewhat normal life. The more he shared the more I listened with all of my being. I didn't want to miss anything. I started to identify myself in some of his story and I started to feel some sort of relief that there was hope for me. Then he shared how he found the Midwest Center for Stress and Anxiety program and how he admired the president and CEO whose name was Lucinda Bassett. He shared a bit of her story and then proceeded to tell us how he helped himself with this great program called "Attacking Anxiety and Depression, A Self-Help, Self-Awareness Program for Stress, Anxiety, and Depression." He described the program to a tee and what it could do for all of us who were suffering from this debilitating condition.

His story and the way he described the program that helped him sold me. I wanted to be able to get to the place where I could go out again and feel comfortable and not afraid that something was going to happen to me. I wanted to get rid of those feelings of dread and fear every time I drove my car. But most of all I wanted to live life with freedom and fearlessness. I knew it would be work because he said it doesn't happen overnight and he said he struggled at first and would go two steps forward and five steps back. That sounds familiar, doesn't it? So, I spoke to Michael and asked him what he thought. He just wanted me to be free of all the fears and anxiety and enjoy life with him and our girls again. That's what I wanted too, more than anything, but I knew at this point I needed help and guidance. So, we bought the program. It consisted of a big workbook and a case that held sixteen tapes filled with ways to help ourselves get through these overwhelming feelings of dread and panic. The tapes also had testimonies on them from others who suffered from panic and depression and who came through it with the help of this program. And it was a huge bonus to hear Lucinda Bassett talk to us on the tapes with such inspiration and love for us and she didn't even know us, but she did know what these feelings felt like. She knew because she lived with these feelings for many years and she spent her life trying to help herself and then others. The program also came with several VCR tapes of Lucinda talking to us and giving us more ideas and hopefulness. I also received wonderful newsletters from the Midwest Center called *Less Stress Press* which were full of great letters from Lucinda Bassett and articles from other members and letters from readers. I am telling you, this program was the best spent money to save my life from so much turmoil and fear.

I couldn't wait to start the program and get better so I jumped right into the work book. I wanted to feel better, and I wanted it immediately. Needless to say, that was not going to be the case. I was going through the tapes and the work book so fast that I wasn't actually working the program. I would listen and answer questions and read but I was rushing it and not allowing myself to work through each chapter to the best of my ability. It took me at least three times of working the program before I realized what I was doing wrong that was keeping me from learning what the program was trying to teach me. And if I thought I could just skip a few things that I thought didn't pertain to me well that was a mistake. It all pertained to me and as I was doing the program over and over I would usually find out that what I always thought about myself and what I was really like was now being shown to me in big capital letters. Sometimes there are things we just don't want to admit about ourselves. I know I have heard myself say to myself, "I am not like that." Oh, but yes you are, honey, and that doesn't mean you are a bad person, it just means you need to work on those qualities that stand in your way of being panic free.

The one thing that I learned about myself was that I was a very negative thinker. Where this came from, I don't know. I cannot put the blame on anyone because I really don't know where it came from. I thought I was a very positive person but I confused that with being a nice and kind person. I treated people with respect and would help anyone whenever I could and I always tried to lift other people up. But when it came to me I was very negative. I didn't talk to myself the same way I would talk to my sister or friend with love and praise if they were down on themselves. I never gave myself a break and I was hard on myself. And when I realized this and accepted the fact that I was a negative thinker, I had to change my way of thinking and trust me this does not happen overnight. So, through the help of the program, I was taught how to do this. I was so surprised at how much better I felt about myself. Ever so slowly I started to praise myself and call myself honey and sweetheart whenever I was frustrated. It would go something like this: "Good job, honey! You may not have gone into the store today but you did drive to the store." Or, "You deserve a treat, sweetie, for all you are accomplishing today you actually went into the store by yourself today. I am so proud of you." Or maybe I would say, "Well, you didn't do all the groceries today, honey, but you can try again tomorrow. Look at what you did do. You went to the grocery store by yourself and picked up a few things. Well done." The old me would say, "What the heck is wrong with you? You were at the store why didn't you finish the groceries. You suck." Or, "You are useless. No wonder people leave you."

Now to a person who has no problem driving anywhere and living life to the fullest, these conversations may sound ridiculous. But for those of us who suffer from panic and anxiety and even agoraphobia we understand only too well what these conversations mean to us. Agoraphobia is extreme or irrational fear of crowded spaces or enclosed public places. It is an abnormal fear of being helpless in a situation from which escape may be difficult or embarrassing and usually leads to a panic attack. This definition of agoraphobia is from the Merriam-Webster dictionary. For me when I was in my depression and especially after my depression, I was experiencing agoraphobia to the extent that I didn't want to leave my house. I remember when I was in that state and Michael would ask me if I wanted to go for a drive in the country (which was one of my favorite pastimes). I would say no out of fear. What if we couldn't get back to the house? Michael had a really hard time getting me to leave our house. It was a very frustrating time for both of us. So, when I give examples of the grocery store or even down to the mailbox, I am not exaggerating the fact that I was full of panic. It was not a nice place to be. But the good news is that we can get past it. There are so many good programs out there to help us. We don't have to do any of this alone. And another amazing thing I learned through the Attacking Anxiety and Depression program was that I could control the thoughts I put in my mind. This was a huge eye opener for me as I thought I didn't have any control at all. But I was so happy to learn that I had all of the control. I was the one who could change my thoughts around to positive self-talk and not the old negative thoughts that just made me feel so helpless. I could change my way of thinking and the old way of thinking had no choice but to leave. This was such a relief to me. I worked very hard to change my thought pattern and would write a lot of my fears and panic down on paper. I thanked God every day for bringing this program to me and Michael. I say Michael because it is hard on the spouse of the one who has this condition and this Midwest Center program has wonderful ways in which the spouse can help their loved one through the changes they are making. There is a section in the workbook that tells the spouse what they should do for their loved one. These suggestions make it easier for the couple to stay together and not run for the hills. So, as you can tell by my praises for the Midwest Center and the person who started it all, Lucinda Bassett and her doctor, I highly recommend this program for anyone who is experiencing any panic, anxiety, depression, or agoraphobia. You will not be disappointed. It took me many years to finally be free of constant anxiety because it took me longer to get it and to actually believe in myself. But once I finally came to a place where I loved myself and forgave myself for all my past mistakes I was able to work through the anxiety, change my way of thinking and move through the fear that had a hold on me.

Eventually I purchased a book by Lucinda Bassett and read it several times. I loved this book. It was Lucinda's amazing story of how she suffered from panic, anxiety and depression and how she helped herself get to the other side. The name of the book is *From Panic to Power* and it is written with such honesty and intelligence. Her program and this book became my life line that I fully believe God brought into my life. I was so lost, and even though I knew I had a long way to go I also knew that I would be okay. First of all because God always had my back and would put these amazing tools in my hands, and second of all Michael and my family and friends would always be there for me.

During this time in my life, I was starting to get out a little more with my friends Tat and Kevin again. We all decided it was a good idea to start golfing. Yes, I said golfing. Hitting that tiny little ball as close as you can into a tiny little hole and if you are lucky maybe it will go into the hole. This was good for me because we would walk the golf course and I was outside enjoying the fresh air. We went golfing a lot. We eventually joined a league for a couple of years too. We had a lot of fun and our friends Tat and Kevin had introduced us to their friends Lily and Thomas a couple years before and we all started golfing together. They were a great couple to golf with. Thomas had a great sense of humor and was always joking around. Lily was fun and was a great golfer. I enjoyed myself immensely hanging out with the six of us. And not only did we hang out with the six of us but there were two other couples we hung out with altogether. We would play cards and get together for dinner theatres for several years. We had some really good times because Tat and Kevin brought us into their circle of friends and they were a great bunch to hang with.

While I was still working through my anxiety issues, my daughter Charlie and Jacob gave me the great news that they were getting married on August 7, 2004. I was so happy for them. I was so excited to hear all the details and when Charlie asked Michael to walk her down the aisle I was overcome with tears. He said, "I would be proud to walk you down the aisle." It was so great to have some happy news and be distracted with showers and the stag and doe. There was a lot for them to do and I tried my very best to help them as best I could. I was so determined not to let this dam panic situation keep me from being there for my daughter. I took the time over the couple of months before their wedding to write her a beautiful heart felt poem to read on her wedding day with my speech.

The professional pianist was a close friend of mine and he played a beautiful rendition of "Canon in D Major" as Charlie's entry song. The tears rolled down my eyes when I saw Charlie walking down the aisle with her arm through Michael's arm. It meant the world to me to see the happy smile on both of their faces. Who would have thought that I would be watching the man I loved walking my Charlie to the man she loved? It was a mother's dream to see her daughter marrying someone I was proud to call my son. It was a great day filled with lots of laughter and joking around. And even though I had a few moments of anxiety I just put one foot in front of the other and refused to let anything get in the way of my daughter's happy day. They had a big wedding and lots of people in their wedding party. It was a big day for them and for Michael and me. Other than the minister calling me by a wrong name, the ceremony was very nice. Jacob's sister sang a beautiful song by K-Ci and Jojo called "All My Life." Their first dance together as husband and wife was "If I Ain't Got You" by Alicia

Keys. All eyes were on them and they looked so happy in love. And although Charlie danced with Michael for the father-daughter dance and had me in tears again, I was beaming from ear to ear when I surprised Charlie with a mother-daughter dance to an amazing song called "In My Daughter's Eyes" by Martina McBride. We held onto each other and laughed and then the neatest thing happened as we were dancing to this very touching song. Charlie's sisters Ava, Bree and Ella and my best girlfriends and my sister Rose and adopted sister Lindsay and a few other beautiful women made a circle around us and held their hands together swaying back and forth to the music. It was a very happy and heart-touching moment. Mother and daughter surrounded by the women they loved. We had an amazing time and we couldn't be happier welcoming Jacob and his family into our lives.

I would like to share with you the heartfelt poem I wrote for my daughter Charlie on her wedding day:

Face of an Angel

As they laid you across my chest, I thought how can this be?
For as I looked into your eyes: the face of
 an angel looked back at me.
And time stood still for a moment as I held you close and cried,
She's so beautiful, God heard my prayers, she's safe and by my side.

As time moved on so did you, I watched you grow each year,
I was with you every step you took and
 wiped away every falling tear.
Then there came a time in your life your choices were not the best,
I like to call these the "learning years" when you put me to the test.

But through it all I stood my ground and
 helped you to get through,
For you were still my little girl, I could never stop loving you.

So here you are how you have grown, I'm so
     proud, I couldn't ask for more.
You've added to my list of joys. Two little girls I adore.
And now today another joy a gift from god above,
The blessing of a son-in-law; whom I have grown to love.
So may God bless your marriage and guide
     you in each coming year.
Fill your life with joy and laughter and wipe away all your tears.

Remember the love you have from your family and friends,
For this is just the beginning, they're with you 'til the end.
Just one last thing before I finish, one last
     thing that will forever be,
I thank God for the day you were born, when the
     face of an angel looked back at me.

CHAPTER 24

Four months later, Charlie becomes pregnant with her third child. We are all so excited to find out whether it will be a boy this time as she has two daughters. But Charlie doesn't like surprises and decides to ask the technician at her ultrasound what she was having this time, and guess what? It's going to be a girl! And guess what else? This will be her last child. Jacob and Charlie decide that three children are enough and get ready to welcome their third baby girl to their family. And while they are waiting for the baby to come Michael and I and our good friends Tat and Kevin are planning a trip.

What better way to test out the anxiety than to go on a big two-week vacation to Las Vegas and the Grand Canyon. Whoa, there a minute, do you think I can do this? I don't know, just thinking about it makes me feel jittery. I am not sure if this is a good idea but Michael is so excited and looking forward to seeing the Grand Canyon how can I ruin this for him? Our best friends Tat and Kevin are the culprits who put this idea into our heads. They want the four of us to go to Vegas and rent an RV and drive to the Hoover Dam and over to the Grand Canyon and maybe a few other areas along the way. I would love to see the Grand Canyon. Oh, what the heck, what's the worst thing that could happen? Did I mention that it is a five-hour flight? Yup, no big deal (squished into little seats). No big deal at all. I can also see that big door hatch closing and now I have no way out, but, hey, I can do this!

So, I decided that I needed to go and see my doctor again because the feelings of anxiety are now back again, and although I have this wonderful program for some reason I must be doing something wrong because I still haven't quite gotten it. I felt like I was missing something. Maybe my problems are deeper than what this program can help me with. So, I go see my doctor and she suggests a woman Psychiatrist that she highly recommends. I am leery at first but then decide I need to do something more than the program I am doing. So, I start seeing this lovely woman Psychiatrist and she goes deep into my child hood and we talk about some things that I truly did not understand what they had to do with my anxiety dilemma. I really liked her but I wasn't sure if I was in the right place. I saw her for about three months or so and then on the last session she said I was doing very well and she felt I was headed in the right direction. I shared with her that I was going on this trip soon and asked her what she would suggest I do to keep calm as I was nervous to fly. She told me that she was nervous to fly too and so instead of putting herself through all the turmoil and anxiety of flying she would take an Ativan. For those of you who don't know what an Ativan is, I can tell you it is a narcotic pill to help people in times of stress. She said it would help me relax and maybe sleep on the plane. I was very surprised that she suggested this pill and to be honest I was very disappointed that this was her suggestion. I left there feeling that my time spent with her was not what I expected it would be. The last thing I wanted to do was take a pill to solve my problem but I understood what she was saying about why put ourselves through all that turmoil when a pill could make us feel better. I must say here that I have nothing against anyone else taking a pill when experiencing a full-blown panic attack and you are out of control. I know how hard it is to calm ourselves down and it can be very exhausting to say the least. But I always thought you would take something like Ativan prescribed by your doctor if you were experiencing something traumatic like the death of a loved one. Then I felt like all this work that I had been putting into working the program that I purchased would have been for nothing and I also felt it wasn't the program that wasn't working, it was me. I had to trust in the program and know that one day I would truly get what I just wasn't getting yet.

So, because I was torn between taking this pill or not, I decided to go and see the minister at my church and get his opinion on this pill I could take. I explained to him the situation and how we were going to be on the plane for five hours and how my psychiatrist suggested I take Ativan and she gave me the prescription to fill. My minister was very careful in his reaction to my question of should I take the pill or not. He told me a story of how he had taken Ativan one time from his doctor many years ago when he was flying somewhere and it didn't work out too well for him. He said he was so out of it he didn't know if he was coming or going. He said it scared the heck out of him. He suggested that I continue working on my program for anxiety and have faith in God and myself that I could fly without any medication at all. He said I could fill the prescription and have it in my purse and if I truly couldn't do it without it then at least I knew that I had it if I needed it. I agreed with him and that is exactly what I did. I filled the prescription and put it in my purse in case of an emergency on the plane. I just find it so funny how I had no idea that my minister had ever taken Ativan and that he was nervous of flying too. When I hear things like this, it reminds me that no matter who you are, there are times in our lives when we all have fears. Every one of us has a fear of some sort even those who are ministers or priests. It is how we work through them that make us stronger and wiser.

Meanwhile, my daughter Charlie is about to give birth to her third daughter, my third granddaughter. Around this same time, my sister and I are having a lot of conversations about our Mom and dad. We live an hour and a half apart at this time but we keep in touch on the phone quite often. We have become very close over the last thirty years since I moved up here and I tell her one day that I admire that she always talked to our mom even though she was in heaven

(I chose to believe this since the day she died). My sister never had a problem believing mom was always with her. I on the other hand never let myself think of mom that way. I always thought of her way up in heaven and I wasn't real sure if she was with me or not. But we got to talking about it one day on the phone and I decided when I got off the phone that I would try to be more aware of the possibility that mom was here with me whenever I called her name or spoke her name to someone else. So, you could say I was testing the waters. I would say things out loud or sometimes to myself like, "Hi, Mom, it's your daughter. Just wanted to say hello today and let you know I am thinking of you." Or I may say, "Hi, Mom, this is all new to me but I do hope you can hear me and maybe you could be with me while I go away on vacation, I am feeling nervous and anxious about going too far from home." So, I talk to her for several days like this. I basically would just try to talk to her like she was there with me and ask her if there was any way that she could possibly show me that she was with me (only if God approved this, of course). I am smiling as I write this part of my story. Just a side note; on November 10, 2005, my mom would be gone now for thirty five years.

On November 11, 2005 I went up to the hospital to see my daughter as she was overdue and being induced. She just happened to be going in on the same day we were leaving on a jet plane and heading to Las Vegas. We went up to see her in the hospital and while I was waiting in the hall to get in I was pacing back and forth. I do this when I am nervous. As I am pacing I am praying to God in my head to keep Charlie and the baby safe and also please keep Michael and I and our dear friends safe as we travel to Las Vegas. Shortly after that I am pacing again and praying quietly again but this time I speak to Mom and ask her if there is any way for her to show me that she is with me and I would really appreciate it. "Any time now, Mom, it would be great because I am going on this big trip and it would really help me emotionally to know that you have always been with me." Eventually I am allowed to go see Charlie in her room and when I go in I am so happy I get to see her before I have to go to Las Vegas.

I stay for as long as I can and then I tell her, "I am sorry, honey, but I have to go." We had a bus coming to pick us up at four to take us to the airport. I was pressed for time but it meant the world to me to see her before I left.

I arrived home, got ready, and then took a quick walk next door to say good-bye to my neighbor/friend Karen. She always had a positive outlook and she had told me when I was nervous to "remember God will be with you wherever you go, he's not just here in our little city, he will be in Las Vegas and the Grand Canyon and wherever else you go." Then as we are visiting, my daughter Ava comes to the door and says, "Mom! Charlie had her baby girl!" I was over the moon happy that the baby was born and Charlie and the baby were doing well. I knew without a doubt that I had to drive over to the hospital and see our new granddaughter before I got on that plane. So Ava and I ran home and told Michael we were going to see the baby. He was concerned that I did not have enough time and I told him I couldn't leave without seeing the baby. I had an hour and a half to run to the hospital and get back before the bus got to our house. I jumped in the car with Ava and we headed to see the baby while Michael finished getting things ready for our trip.

When I got to the hospital, I was so excited to see our new little granddaughter. We went inside to see her and she was in the incubator so we had to wait a few minutes before we could go and see her and of course only the parents and grandparents were allowed to see her at first.

While we were waiting, my daughter looked at me and said, "Mom, ask Jacob what we named the baby."

"Well, I thought you were naming her Allie?"

"Yes, we named her Allie, but ask Jacob what her middle name is."

I looked at Jacob and said, "Okay, Jacob, what is her middle name?"

He looked at me and smiled and said, "Her middle name is Josephine!"

All of a sudden, this amazing sensation came over me like I was being doused in love and joy from the top of my head down to the tips of my toes. And in that moment, I knew my mom "Josephine" was with me. I walked over to my daughter Charlie and whispered to her, "Your grandmother Josephine is here with us right at this very moment."

My daughter said, "Mom, stop, you're going to make me cry."

"Go ahead and cry, dear. She is here."

Then when I pulled myself together I asked Charlie and Jacob how they came up with the name Josephine.

Charlie said, "We were both getting frustrated because we couldn't come up with a middle name for our baby girl and I told Jacob that he had to pick the middle name because I couldn't think of anything I liked. So, this morning before we came to the hospital Jacob was in shaving and the name Josephine kept popping into his head. He was thinking, 'Why does the name Josephine keep popping in my head?' He wasn't even sure if he liked the name. It was not a name he would have chosen. He couldn't understand why he would even think of this as a middle name. Then when he was done with his shower and dressed he came out and told me he thought maybe he had a middle name for the baby. I asked him what it was and he said, 'Josephine.' I said, 'Are you kidding? Why would you choose Josephine?" He said, 'Because it is the only name that keeps popping up in my head.' Then I gave him a weird look and he said why and I said, 'Because Josephine is my grandmother's name.'"

They both decided that they had to call her middle name Josephine! Now I don't know about you but I am 100 percent sure that the little voice inside my son-in-law Jacob's head was the voice of someone very special and that was her way of showing me and telling me that she was always with me and would continue to be with me. I couldn't wait to see Allie and so Jacob and I walked arm in arm down to see her. When we got there the nurse was very adamant that only the grandparents could see her.

I said, "But I am her grandparent, I am her nanny!"

The nurse looked at me and said, "Really? I was expecting someone older."

I had a chuckle and said shyly, "Yeah, I get that all the time."

Jacob laughs and we proceed to the incubator. And there she was, Allie Josephine! My third granddaughter, and I beamed from ear to ear. I can't even describe to you in words what I felt at that moment but let me just say I was happy. We were only allowed to stay for a few minutes but I was so glad I got to see her before I went away. I wished her well and then went to say good-bye to my daughter. Well, don't you know that I could have flown the jet to Las Vegas myself, I was on such a high! Nobody and I mean nobody could have ruined my day because I was so happy to know that my mom was and would always be with me whenever I called her name.

CHAPTER 25

Okay, I am in the airport waiting for the flight attendant to tell us when it is time to board the plane. I am still on a high from my mom's message to me but I must say I was starting to get a wee bit nervous. It all starts with the search as Canada is on high alert at our airports these days more than normal since the horrific attack in New York City on 9/11. I am totally okay with this as I want to be safe and so we go through the process at the gates and then walk a mile or so to get to our terminal. By the time I get there I am tired. My body has been through such a rollercoaster the past couple months working through my anxiety and having sleepless nights thinking about getting on the plane and being so far from our children and now our new little granddaughter. My mind starts to get negative and I hear myself saying, "What if I have a panic attack on the plane? What if I pass out on the plane? What if I scream and tell them to let me out of the plane?" Then I start saying things like, "Holy crap, honey, you're not even on the plane yet. Why are you getting so worked up? What if you have a great flight and you do not have any panic or maybe you just have a little panic? You know what your steps are to work through it. You know this is your mind's way of scaring you into not taking this trip. Trust in yourself, honey, you can do this! If you do have a panic attack, do not make a big deal out of it. Listen to your tapes from your program. Enjoy a conversation with Michael. Play a game with Tatiana. Just do your breathing exercise and give yourself positive self-talk that you learned from the Attacking Anxiety and Depression program. You can do this, one minute at a time if need be. So, get on that plane honey and show yourself that you are in control of your destiny. And besides, don't you want to see the amazing Grand Canyon?"

Needless to say, we get on the plane and thanks to Tat she had booked the first couple seats on the plane. I was happy to see how close I was to the door. Not that I would open it up during flight (or would I?). And on a scale from one to ten, my anxiety was a five, and it eventually went down to a comfortable three, especially when I would think of my mom and my new granddaughter's middle name. And the best part was I didn't need to take any Ativan. I was so proud of myself.

Now unbeknownst to me, my dear friends and husband were secretly making bets on whether or not I would even get on the plane. You got to love their faith in me. They really thought I wouldn't get on the plane and they were all very surprised that I got on the plane and sat down and proceeded to do what I needed to do in order to make myself feel comfortable. It was a number of things though that I realized that had gotten me on that plane. I was still so happy about my mom's visit (not a real visit in the live sense) and that gave me hope and courage. I pictured my new granddaughter and how beautiful she was. I realized that no matter where I was that God was always with me and if he was busy then my angels were with me. I would never be alone. I was blessed that I was with my wonderful husband and my best friends. I thought about all the good stuff that was waiting for me when I got off the plane. I wanted to experience the beauty and wonder of the Grand Canyon and feel a spiritual connection with God while I was there. I knew our kids were safe and there for each other if need be. And I realized even if I had another panic attack (which I did), I would be able to get through it. If I wanted my life to change then I had to continue working the anxiety program and have faith in myself that I was worth the work.

The landing was pretty good but as soon as those doors were open I hightailed it out of there. I think I even left my posse behind. Well, I swear I just set myself up for anxiety and panic attacks. Before we left for this trip, my job was to book us a hotel for a few nights. No problem, I booked us with a hotel I thought was decent and a good price. The pictures on the internet were nice and it was just outside the strip. When we were driving to the hotel in the cab, we all noticed that the area was sketchy. I am sure that most of you are quite aware of the CSI programs on TV. Well, okay, then you would know that some of the footage they take where the murders take place will show a beat-up motel in the back ground. Well, we went into the hotel, I gave them our confirmation numbers, and the man at the desk was absolutely no help in giving us our rooms. We argued politely with the man and he said the only thing he could suggest was a motel just five minutes down the street at his cousin's place. What? We had given a down payment over the phone to hold these two rooms and it didn't look like we were going to get our money back but by this time it was eleven their time and we were exhausted. So, we drag our suitcases down the street past some very sketchy looking buildings and people. There were a lot of ladies of the night and some odd characters staring at us (absolutely no problem with ladies of the night, I was more concerned with the other characters). We must have looked out of place. We got to the motel and holy crap was it a dive! Now I wasn't born with a silver spoon in my mouth, but I did expect to see something a little more taken care of. As the men went inside to pay for our rooms my friend Tat and I stood close together and felt like someone was watching us. We both looked up to the second floor of the motel and there was a man looking out the crack of his door at us. We both clung to each other and felt very vulnerable standing there. As soon as the guys came out, we quickly went to our one room (only one room left) on the second floor. We opened the door and went inside and couldn't believe our eyes. It was seriously like a crime scene. The door was two inches up off the floor casing. We closed it and latched it as best we could. We pulled the dirty curtains over to close them and they left about four inches of window on each side. The best was the bathroom. The toilet was disgusting and the shower tub was no better. The shower head was missing and there were no towels but we had no intention of showering there anyway.

We were so tired we just looked at each other and said we would find a decent hotel in the morning. We checked both beds for bugs and were pleased not to see any. Then we left our clothes on and slept on top of the blankets. When we all climbed into our beds and said good night, I turned to Michael and said, "Hold me, honey, I'm scared."

Michael, without missing a beat, said, "Hold me, honey, I'm scared too."

Well, that was it, we all started laughing our heads off. Then I was the brunt of the jokes for booking the first hotel in the first place. Let me just say that we rested for a couple of hours and by six in the morning Tat was on the floor looking through the huge phone book for a telephone number to another hotel. We finally found two rooms at the Circus Circus Hotel and called for a cab to take us there. The cab driver asked us why we stayed where we were and we told him it wasn't our choice and he said, "Wow, I can't believe you stayed there!" When we arrived at Circus Circus we were pleasantly surprised at the size of the rooms and how cheap they were. We were very happy with this hotel and we made some wonderful memories there.

Let me just say that Las Vegas was never on my bucket list, but I must say that I loved the amazing unique hotels! We went to every hotel and enjoyed the nice weather and all the funny things we would see on the strip. Eventually I did have a panic attack and that was in the Venetian, the beautiful Venetian Hotel. We were looking at the beautiful artwork of the walls and the bridges where the gondolas were passing under the waterway when all of a sudden I felt claustrophobic with all the people and my heart started racing out of my chest. I looked at Michael and told him I needed to get outside. I could tell he was frustrated as he took my hand and led me out of the huge building and out into the front of the hotel. I felt so alone and down on myself and I became angry that I was doing this again. I was also angry at Michael for not understanding and having patience with me. But in the big picture, I knew it was hard on him to see me like that. After being angry for about an hour, I decided I better change my attitude or I would miss out on all the amazing things to see. Tat gave me a pep talk and then I gave myself a pep talk and told myself I was okay. I was just tired and feeling overwhelmed with all the activity and I just needed to breathe and enjoy the outside for a while. And that's what we did. We enjoyed the outside for a while and then we would go into another huge hotel. I started to relax and I was able to go into the buildings with more ease.

Living with anxiety and panic can really take a toll on you if you don't work a program. I was so glad that I brought my tapes and reading material with me. I was able to fill my mind with positive and uplifting information that made the next part of our trip so awesome. It was time to get our RV and travel to the Hoover Dam and then on to the Grand Canyon. I was so excited about this part of our trip. When we got to the Hoover Dam we had to stop at a checking point and have our RV checked out by the police and special guards. This was no problem for us as we totally understood the reason behind it. When they were done, they waved us on and we went to see the Hoover Dam. Wow, I was so amazed at the size of this place! It was so incredible to see this dam and hear the stories behind the building of it, but the loss of men was so sad. Michael and Kevin went down under to see the dam and Tat and I just stayed up top to shop and walk around. That was when Tat surprised me with a beautiful small white angel inside a piece of hard glass. It was oval and fit in my hand perfectly. I loved this angel and she traveled with me everywhere after that. And she was also tucked away in my hand whenever I was nervous or afraid of something. I thanked Tat so much for the thoughtful and perfect gift.

The guys told us it was unbelievably huge inside the dam. I was very impressed and was so glad we got to see it. We were there for several hours and then we headed up the switchbacks toward the Grand Canyon. If you have never seen the Grand Canyon, then you are missing something so incredible and expansive. We were on the southern rim and we stayed in the campground. Every day was beautiful and warm and at night it was quite chilly. We were there in November and we knew enough to bring big warm jackets and sweaters. We got to see the sunset and the sunrise at the Grand Canyon and it was worth every minute of it. I remember saying a prayer to God in thanks for such a beautiful place to behold. I felt so humbled and honored that I had this opportunity in my lifetime to see this magnificent natural beauty of a place. I was truly in awe and felt tears coming down my face at one point because I almost missed this adventure because of my anxiety and fear. To live in the moment became so real to me and I knew that no matter how long it took me I would keep working this program that God had brought into my life so I could live a life free of fear and see the beauty that was before me.

The rest of our trip was truly breathtaking. We saw so many red mountains and pure raw nature at its best. We drove through a mountain which made me nervous but again I just breathed and held my friend Tats hand and when we got through it I looked back at the mountain and was simply in awe that we just drove through it. We stayed in an RV park in Mount Zion and enjoyed getting up in the morning to see a huge red mountain behind us. I was in heaven with all the beauty I was fortunate enough to see. We took pictures of everything and laughed so much during this trip. I just felt so blessed and thanked God for all that I was experiencing.

It was bittersweet when it was time to leave. Our friends made our trip so memorable and we had so much fun but it was time to get on the plane and go home to reality. I was sad to leave this time behind us but I was excited to see our family. We got on the plane and I had minimal anxiety which I believe was because I knew the only way to get back to my beautiful family was to take the plane.

I continued working this program for my anxiety. I was able to work full-time hours again, and even though I found it really stressful, I knew I had to be out in the working world and not locked up in my house. I had started going back to church on a regular basis again many months before our big trip and I even joined the choir. I was still going to a low aerobics class that my friend Karen held twice a week and I was practicing driving to more places by myself. I was on a mission to get over this anxiety and fear that caused my panic attacks and I just kept moving forward. I even started taking piano lessons with one of the ladies from my church. I even went as far as going to my coworker's house down the street to practice on his piano. Eventually he talked me into taking his piano to my house so I could have the piano right there in my home to practice anytime I wanted. I did not want to take his piano but he said nobody ever played it and so I agreed. I was still having a few panic attacks and I found I would not put myself in certain places in case of having a panic attack and I was still avoiding certain things. I still wouldn't go shopping at the mall by myself or take my grandkids very far. I always had to have someone with me to go most places. But I still never gave up I kept going over everything I was learning through the Attacking Anxiety and Depression program.

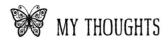 ## MY THOUGHTS

You must be the change you wish to see in the world. (Gandhi)

CHAPTER 26

I still continued to work on myself concerning my anxiety and panic. Although my bouts with these conditions were getting fewer and fewer I stilled worked hard to put positive thoughts in my mind constantly. I continued listening to my anxiety and panic tapes and they helped me tremendously. My life was getting better and better. As a matter of fact, in January of 2007, we planned another trip with our good friends Tat and Kevin and also opened it up to anyone else who would like to go. We ended up with twelve of us and we had a blast. We went to Puerto Plata in the Dominican Republic. My anxiety on the plane was minimal and the flight wasn't as long as it was to Las Vegas so that was a plus. But I was not prepared for what I saw when we traveled on the bus to our resort. I saw some very poor parts of the country and I saw a lot of policemen with small machine guns in their arms. It was very disconcerting to me and I really had to breathe and tell myself this was a different country and they all have their own way of doing things. The resort was very beautiful and everyone was so friendly that we felt very safe where we were. We went off the resort almost every day to get a feel of the country. It was so eye opening to go off the resort. We went in to the city and shopped and bargained with people and that was a new experience for me. Of course, everyone watched out for me because when they left me I got myself into situations.

For instance, when I was just walking along minding my own business and sightseeing, this really nice woman with braids through her hair stopped me and sat me down in a chair and said, "Pretty lady, I will give you braids in your hair to go with your pretty face."

I started to say no and she was so fast I swear she had three braids already on the one side of my head and was starting on the fourth one on the other side. I just sat there and smiled and figured someone would notice I had stopped sooner or later. Just as the nice lady was finishing the three braids on the other side of my hair, my friend Tat came walking over to me. She asked me what I was doing and I said this nice lady decided I needed to have braids in my hair. Tat was not impressed and said to the lady something like, "Hey, my friend did not ask for you to do this, you can't just grab people and put them on this chair and start giving them braids!" The nice lady argued with Tat and I started getting nervous. Tat looked at me and said, "Come on, we are leaving." The nice lady said I owed her something like six dollars. I went to pay her and Tat said, "No, put your money away. This is not the way we do business."

The nice lady said, "She give me six dollars, I do braids for her."

Tat said with a big smile on her face, "I don't think so, she didn't ask for this, you sat her down and did it on your own."

They started to argue a little bit and I finally said, "I just want to catch up to everybody. I will pay her, it's no big deal."

Tat was not happy and told me I shouldn't give her anything because of the way she did it but she knew I just wanted to get out of there so she said, "Well, okay, but give her less than six dollars." So I handed the nice lady four dollars and said thank you and she was happy and we walked away. Tat was still not a happy camper but eventually we laughed about it and our crew made fun of me and said I had to stay in the middle of the group so they didn't have to keep saving me. Needless to say, when we went to the market, nobody left my side and they babysat me. I didn't mind, I just thought the whole situation was pretty funny and I liked the colorful beads in my hair.

We went out on dune buggies early one morning and stopped at a school to give the children lots of supplies and candy and hats. It was overwhelming the amount of children who put their hands out to us and surrounded our dune buggy. I couldn't get the stuff out fast enough. I felt so happy to give to these children (with our friends) some very much needed supplies and the children were so happy. It made our day. We saw a lot more of the country that day and enjoyed every minute of it. We were completely filthy when we came back to the resort that day but the smiles that were on our faces outweighed any dirt we had to wash off.

Then one evening, most of our crew wanted to go into town to a small casino. I truly did not want to go but I felt I would be alone and I didn't want that either. So, I went with the crew to the small casino. We were only there about an hour or so and decided we needed to go back to the resort. So, we got two taxis and started home. The streets were very narrow and packed with vehicles. I was very nervous and was getting cranky because people were hollering and cursing each other as the traffic was brutal. Finally, we get back to the resort and I am extremely relieved. Our taxi arrived first and then two minutes later the second taxi pulled in. Most of the young people (sons and daughters) were in that taxi and when they got out they told us to sit down because they had a story to tell us. We sat down and I thought, "Oh, no, what happened?" The one young person was Tat and Kevin's son Christopher. He proceeded to tell us that their taxi driver almost got in a fight with another driver they were passing because of the other driver being too close to them. Christopher told the story with theatrics and humor but I wasn't laughing. He told us when the taxi driver and the other driver stopped arguing, Christopher asked the taxi driver, "Um, is there a problem?" The taxi driver smiled at him and reached under his seat and pulled out a gun and said to Christopher, "No problem at all, friend. You are safe with me." Then he shoved the gun back under his seat and continued driving. Christopher had most of us laughing the way he told the story but it was still upsetting to me. I said no way in hell was I leaving the resort at night again.

The last thing I will tell you about that trip was the day we all went to a place that was two hours away to swim with the dolphins. I was so excited to do this but I was nervous too. But every time I started to feel nervous or anxious about something new, I told myself that I would probably never have this opportunity again and to enjoy the new things I am seeing and doing. And so I did. I was able to go and swim with the dolphins. It was very well done as far as safety was concerned. It was just a small blocked off pool with sides and seats around it in the middle of a small lake. We got into the water which was only up to my hips and then the dolphins would dance in front of us. They also got the dolphins to kiss us one at a time and boy was that fishy. The dolphins were so smart and would get up on their fins and give us a hug so the photographers got many pictures. When it was all done, I looked over at Michael and I was beaming like a Cheshire cat. I was so proud of myself for not backing out at the last minute. I was so happy that I got into that water and let the dolphins swim around me and in front of me. Several of us did it and it was a wonderful memory for me. But my excitement was short-lived. When we were all walking together at this place and heading to see some more sights, Tat's son Christopher had pulled his shoulder out of its socket. Holy crap! The poor guy was in pain and we needed to get him to the doctors. He was taken to the hospital with his parents and the rest of us stayed as we had to get on the bus back to our resort. We all felt so bad for him and hoped that he would get good care. And that is exactly what he got. The doctors and nurses took good care of him and had him back to normal. The bus finally came to get us and on our way back to the resort it stopped at the hospital and picked up Christopher and his family. We were so happy to see him. He had a sling on his shoulder and looked a little pale but was happy to get back to the resort. Eventually it was time to go home and I went home with so much confidence in myself and in my being able to handle things that came my way. And wouldn't you know it, that confidence was tested.

It was late winter of 2007 and the pain in Michael's chest was getting worse. We weren't sure what it was but I knew it had to be bad if Michael was complaining about it. We had gone to bed but his pain wasn't getting any better so we decided we better get him to the hospital and get him checked. I wanted to call an ambulance but Michael insisted I drive him. By the time we got there, he was in excruciating pain and they took him in right away. I was beside myself with worry as I wasn't sure if he was having a heart attack or what. When I got to see him, they had him hooked up to drugs for the pain and were getting him ready to go for an ultrasound and blood tests. When he came back I just sat beside him and waited for the doctor to come and tell us what was going on with him. They had already ruled out a heart attack earlier and were looking at his gallbladder and surrounding area. The doctor finally came and told us his gallbladder needed to come out right away. We were both surprised it was his gallbladder but the doctor assured us that once the gallbladder was gone Michael would be fine. His pain just kept getting worse by the minute. He was in so much pain and it bothered me to see Michael like this. He was always so strong and healthy and I felt so bad for him. I stayed with him the whole night and the nurse put a warm blanket over my shoulders when she saw me with my head down on the end of his bed. I was so worried about Michael I refused to go home. The next morning I called the girls and explained what was happening and that he was okay. I called Tat and asked her if she could come and sit with me while Michael was having the operation and she said yes of course. When Tat got there, I was exhausted but I was happy to have her there with me. She was always there for me.

It seemed like they were taking a long time but finally someone came down to us and told us that he was in recovery and everything went well. We were able to see him and he was just glad that he wasn't in any huge pain anymore. They gave him a laparoscopic and he had four small incisions in his stomach but he was doing great. The doctor told us they were sending his gallbladder away to have a biopsy done which was normal protocol and he said that everything was probably okay but they had to do this for precaution. Other than that, we were able to take him home and he would be off for a few weeks. A few weeks later we got news that Michael was to go in to see this doctor for the results of his gallbladder biopsy. We were both surprised at this appointment because the doctor was sure all would be well and we probably wouldn't hear from him. But that was not the case and we both knew that whatever the doctor had to tell us was important. I came home from work and immediately asked Michael what the doctor said. He told me to sit down and as soon as he said that I started to panic. Then he told me that they found cancer cells at his bile duct that was connected to the gallbladder. I know he told me more but all I heard was cancer! Cancer was the one word in my life that I absolutely hated with a passion. Cancer took my mom and it took my dad and it took countless other people. I started to cry and went to Michael and we held each other. We never said a word for a while and just took in the information that was laid before us. Eventually I asked him what the next step would be and he told me they were sending him for several big tests at one of the best cancer hospitals about an hour away. From there they would set him up with a specialist who would tell us the best course of action from the result of these tests.

And so it began. Michael went for so many tests and he was such an inspiration to me. I always saw my husband as a very strong and fearless man. When he would tell me about the tests I would feel sick to my stomach. I tried so hard to be strong around him but inside I was falling apart. Why was this happening? Why was it happening to Michael? He stood by me when I was at the lowest part of my life. He watched me fade away into the walls of depression but he never gave up on me and he never left me. He didn't abandon me when I was not sure if I would ever come out of it. And now Michael was facing his own demon of cancer, the demon that tries so hard to take so many people's lives. I hate this dear God, I hate that he has to go through this!

Michael wanted to wait to tell our four girls until he went to see the specialist. So in the meantime it was hard not to tell them but I knew he needed to know what the plan would be before we could tell the girls. Only one day our daughter Ava had answered the phone when we were out and it was the nurse calling from the cancer hospital with a date for Michael to see the specialist and she was devastated. She asked us what was going on and we had to tell her that Michael had cancer. She ran upstairs to her bedroom and started crying. I told Michael that he had to talk to her because it was his story to tell and we went up to talk to her. Michael couldn't handle it when she started crying hard and it made him upset and so he raised his voice and said something like, "I am going to be okay. You need to calm down!" I knew this hurt Ava that he was angry but I also understood that Michael was not in a good place and couldn't handle Ava being upset. It was hard on him and it was hard on me. Michael is a very private man and does not like any attention on him and does not like anyone to worry about him. So, I had to try and not show my fear and be as strong and positive as I could around him. He needed me to be strong and I did the best I could because I loved him so much and wanted to be strong for him as he was for me.

We went for his appointment at the cancer hospital and saw his assigned doctor. There were a team of doctors who decided on the best course of action for Michael's condition and it ultimately came down to a major surgery to restructure his bile duct to his bowels. If everything turned out the way they hoped it would then he would not need any chemotherapy or radiation. Of course, this is what I prayed for and begged God for a perfect surgery. So now we had the plan and it was time to tell the girls. By this time, Ella lived with her fiancé Scott and Bree was going to teachers college. Michael told them he had some bad news and then told them he had cancer and all the particulars about it. He was able to tell them by now that he had a date for surgery and that everything would work out okay. The girls were upset of course but took it pretty good in front of their father. They were very strong and positive that everything would be okay. I was very proud of them for taking the news the way they did and showing their father their strength. Of course, I am sure in their own private moments they shared their concerns and tears for their dad. Charlie on the other hand broke down in front of Michael but she is a lot like me. We both wear our emotions on our sleeves. Needless to say all the girls were shocked by the news but held it together when needed.

We were lying in bed one night and just cuddled up holding each other. Michael decided we needed to talk about the "what if something happened to me" talk. I didn't want to talk about that but I knew we needed to just in case something happened. Michael told me what I was to do and he said he would write a list of all the financial stuff I needed to know. He told me his wishes of what to do with his body and we discussed it in length. I told him my wishes and he concurred. I would cry and he would hold me and tell me everything would be okay. I told him I couldn't imagine my life without him and he wasn't allowed to die before me. I told him he was the strong one and I was supposed to go first. We said silly things to each other and laughed. We talked for quite a while and even though I knew we had to have this talk I silently cried myself to sleep. The next morning when I got up he handed me a piece of paper with all the important financial information on it. I found it very hard to look at this piece of paper and so I put it away hoping I would not have to use it for a very long time.

The day came for the major surgery. Our dear friends Tat and Kevin were there with us. Of course, we all know that they were not only there for Michael but they were there to keep me calm and support me while I waited for Michael to come out of surgery. To me, this day was a very strange day. My body was definitely there and my friends kept me busy but my mind was not there. It is very strange to describe how I felt. I was so full of anxiety but I kept shoving it down and telling it not to bother me because I have to be strong and confident for my husband. So every time I would get nervous or feel sick to my stomach I would do my breathing exercises or read *From Panic to Power* by Lucinda Bassett. I was determined to stay strong and not fall apart. Michael needed me to be strong, as I said in my vows to him and to God "in sickness and in health" and he was truly the love of my life.

Each hour that went by was dreadful to say, the least. I knew he would be in there for about six hours, but by the time six hours came and he wasn't out yet I started to panic. My mind would throw in some awful thoughts and I would start to sweat and feel so sick to my stomach. I didn't know how much longer I could hold on until I heard that Michael was okay. I watched the minutes move on the clock, and the more I watched the more I got anxious. I started pacing and pacing. My friends were so patient with me and tried their best to keep me occupied. We moved around to other areas to sit to break up the monotony. Finally, after six and a half hours, the doctor came out to me and I jumped up and ran to him (almost knocked him over I was so glad to see him). I blurted out the words, "How is my husband?"

He told me, "The operation took a little longer than expected but everything went perfect and your husband is in recovery. The next twenty-four hours he will be in intensive care to make sure he is doing well."

I started to cry and said to him, "Can I hug you?"

He smiled and said, "Yes, you can."

I hugged him so tight and for a long time and then said, "Thank you so much, Doctor. I appreciate everything you did for my husband. Thank you, thank you."

When I let him go, he just smiled and told me it was his pleasure to help my husband. Then I sat down and put my head in my hands and thanked God that everything went so good for Michael and I thanked God for watching over the doctor and the nurses when Michael was in the surgery and then I prayed that God would continue to watch over Michael over the next twenty-four hours until he was out of any danger.

After we saw the doctor we were so relieved and we were able to relax and wind down from the long day. It still took almost two hours before we were able to see him. Ella and her fiancé Scott showed up just before we went up to see Michael. We were all sitting in the waiting room on the floor Michael was now on and the nurse came to tell me I was able to see him. I got up and I felt so unsteady and I was scared to see him. Ella said she would go with me and if I started to feel stressed to just look at her. And so we went to see him. I was filled with so many different feelings when I saw him I found it hard to breathe but I just kept asking God to give me courage and strength. Ella was so good with her dad and as I watched her I felt so blessed that she was there with me. When I looked at Michael I was overwhelmed with sorrow of how he looked. He was always my big strong man but now he couldn't even move any part of his body. He looked so pale and helpless and my heart was breaking. We stayed with him only a short time as he needed to rest and be watched by the nurses. I had a hard time leaving him but I knew I was just in the way and I wanted him to be well taken care of and monitored every possible moment. I thanked Ella for being with me and told her I loved her very much and then we all went to our cars and drove back home.

I wasn't even in my friend's car for five minutes and I just started balling. I was so happy Michael was okay but I was finally letting go of all my pent-up anxiety and boy did I cry. I didn't stop crying until we got home (which was fifty minutes later), and then both Michael's sisters called to see how everything went and I started crying again. I couldn't even talk to them. It was like this tap was turned on and water just poured out of me and I couldn't stop crying. I felt so bad but I just let it go. As a kid, I was told not to cry and be tough, but no way was I holding all these feelings in. All my fears and anxiety just poured out of me and I had no control once it started. Eventually I settled down and my friends left to go home and get some well needed rest. Thank God they were with me. I was so thankful for my dear friends Tat and Kevin and their constant support.

But now it was time to go to bed. I couldn't sleep. I just felt so afraid that something was going to happen to Michael through the night and I just filled myself with so much fear and anxiety I made myself sick. I didn't want to be alone but I didn't want to call Tat as she needed her sleep too. So, I called my good friend Bridgette from church (who lived three minutes away by car) and asked her if she would mind terribly to come over and spend the night with me as Ava wouldn't be home until late in the night. I was beside myself and I needed the prayers and the company. My friend Bridgette agreed to come over and stay the night with me and I was so thankful she would do this for me. She even had to work the next morning but knew that I did not want to be alone and still came to stay with me. I was so happy she came to be with me and I will always remember her kindness.

A week went by and then Michael came home with Tat and me which was a difficult ride for Michael as he was in pain off and on during the car ride. We helped him into the house and up the stairs to bed. It was so hard to watch him like this but I kept saying my prayers and asking God to give me courage and strength to help Michael. I did my very best to be there for him but I really wasn't a nurse in any way, shape, or form. Ava and I were not the best at changing his dressing and neither one of us wanted to see the staples in his stomach. Poor Michael had to put up with us trying to take care of him. He was off work for three months and eventually went back to work doing light duty at first. But the really good news came on his three-month check-up and we were told he had no cancer anywhere in his body. The doctor said he was cancer free and we were over the moon happy with that news. I thanked God over and over for Michael's prognosis.

You know when you have someone you love as much as I love Michael, you really appreciate all the little things in life. You realize that everything that you thought was important to be happy are not even in the running when it comes to almost losing someone you love. I took for granted that Michael would always be here with me to grow old with and now I had to accept the fact that one day one of us would be gone. We always joke that neither one of us want to be the one left behind. I will tell Michael that I was going first because I couldn't bear to be without him and he says he is going first because he couldn't handle life without me. But we both know that it isn't up to either of us which one will go first. Life has no guarantees and we are not in charge. So, for now we enjoy every day we have together. Even when we disagree or argue about something ridiculous it is short lived. Of course, I am usually right. Okay, maybe not always right but pretty close. But seriously, we are both blessed to have each other through the good and the bad and I am really thankful for the day Michael decided to stalk me.

CHAPTER 27

Ava called me at work in April of 2008 and she sounded very distressed. I felt sick to my stomach when she told me she was feeling tightness around her heart. I tried to be as calm as I could but my anxiety and panic were starting to swallow me up. At first I suggested that maybe she was stressed and was having some panic issues but she said she was actually feeling a physical tightness around her heart. I myself would feel physical symptoms in my body with my panic attacks and so I was still thinking she was having panic symptoms. We talked for a few more minutes trying to figure out what was going on and if we should call the ambulance or not. Ava didn't think she needed an ambulance so I told her to call my next-door neighbor Karen and ask her to drive her to the hospital and I would meet her there shortly. She agreed and then called me back to let me know that Karen would take her up. I had to ask my coworker if she would bring me to the hospital to make sure Ava was fine. I still wasn't driving anywhere too far by myself and as embarrassing and frustrating as it was for me not to drive myself I knew I was no good to Ava when I was panicking.

My coworker took me up to the hospital and before I went in to the room where Ava was admitted I said a prayer for courage. As I walked into the room I could feel my heart racing and panic was setting in but I tried my very best to be strong for my girl. I felt so bad that she was there and just seeing Ava in the bed made my heart swell. It didn't matter what age she was she was still my baby girl and it broke my heart seeing her all alone in that hospital bed. She looked pale and although I knew she was probably scared she put on a face for me. She acted brave and proceeded to tell me what was wrong. I introduced her to my coworker and felt bad that I didn't have the courage to drive myself there. But I shoved my own feelings down and tried very hard to just be there for Ava. I couldn't bear to hear any bad news and beforehand I told my coworker that I was happy she came with me for support. My coworker had been a big part of my life for a couple years now and she was so supportive about my panic issues. Ava proceeded to tell me there was an infection around her heart and they were going to keep her a couple of days to make sure the infection cleared up. I felt so sick when I heard the news. I had never heard of anything like that before. She assured me that the doctor said once the antibiotics worked through her system that she would be okay. We stayed with her for a little while and then we had to get back to work. Of course, I just wanted to stay right there with her but I knew we had to get back to work. So as bad as I felt for leaving I left her there and told her I would be back up with Michael later.

When I went back to work I felt like such a failure. Why couldn't I have just driven up to the hospital by myself and why couldn't I just have stayed right there with my baby girl. My heart broke and I was so angry at myself that I still let the anxiety and panic get the best of me sometimes. Later when I followed my friend home I was not a happy camper. When Michael got home from work, I told Michael that Ava was in the hospital and he was shocked and quite concerned. We had a quick bite and went up to see her. I picked up a few things for her from the gift shop and I was so happy when I found this beautiful flat stoned angel in the gift shop. I put it in a card that I gave her. I told her to hold the angel if she felt scared or alone. When I left her that night I knew I had to work harder on the program I purchased and get a handle on my life. I couldn't go on the way I was.

I was ashamed and my heart was breaking for Ava. I didn't want to leave her that night but I knew I had to. I cried quietly to myself that night in bed. Michael hugged me and told me Ava would be okay and I knew she would but I just felt so helpless for my daughter. We did tell her to come and stay with us for a while when she got out of the hospital and she did which made me very happy. Eventually she went back to her apartment but all I wanted was for my baby girl to come home where I could take care of her.

I bring this story up not only because it was important to share my daughter's experience but also to show others that anxiety and panic can take so much of our life away and we can't get it back. Yes, I had gone on a few trips and faced my fears of flying and seeing new things that I was so thankful for. Yes, I was working again and I was driving to work again but I wasn't putting myself in uncomfortable situations either. I was only doing what I felt comfortable with. I was at a standstill and I was letting myself just get by. But when I saw my daughter Ava lying in a hospital bed and I wanted to be strong for her but inside I was falling apart I knew it was time for me to stop just getting by. I needed to find out what the hell was holding me back with my program. I knew the program would work for me because I listened to so many people talk on the tapes of how the program had changed their life and they were doing anything and everything that they couldn't do before the program. And so again for probably the fifth time I started the program again and worked it harder and listened more intently and I didn't rush it. I was determined to be free of all the anxiety and panic that always seemed to come back and haunt me. I couldn't just say the words anymore I had to be the words that I read. And that is what I did, I started to practice driving to more places by myself and walk in to more stores by myself and go for walks by myself. I would drive for about fifteen minutes around to areas further than my neighborhood. Then the fifteen minutes turned into a half hour and then the half hour would turn into forty-five minutes and then an hour. This all happened slowly but surely. I needed to show myself that nothing was going to happen to me when I was by myself and I had to get over the time I had my first panic attack in my car. I had to drive through that wall of fear of driving by myself. Many people before had done it and I was going to do it too. Every time I would start to panic I would pull over and listen to my tapes and then proceed to my destination. Eventually I was able to drive without listening to my tapes because I knew them almost word for word and I would just tell myself that I was worth it, I was beautiful inside and out, and I was not going to let the fear be the thing that stopped me from driving. It took months and months but eventually I told my coworker that I was going to drive myself to work and back and if I started to panic I would work through it. That was a big deal to me. I could finally drive myself to work alone. I was so proud of myself and I thanked God for bringing this wonderful program into my life. The program wasn't the problem, *I* was the problem, and once I figured that out I knew I was on my way to a new way of living.

As I was working on my program my daughter Ava was moving in with her two dear friends Cindy and Nick. And through her two friends she met a guy named Joshua and they started dating. I was so happy for Ava as Josh seemed like a great guy. To see her happy made me happy.

On October 4, 2008, our daughter Ella and her fiancé Scott were married. I was so happy on that day. Ella had asked me a month or so earlier if I wanted to say a speech on their wedding day. I was honored to be asked to say something and I started working on a poem that I could share on their special day. Both Michael and I were so happy to welcome Scott into our family even though he had been a part of our family for five years now. We knew Scott quite well and loved him dearly. He was a good match for Ella. Because Scott had a great sense of humor I decided I would write a funny poem and also have two pairs of underwear made up for the bride and groom. It was an inside joke between Scott and I and I was so excited to do this with Michael. Of course, Michael would have his own speech and I would follow him but I felt important when Ella included me. The day was beautiful and the wedding was very sweet. Ella walked down the aisle arm and arm with her dad to a song being played on a harp. The harpist played "The Prayer" by her favorite female singer Celine Dion. At the end of the aisle, Ella's mom took her other arm and together her mom and dad walked her to her groom. Ella's new sister-in-law sang a beautiful Celine Dion song called "Have You Ever Been in Love" that brought tears to my eyes. Michael was so proud and did an amazing job on his speech, talking of how he used to hold Ella's hand as a little girl to keep her safe and now he was giving her hand away in marriage to a great man, Scott. And then I found myself tearing up when Michael and Ella danced together for the father and daughter dance. We were very proud of Ella and Scott and had a wonderful time at their wedding. We danced the night away and laughed with our family and friends. I just love weddings!

At the end of the night, I was so proud of myself because I was the designated driver. Yes, I had to drive back to town at one thirty in the morning and I did it! It was my first time driving at night in a lot of years and I was so happy I did it. I proved to myself that I could do it if I had to and that meant a lot to me. It was always easier for me to have faith in God than having faith in me. I was starting to learn to have faith in myself and I was testing the waters by putting myself in situations that I had no choice but to do it. I learned that if I just lived in the moment and not think about the future I could do things a lot better. I enjoyed myself at the wedding and didn't let myself think about the drive home that was coming up later in the evening. And because I only thought of it when it was time to go, it was a success. I didn't over think it whereas before I did any-thing out of my comfort zone I would think way too much. I would obsess and worry myself sick until I had myself in such a dither that I couldn't move. I would think to myself, "What if I have a panic attack?" Now I change that around and say, "What if I don't have a panic attack? Awesome!" Or I think to myself, "So what, I will just breathe and it will last a few minutes, I can handle that." I love the fact of knowing that I am the one in control of my thoughts and if

I don't like the negative thoughts in my head I just change them to positive thoughts.

Someone who has been positive all their life or haven't been through a dysfunctional childhood might say, "What is all the fuss about? I don't get it." But why would you get it? Unless anyone has ever walked in another's shoes and only grew up in negative situations, no one else could possibly get it. But that's okay, those of us who lived with anxiety and panic, we get it. And because of that, we are the best people to help others who are going through panic and anxiety and agoraphobia. These conditions are real and those of us who have these conditions need support from our family, friends and strangers. We didn't ask to be like this. It is embarrassing and debilitating and we need to know people stand beside us and believe in us. Support us, for we would help you in a heartbeat. Love us unconditionally and know that we love you too. With help from the right sources and trust in ourselves and others and for me a huge faith in God, we can overcome these horrible conditions. When someone breaks their arm or foot for example everyone can see it and they know that the person is probably in pain. But when someone shows anxiety or panic, you only see a person acting strange and may not be as sympathetic because you can't see it. Let me tell you, the person who is in a panic attack feels this: racing heartbeat, sweating hands, not being able to focus, feeling helpless and scared, contemplating running or not moving. Everything around them feels unreal and they feel lost. These are a few of the symptoms that someone feels when having a panic attack, you may see the sweat and the look on their face but you cannot see the inside of their body or their mind which is where it all comes from. Eventually the person with the broken arm gets the cast off and needs therapy and then eventually through patience and taking care of themselves they are back to normal. Someone with panic attacks doesn't get to take their mind off or their insides out (which sounds ridiculous I know), but it's true in a sense. So all I am saying is when you see someone having a panic attack give them your support ask them if they need help, take care of them as you would someone walking in crutches. We need to know you are there for us. Thank you.

The time frame is now November of 2008, and Michael was feeling pretty good now and so we decided to go on a two-week vacation to Myrtle Beach with our dear friends Tat and Kevin. Life was too short to not get out and see as much of the world as we could. So, we planned a two-week trip which included golfing as much as we could and sightseeing on the days we didn't golf. We had a great time. We drove down through the mountains and saw many deer and beautiful scenery. It was breath taking through the mountains although I wouldn't want to drive through there during the night with all the deer running around. We stayed in a two-bedroom, two-bathroom condo. It was quite fancy with lots of room. Wow, was this really happening to me? Were these the kinds of things I could do and enjoy when I didn't let my anxiety take over? I was so blessed and appreciative that I was reaping the rewards of amazing vacations when I trusted in God and this program I was given. In the two weeks we were there, we didn't stop. We went everywhere and did everything we could in those two weeks. Michael's sister and husband were down in Myrtle Beach the same time we were and we met up with them for an evening of dinner at a Japanese restaurant. It was a lot of fun watching our dinner being cooked in front of us with such a great show by the chefs. Lots of laughter and good food with my sister-in-law and brother-in-law made it a special night. We golfed, we dined, we saw a couple of great shows, we played, and we just enjoyed ourselves immensely.

When we came home I thanked God so much for all of my blessings—my family, my friends, and this newfound freedom of minimal anxiety. Would I ever be totally free of anxiety? Probably not because life happens and there are no guarantees that life will be free of pain and sorrow. But what I do know is that God was with me every step of the way and my life was changing for the better. I was looking forward to more vacations and even the flying would be okay because I was doing everything I needed to do to have as less panic as I could have.

Life was going on with or without me so I chose to work on my anxiety program to the best I could. I kept myself busy and I continued to work hard at my job. At this time in my job I found it to be getting more and more stressful but I held on because I liked the people I worked with and the job was like second nature to me. I knew my job quite well and I was good at it. But I did start to question if this job was what I really wanted to do with my life. I didn't feel like I was accomplishing anything important in my life in the job I was doing. So, I did start looking here and there for something else, something meaningful but nothing seemed to jump out at me. And while my life was moving forward there was something else happening to Ella and Scott. Ella was pregnant with her first child and we were so excited. And on January 9, 2010, Scott called us and told us happily, "It's a boy!" He was over the moon happy and so were Michael and I. We had three beautiful granddaughters and now our Ella was giving us a grandson! We were ecstatic, to say the least. They named him Jacob and he was so adorable. Michael and I went to the hospital as soon as we could and held him in our arms. It was so amazing to have a grandson! We had no idea what to do with a little boy but we were ready to enjoy this little guy. It was so nice to have another baby in the family. Jacob would bring so much joy and love to our family and all I could think of was how blessed I was. I was a proud nanny that day and when I held him I knew he would fill my life with laughter and happiness. I was his nanny and he was my grandson!

So now my life was going pretty good with a new baby and new hope in myself. But then life has a way of letting you know that there will always be something to get through, something horrendous happened not to me but to people I loved dearly. Life reminded me that no one is exempt from hell on earth.

CHAPTER 28

Charlotte was an amazing, free-spirited woman. She didn't hold back on how she felt about things and lived her life to the fullest. She was a beautiful girl with big brown eyes and her smile and laughter lit up a room. I first met Charlotte at Charlie and Jacob's wedding and I immediately liked her. I had hoped I would see her again and get to know her better and I did see her again at Charlie and Jacob's annual barbecue. Charlotte was with her fiancée who was a quiet guy but seemed friendly enough. My favorite memory of her was when her sisters, cousins, my granddaughters, and I were dancing up a storm in the living room. I remember Charlotte laughing at me as I tried to dance the same way the rest of them were which was with a lot of jiggling of our butts. I couldn't quite get it but Charlotte said, "You're doing good, Charlie's mom!" And it is those words and the sound of her laughter that I will remember Charlotte with love and admiration. For you see, as hard as it is for me to write these words, you need to know that Charlotte was murdered while she slept by her fiancée.

As much as this affected me and my family, my devastation was nothing compared to the devastation of Jacob and his family. Charlotte was Jacob's older sister. I can't even begin to tell you how it tore out the hearts of Jacob and his parents, his siblings and all those who knew and loved Charlotte. To watch this story unfold was heart-wrenching. I listened to family members share their stories of Charlotte and memories of her as a young girl at the celebration of her life. I watched Jacob's mother fall to the ground crying out to God for her beautiful daughter at the cemetery. I watched as this horrendous murder tried to tear apart Charlie and Jacob and tested their marriage. I listened to my daughter Charlie tell me that my twelve-year-old granddaughter was having a very hard time with this and she was seeing a counselor at school. And I listened quietly and sometimes angrily at the conversations my children would tell me that were happening in the courtroom. This senseless murder affected so many people and it affected me deeply as I watched it all unfold. The court sessions went on for a long time and they were hard on everyone that witnessed these proceedings. I had known Jacob and his family for many years and I loved his family very much. I felt so helpless with what to do for his parents except for praying for justice and for God to carry them through this malicious act of murder. And so I reached out to my church and for many, many weeks and months we prayed for Jacob and his family. My church reached out to me and gave me a prayer shawl which members of the church had knitted together and had it blessed. I would put this prayer shawl around my shoulders and cry and pray for Charlotte's family. I thought this idea was wonderful and even for just a few minutes I was filled with comfort. My good friend Bridgette suggested I could give a prayer shawl to Jacob's mom and I thanked her for the great suggestion. I had to do something to show her that as a mother I felt crushed inside for her pain. I knew Jacob's parents were strong faithful people of God and spent a lot of time at their church so I knew I could offer them my prayers. And so I met with her at her home and we talked and shed some tears and she wrapped the prayer shawl around her shoulders and we hugged. I didn't want to let her go but eventually I gently let her go. My heart ached for her and her family and my mind was so angry at the one who took Charlottes life. She had so much more to do and so much more life to live. She was smart and funny and loved by many. She didn't deserve what happened to her. It was said that she had confided in someone that she was going to leave her fiancée. It was said that things had gotten bad between them. These statements came from reliable people and there was no reason not to believe them whatsoever. But the sad thing was, Charlotte never got the chance to leave. He took that freedom from her and all he had to do was let her go. But instead he chose to kill her. And that leaves us with so many unanswered questions. What happened on that fateful night?

I will refer to Charlotte's fiancée as he. And first I will say that he got eight years for his crime. And as I am writing this he is now out of prison. He did six years for his crime. Six lousy years. His lawyer used the fact that his client had mental issues and was not in his right mind when he committed murder. Obviously, I am giving a short version of what went on in the courtroom but he had a psychiatric evaluation and the doctor said he should not be tried for murder. That is what the parents and the family had to hear while sitting in the courtroom and grieving the loss of their daughter. Those courtroom sessions were very hard on the family and friends who supported the family. My daughter Ava and her boyfriend Josh and of course Charlie were there with Jacob and his family through it all and it was such a disturbing court case. And to make things worse the sister of the accused would act very rude by making cold remarks and smiling an evil smile at the family. Many times my girls would come home and say how they just wanted to smack her. Whatever reason she had to do this to the grieving family is beyond me, but at least the mom and grandmother of the accused showed remorse for his actions.

Did the accused have mental issues? Did he have any remorse for what he did to someone he once loved? I don't know the answers to these questions. What I do know is he got off with only six years. What I do know is that his life will go on and Charlotte's life will not. What I do know is that six years later Jacob and my daughter Charlie's marriage is the strongest it has ever been, Jacob's family has moved on with weddings, grandchildren being born, birthdays, and anniversaries. They are living their lives the best they can and are smiling and laughing again. I am sure there is not a day that goes by that they do not think of Charlotte and how much they love her and miss her and I believe that a person can never get over something as horrible as losing a daughter, sister, to a senseless act that should have never happened. But if I may be so bold to say that when I see Jacob's amazing parents I see new light in their eyes and it makes me think that they are moving on because Charlotte would want them to live life to the fullest and their strong faith in God has helped them to do this. It is people like these who are heroes to me. I admire and love Jacob so much and I have been so blessed to have him as my son-in-law. My life is better just by knowing his family and I thank God for holding all of them in the palms of his hands all of these hard years to get them to where they are today. And when I think of Charlotte today, my hope is that she is dancing and laughing and living life to the fullest in the presence of those who have gone on before her and she just might be telling us to live life to the fullest and be sure to dance and be happy.

CHAPTER 29

Two months after Charlotte's death, still in the midst of grieving for my son-in-law Jacob and his family, we were to go
on a two-week trip to the West Coast in beautiful British
Columbia! As much as my heart was still hurting I knew this would
be a good trip and a well needed trip. I told myself to concentrate on
the beauty I was going to see and allow myself to be happy. I actually
brought my prayer shawl to comfort me on the plane ride. We went
out in August of 2010 for my nephew Christopher's wedding to his
beautiful bride Crystal. Remember, Christopher is Tat and Kevin's
son, and even though he was not my blood nephew I adopted him as
my nephew. I couldn't love him anymore than if he were my blood.

It was also Michael's and my tenth wedding anniversary and
what a way to spend it. I can't even describe to you in words the
beauty I saw. The mountains were bigger than life and the valleys
were a spectacular green. I was in awe. The fresh water lakes and riv-
ers were a sight to be seen. The wedding itself was at a resort in a town
called Campbell River. The resort was nestled on a small hill that over
looked a water passageway called the Discovery Passage and it flowed
out into the ocean. We watched the big barges go through and were
lucky to see a couple of cruise ships making their way through the
passage. We woke up every day and looked out to some very nice
views. The wedding was beautiful and the bride and groom were so

happy and we all danced late into the night. When the wedding was over a few days later we went on to Whistler Mountain. I could have cried with the beauty. We saw a big black bear running along the side of the road which was not something you see every day. Nature was at its best and it was all so breath taking to say the least. We stayed right in Whistler village and enjoyed the most amazing views.

But the best view would be the view from the top of Whistler. Oh, yeah, for sure! Let's do it. We get on a small gondola that was enclosed and it took you up twenty minutes to the next stop. Okay, not liking the closed-in feeling but I can't get up there any other way so suck it up butter cup. Okay, why are we stopping? I am not an expert but I do think we need to go a little further up the mountain. Okay, we have no communication but we now have to trust that we will be okay hanging in the middle of the air in a small closed-in gondola. It would only happen to me. I am not impressed but I am doing my breathing exercise and holding on to my sanity. Whose bright idea was this anyway? I could have just let Michael and our dear friends and their daughter go up and I could have just waited at the bottom and let the fear take over. Oh, yeah, I wanted to see the top of the mountain. Ten minutes have gone by and I have taken off my jacket and ready to take off all my clothes if this gondola doesn't get going. But just as I am contemplating taking off my clothes the gondola starts going up the mountain again. Yahoo, we are moving and almost to our first destination. I am happy now.

We get off the gondola and now we have to get on the open-air ski lifts. They are quite big and have a lid that comes down over you if you are cold. I am far from being cold. Michael and I get to have the ski lift to ourselves and Tat, Kevin, and their daughter Melanie are on one together. The ski lift moves at a good pace up toward the mountaintop and at this time we still cannot see the summit. We see bears running on the mountain side and enjoy the scenery as we climb higher and higher. Eventually we see the summit. I was so quiet and in awe of the height and splendor of the snowcapped summit. It was too incredible for words. We got off the ski lift and just stood beside each other in complete awe of the beauty that beheld our eyes. It was absolutely incredible. I had anxiety on the journey up but that was all gone when I stood there and did a complete circle with my body and had an amazing view of so many other mountains in close proximity. My heart was filled with love and my eyes were filled with tears. And the quietness of it all was ridiculous. We saw planes flying underneath us and just couldn't fathom how high we were. A half hour had gone by and we decided to go inside this big building and have lunch. It was just so crazy to even think of how they got all this stuff up there to the top of this mountain. It would have been a treacherous drive up to the summit. Once our lunch was over we decided to walk down to the next part of the mountain where you could get on another huge gondola over to another mountain. It took us a good while to walk down to our destination but we were stopping along the way to have fun in the snow and take pictures. When we finally got to our next destination I started to be nervous again because this gondola was so high between the two mountains and it took twenty-five minutes to get to the other side. I wasn't sure if I could last twenty-five minutes and not get out. But I gave myself a pep talk and just went for it. When we were on the gondola there was a man on it who was quite afraid. He had his head in his hands and he wouldn't look out the glass windows. I went over and sat beside him while his wife and kids were looking out the windows. I quietly introduced myself and told him I was afraid too and I had panic issues but I suggested that he may never do this again and while he was here he could tell himself he was missing out on the beauty that was around him. I told him he wasn't alone and told him it was a sight to behold. He didn't get up from his seat but he did turn around and look out the windows behind him and he was amazed. He eventually stood up and I saw a smile on his face. His wife came over to him and put her arm around him and I was filled with joy for him. When we reached the other side we all couldn't stop talking about what we just did. When it was time to go down on the ski lift, I was so relaxed and I thanked God for the beauty of our world. I also thanked God that I had this amazing opportunity and I would never forget it as long as I lived.

Okay, day three of our Whistler trip, and what was on the agenda that day? Did I hear someone say zip lining? Of course, what else? Okay, I guess we are going zip lining, and walking off the edge of a tall tree is no big deal and then another one and another one. I was scared shitless! But I was doing it if it was the last thing I ever did. I was stepping through that wall of fear again and telling it to go blank itself. Best thrill ever! I absolutely loved it! I was one with nature and I was flying over water and going from tree to tree. Excellent adventure for sure!

And just when I thought this trip couldn't get any better, our group decides we should go whale watching. We went out on a big rubber boat into the Pacific Ocean. We were dressed with one-piece suits that the crew gave us. The ride was fast and exhilarating. The water sprayed our faces and we soaked it all in. When we finally saw a family of whales we were captivated by their size. We saw hump back whales and we saw the great killer whales. Wow is all I can say. It is very humbling to see these creatures in their habitat. They are huge but majestic when they swim in these deep and cold waters. Well worth the money and time to see them. Our time in British Columbia was incredible. Canada is incredible. I always think we should be going to the States or the Caribbean or Mexico or Europe, and don't get me wrong, I have been to some of these places and they are amazing too. But if you ever have a chance to see British Columbia, just do it. You will not be disappointed. There is a lot to see and it is so worth seeing a piece of our beautiful country of Canada.

So, back to work it was for Michael and me. I showed my coworkers my amazing pictures from the west coast and got back into the everyday work life. And let me say here that the reason Michael and I could afford these trips was because we both worked hard at our jobs. Every week, money went into our "vacation fund" and by the end of the year or sometimes longer we would have the money to go somewhere. Michael and I worked hard for everything we had and it felt good to see our hard-earned money bring us some well-earned vacations.

I was back to work for a couple of weeks and this one day, my one coworker asked me if I had a sore throat. I said, "No, why?" He told me that before I went away he noticed I had a bump on the side of my throat. He touched the spot to show me and I did feel a bump that I had never noticed before. He told me you could really notice it when I stood sideways. He also told me I should go see about it and have it checked out. I agreed but I kept forgetting to make an appointment. Another two weeks had gone by and my coworker asked me when I was going to the doctor and I told him sheepishly that I hadn't made the appointment yet. He gave me a look of concern and said, "You need to make the appointment now." And so I did. I went in to see my doctor and she had me go for blood work and an ultrasound. To make a long story short she then sent me to a specialist for the throat area. The specialist was young but very up with all the latest gadgets and information and I felt very safe with his decisions. He met me at the hospital one day to have a special throat test done. He had to take fluid from my throat with a long needle, which was fun. Not! Then he had to put a camera down my nose to take pictures of my throat. Well, I was not prepared for that but I didn't have time to get scared as he did it so quick that before I knew it the long tube with the camera on it was down my throat. I must admit after that one I felt like fainting but I just lay down on the gurney.

The specialist found that I had a huge tumor on the left side of my thyroid. Okay, I am a big baby when it comes to hospitals. I faint at the sight of blood and just the mention of needles turns me green. So, it wasn't a surprise to me or Michael that I was upset that the tumor had to come out. And the only way that was going to happen was to have my throat opened up and my specialist performing the removal of the tumor. Man, are you freaking kidding me? "Okay, okay, I will get it done but I am not a happy camper," I said. I have to admit I was afraid at first of what they may find with the tumor but all I had to do was think of the loss of Jacob's sister and what his family went through and I told myself it could be a lot worse and to suck it up. It was mentioned that the tumor would be benign or malignant. I was confident that it wasn't malignant which surprised me because I was a person with anxiety issues. But more than anything, I was nervous about the area he was going to open up. And on the day of the operation as they wheeled me away from Michael and my daughter Charlie I began to feel panicky. I asked God to be with me and keep me safe but I had tears running down my face when I lay there waiting in the hallway for my turn. Then out of the blue I look up and over to the right of me, and what did I see? I saw a tag attached to a pipe with my husband's work name on it. I was so happy to see that tag and that to me was my sign that I was not alone. Of everything else I saw in that hallway, that was where my eyes went. I slowly smiled and said thank you to God for pointing that out to me. To someone else that may have been a coincidence but I took it as a sign and that made me feel much better. Okay, so I know that God is probably busy with everything going on in our world but I do believe in angels and I choose to believe that whenever I need help God sends his angels.

When I woke up in the operating room, I was in a lot of pain. They gave me some drugs and then I woke up in the recovery room. The pain was bearable then, just a small throbbing but I was just happy it was over. Michael was there by my side and of course my besties Tat and Kevin were there too. My girls came to visit me with their better halves and I was so happy to see them. Apparently, the tumor was bigger than they thought and was touching one of the main arteries in my throat. The doctor told Michael it was quite extensive to do as just one slip of the knife hitting the artery and it was game over. It was as big as a softball and growing down into my throat. The doctor said he had to send it away for tests to see if it was malignant or benign but he thought it looked good and wasn't concerned that it was cancerous. And to be honest, I don't know why, but I really didn't believe it was cancer. I really had faith that it would come back benign. And it did. It was such a big relief to hear those words that it wasn't cancerous. I thanked God and I thanked the doctor for taking such good care of me. He was an amazing doctor and I was really impressed with his work. My throat has a scar but it is right in with a crease and looks like it was always there. Of course, I know it is there and it is a reminder to me of how blessed I was that I did not have cancer. When I went home with Michael and was all tucked in on the couch I noticed that Michael was staring at me.

I asked him, "Why are you looking at me."

"Don't do that again."

"Do what?"

"You are not allowed to go in the hospital again for anything. I cannot handle seeing you there in the bed so helpless."

I smiled at Michael and said, "Now you have a small idea of how I felt when you were in there for your big operation!"

And of course Michael said, "It's okay if it is me, I would rather it was me, I don't like seeing you in there!"

I just smiled again and touched his hand and said, "It's okay, honey. I don't plan on going in again any time soon."

With the operation behind us and everything back to normal, it was time to plan our next trip. The main reason I am sharing with you about our trips in the next few chapters is so that you can see that even though I had anxiety and panic issues with help from the anxiety program I was able to face my fears. These vacations were not only about relaxation for me. They were mainly about the newfound freedom I had inside of me. The freedom from the major panic attacks and the debilitating depression that had consumed most of my childhood and adult years are the reason I enjoy my life now. And that is what I want for you. I want you who suffer from these debilitating conditions to face your fears and enjoy life to the fullest, fears and all. We all deserve to live our lives without the weight of chains around our feet that keep us in one spot all our lives. We deserve to be free from the haunting of our past and graced with the light that is ours if we but open our minds and hearts to it. Reap the rewards you deserve. So please bear with me as I share with you several places I had the opportunity to visit and the amazing things I experienced because I pushed through my wall of fear. And please believe me when I say this is not about bragging about what I could do now, it is about showing others that anyone can do it if they believe in themselves, have faith in themselves, work a program such as the one I worked and for me most of all is my faith in God. Faith that God would put the right things and the right people in my life to help me find my way in my world of darkness.

With that being said, our next stop would be the Mayan Riviera in Mexico. Wow! What an amazing trip! We landed in the city of Cancun. It was a little overwhelming seeing the police with the guns in their hands or hanging behind their shoulder but I knew from the Dominican Republic it was a safety thing. Once we got on the bus to go to our resort I started to relax. I had minimal anxiety, all good. And most importantly I would always pray to God to watch over us as we had our adventure. And what an adventure it was! We went to see the lost ancient cities of the Mayan people, truly a sight to see. At that time, we were able to walk up the giant steps of the pyramid like building. It was very high and intimidating. Kevin and I made it three quarters of the way and Michael and Tat of course made it to the top. It was one thing to climb up it but it was another to climb down. In the end, it was well worth it to be a part of that climb. You really felt what the Mayan people had to go through. It was crazy to say the least. Also on this trip we got to experience the inside of a cenote which was an underground water hole. For me, this experience made me feel claustrophobic. You had to go down through a hole in the ground and on these really sketchy stairs down into this underground oasis of beautiful aqua water. The water looked like a precious jewel. Above the water hole was an opening in the ground that had a water fall flowing through. It truly was a sight to be seen but all I could think of was I had to get out of there. I watched my group jump into the water and I took a couple pictures and then I was out of there. I waited for them outside the entry way and got my breath. That was the only time I had more anxiety but I just let it slide off my shoulder and didn't let it ruin my trip. I was still very proud of myself for going down and at least giving it a try.

We got to experience a traditional Mayan ranch with delicious Mayan food and learned more about their culture. We experienced a dinner show at this huge coliseum where we watched the story of the Mayan people being taken over by the Spanish when the Spanish invaded their territory. It was quite vivid and sad but it was well done. The story gave you more insight into how the Mayan lived and what they went through when the Spanish stripped them of all they knew. The show itself was well done and shocking when you learned the story. We visited an old Mexican city that made you feel you were back in that era it was so authentic. We also went in this glassed-in circle tower that went a couple hundred feet in the air and gave us an amazing view of the one big park we went to. This was a big deal for me and I did it and enjoyed the view. I must say here that I was so impressed with everything I was learning about the Mexican and Mayan cultures. We felt very safe and welcomed where we were and that made the trip a good one. We also went zip lining in the Mayan Riviera and it was so much fun! Zip lining was becoming my new loved sport. I was so amazed at myself for the things I was doing and actually enjoying.

I loved the Mayan Riviera in Mexico and I would definitely go there again someday.

In October of 2011, we were Vegas bound to a wedding being held in the Caesar's Palace Hotel and Resort for our daughter Charlie's good friend. We would have her friend over for dinner sometimes and I had known her for many years. Not only did we want to see Vegas again, but we were more than happy to be there for her special day. We thought the world of her. The wedding was beautiful on the Caesar's grounds and the bride looked amazing! We enjoyed ourselves very much and it was nice to spend some one on one time with Charlie.

Now you can't go all the way to Vegas without going down to Fremont St. and we wanted Charlie to experience it. So, off we went to Fremont St. and it was a blast. Lots going on, lots to see and lots of food and casinos to choose from but what did I notice that was crazy to see? A zip line with people flying above us down Fremont St. That's right, I said a zip line! Yahoo! So, Michael held all our stuff and Charlie and I headed for the zip line. Okay, so it was a little nervy, to say the least. You had to go up an elevator in this building that took you to the top of the building. Then you had to get in line and wait your turn to step onto a scaffold. Yes, I said a scaffold. I started getting really panicky standing in line waiting. I wasn't sure this was safe. Charlie was starting to get nervous too when she knew I was nervous so I had to tell her I was just excited and we would be okay. They had it set up so four people could all go at once as they had four separate zip lines set up. It was so cool because then I would be able to go at the same time as Charlie. Well, I got settled into my seat and Charlie was only a short distance from me but she didn't feel safe when the guy told her to go. She looked at me and said she wasn't in the seat right. She told the guy something wasn't right and then he got her to stand up and sure enough he didn't have her tied in right. So, he put her in the seat properly and poor Charlie didn't know if she really wanted to go through with this now and I didn't blame her. I was so excited and I knew if I didn't go now that we might change our mind especially after Charlie's seat not being right.

I looked at Charlie and said, "Let's go, honey. Yahoo!" and off I went. Charlie quickly came behind me and we had a blast! But holy crap when you come in for a landing you're looking at a wall and the dam zip line guy wasn't braking my landing so I hollered, "Holy shit, somebody help me, I'm going to crash!" Well, at the last minute, the brake goes off and you are inches from the wall and apparently that is supposed to give you a thrill but all it gave me was a look of fear and a white face! Anyway, Charlie watched me come in before her and she was prepared for the abrupt stop. She laughed her head off at me and we both just laughed together. We both had our moment of fear but it was worth it! Michael took pictures and was happy that we did it together. We had a few other moments of fun together but that was the most exciting and it really was special to Michael and I having quality one on one time with Charlie. Awesome memories.

In 2012, we flew to Fort Lauderdale and did a seven-day cruise with our besties Tat and Kevin. This time we were meeting my best friends and family from my old home town. We all decided to go on a Caribbean cruise to see my god daughter dance and celebrate her birthday. I was so happy to be able to go on this cruise with my adopted sisters Mary and Amanda and my nieces Diana and Krista. We spent a couple days in Fort Lauderdale and then my adopted sisters and nieces arrived and we all met at the cruise ship. It was so amazing to me to board this crazy ass ship. It was so big and beautiful and only a year old. It was ridiculous how big it was and we were only on a midsize ship! We had a balcony room because I insisted if I was going on the ship I wanted to see the water from my room. And it was worth it to me. I slept quite well with the lulling of the water. I was not sea sick at all and neither was Michael. So that was a plus. All of our rooms were right beside each other and the steward let us unhook our walls and made it one long balcony. It was truly a lot of fun. We all hid ourselves in the seats above the theatre where my beautiful god daughter was dancing. It was an honor for me to get this chance to see her dance. I was blown away. She was amazing and so beautiful. I was in tears watching her. When it was over, my sisters and nieces went up to their rooms and we planned to ask my goddaughter Whitney to come and see our rooms. Then her mom Mary and the rest of her family would be sitting on the balcony and surprise Whitney. And that is what we did. We surprised her with our presence and took pictures together and then we told her to come to our state room and see us. Oh, I forgot to tell you that her boyfriend Sergio was an engineer on the ship and he was in on the surprise. He was awesome! We all just loved him from the moment we met him. And so we surprised her and she cried happy tears when she saw her mom and family. It was such a great surprise.

The nice thing about a cruise to me is the fact that they stop at all these magnificent islands! I believe our first stop was Turks and Caicos and the water was so beautiful. On the island of St. Maarten, we bought a beautiful diamond band for my anniversary. I loved it and I got Michael to put it on my finger. I am not one of those wives who need a lot or expect a lot for our anniversary but this was a nice unexpected gift and when I look at it I think of the beautiful islands we visited and the romantic time we had together. On their private island that the cruise ships stop at, we went horseback riding in the water. I was nervous because I was not a good swimmer and I had a huge horse. First off, the guide took us on short walk up a hill and then down a hill and it was intimidating for me but the one guide stayed right with me. Michael was very good at riding his horse and I was quite impressed with him. They taught us how to hold the reins when we were walking in the water along the beach so the horse could breathe properly. These horses were beautiful and trained very well. It was pretty cool riding along the beach and we took some amazing pictures.

We also celebrated Whitney's birthday on the island of St. Maarten at one of the outside restaurants. The food was amazing and there was a lot of laughter and fun. What a way to celebrate your birthday on a beautiful Caribbean island with some of your best friends and family with you! We were so happy to be a part of Whitney's celebration and to get to watch her dance meant so much to me. I was thrilled to be with all of my dearest friends and being at sea was incredible. We stopped at Puerto Rico and honestly I was taken back with the port. We walked so much that day and none of us complained because there was so much to see. We were very impressed with that city and its surroundings which included a huge fort on one side and a rain forest on the other side. Truly worth the visit, and sitting in the port was the *Black Pearl* from the movie *Pirates of the Caribbean*. Puerto Rico was quite a beautiful place to visit and I highly recommend it as a vacation spot.

When we came back from the Caribbean cruise and the several days in Fort Lauderdale (where we went to the everglades and experienced lots of alligators), we were getting excited to welcome our daughter Ella and Scott's second child. It was a surprise the second time around when they called on June 19, 2012, and Scott said, "It's a boy!" Another beautiful baby boy, which meant we now had two grandsons! Jacob now had a little brother to grow up with. It was awesome and amazing the second time around too. Holding little Sampson was just as precious as the last four times we did this. Our lives were so full of beautiful grandchildren. My favorite thing to do with Sampson was to feed him. He was so cuddly and affectionate. I was one proud nanny. And you know what? Enjoy those moments when they need you because those moments go so fast. In the blink of an eye my grandchildren were growing way too fast for me, especially my granddaughters. Just saying!

And so the next trip we planned would be on January 30, 2013. Michael, me, and my sister Rose had the pleasure of meeting my brother Brad and his wife Christine in the Mayan Riviera in Mexico. We had such a great trip with my brother, sister-in-law, and sister. This was very special to all of us because we were together as a family. We ate together and laughed together and said good night to each other. It meant so much to me. We went on three excursions which were crazy fun! We took them to the Mayan ruins on the beach in Tulum. They were quite impressed as we were this second time around. We did an all-day excursion into the Mayan ruins where we climbed another Mayan temple. We zip lined through a few trees. We had to canoe over to a cenote and a Mayan ritual. Now this cenote was ridiculously scary for me. You had to crawl through a small hole in the ground and try to make sure your feet landed on the slippery wooden step and then proceed down several more slippery steps. The steps were slippery because of the moisture of the underground area. I went down like a trooper but I came back up in a few minutes when I heard our guide say another group was coming down. That was it for me. Up I went and had an outdoor shower and sat waiting for my family. I had a nice conversation with one of the guides and I was happy. My family enjoyed it because it was beautiful once you got down inside but they understood my claustrophobia inside. I still patted myself on the back for even going down. I still stepped through my fear and climbed through that hole and instead of putting myself down I told myself the old me would never have even attempted it before. Good for me, I said!

Wait a minute how could I forget to tell you about the repelling down the side of a small hill to walk through the jungle to get to the canoes. Well, that was something to be seen. I actually panicked when I saw that we had to rappel down this rock-faced hill. There were quite a few of us and we all cheered each other on. My sister Rose was awesome! It didn't seem to bother her a bit. She was always the strong one. I always admired her over the years for the things she did. My sister-in-law and I were the last to go as we had scared ourselves sick and didn't want to step off the edge backward and trust we wouldn't fall to our death. Christine went before me and I was so proud of her and then I realized if she did it I just had to do it. It was my turn and I was shitting bricks. I looked at our guide and said, "If I faint on the way down, will you get me?" He just had this big grin on his face and told me I was not going to faint and to just look at him the whole time and trust him that he wouldn't let anything happen to me. So I did. I looked him right in the eyes and listened as he instructed me to hold the rope with my left hand and hold the other rope in the other hand close to my right hip and he instructed me how to gently let off on the rope and it would bring me down slowly. I turned around and stepped out on the ledge and hung there for a few seconds and he told me to gently let myself go down. Okay, I was hanging on the side of the hill and had no choice but to go down now so I did and let me tell you I wasn't very good at it or graceful either. I went down a little too fast but I made it to the bottom and I burst into tears. The tears were about two things. One was the release of the fear and the other was that I was so proud of myself for doing it. That was way out of my comfort zone, but I did it and I praised myself and gave myself a lot of love that day.

Another excursion took us on a drive to a great beach area for snorkeling. The idea of swimming way out to another side of the area to see amazing species of fish did not appeal to myself, my sister, or my sister-in-law. It was all overwhelming to us three girls and another girl who was in our group. We had to wear flippers and the snorkeling paraphernalia and it became too awkward and uncomfortable to swim with the flippers so we opted to stay on the beach area to snorkel with one of the guides. Michael, Brad, and another fellow went with the one guide way out past where we girls could ever swim. After about twenty minutes, they were out of our sight. They were gone a long time and we were starting to get very concerned about them. Eventually we could see them swimming back and we were happy to see them. When they walked up the beach toward us they looked quite tired, scary tired really. They told us later that this guide was great but he went way overboard in how long he kept them out there. But they told us they saw things they had never seen before which included a huge sea turtle and an even bigger manta ray which was very poisonous. They were so happy they did it. They also said us girls would never had made it. I was not a good swimmer at all so I was so glad I didn't do it. I saw enough pretty fish just off the shore of the beach and that was good enough for me. We were exhausted by the time we got back to the resort but it was an experience and we laughed at dinner about the day. Our resort was quite beautiful and the food was great and our time together was priceless. I would like to think that our mom and dad were watching us from somewhere above enjoying our special time together like we did when we were young and together as a family.

CHAPTER 30

Well, I finally got the courage to quit my job of seventeen years and move onto something else. It was scary because I was so used to the atmosphere at my place of employment and I had been coming here for a long, long time. I knew this place like the back of my hand and it really was bittersweet to leave this position. But what gave me the shove was the fact that they were moving their business to a place down the highway and I really didn't want to go through the move and then find another job. I wanted to just leave and look for something else. And so I did, I gave my notice and said good-bye to many people that were a big part of my life. And the way it worked out I left my job right when our daughter Ava was having a destination wedding. Great timing on my part! November 2013 would find us in the Mayan Riviera again to celebrate the wedding of our daughter Ava and her fiancé Joshua. Michael and I really liked Josh. He was a great guy and from a great family. He treated Ava very well and was very respectful toward Michael and me. It all began when Ava and Joshua had planned this big trip to Europe starting at Portugal and we were so happy for them. The day they were leaving, I went to see Ava and went with her to pick up a few things she needed. While I was with Ava, Joshua stopped at our house and asked for me but I was out with Ava. He wanted to ask Michael and me for Ava's hand in marriage and he hoped he would see me before they left to go to the airport. He asked Michael and of course Michael said yes! When Joshua got back to their house he took me outside while Ava was in the washroom and quickly told me he was going to ask Ava to marry him on their trip. I was ecstatic but Joshua quickly told me not to show any emotion in case Ava looked outside. She would have been wondering what we were talking about. So, I held it in and smiled at him and hugged him and told him I couldn't be happier than to have him marry Ava.

They got engaged in Portugal and had the time of their young lives. And that brings us now to Mexico where they got married. Let me just say that the wedding was so picturesque, you could even say it was like something out of a fairy tale. Michael and I both walked Ava down the path to the Pergola. Arm in arm we walked down to the instrumental version of "A Thousand Years," originally sung by Christina Perri and David Hodges. The music was hauntingly beautiful knowing the words were "I have loved you for a thousand years, love you for a thousand more." I was so proud to be on one side of my daughter while Michael was on the other side. It meant the world to me that she wanted me to walk her down to her groom. On a small hill on the beach with the aqua blue water as their back ground standing inside a beautiful round white pergola with big white columns they said their vows. I looked out at the blue velvet water and thanked God for that day and all the beauty I felt at that moment. I had tears in my eyes and felt so much love and happiness for Ava and Josh. Our four daughters and their better halves were with us and our family members and our best friends witnessing this day and I couldn't be happier. Then about thirty minutes after the ceremony it started to drizzle and then poured. Well, you can't have everything! We all managed to take pictures and laugh and enjoy ourselves amidst the rain. And it rained and rained for the rest of the evening but their reception wasn't dampened by the rain. There were a few of us who got up and said speeches for the bride and groom and of course there was a lot of laughter during those speeches. They had a beach party planned but they had to change that idea into a stunning area on the resort and the staff did a fantastic job in setting up the party area. Other than the rain falling, it was such a fun and memorable time. I would like to share with you the heart felt poem I wrote and read for Ava on her wedding day.

My Beautiful Baby Girl

If I could have three wishes, one wish for me would be,
To go back when you were little and you sat upon my knee.
To watch you play with your baby toys and goo and gaa and sing,
Oh, what a special wish for me with all the joy it would bring.

To sing to you a lullaby and listen as you make not a peep,
While asking God to keep you safe as you drift right off to sleep.
To hold you when you're sick with a cold,
    gently rubbing your back,
Bathing you to keep the fever down and keeping you on track.

I'd just sit back and watch you grow at a much, much slower pace,
And watch you learn new things each day,
    with determination and grace.
Playing this little piggy went to the market on your tiny little toes,
Playing peek-a-boo with you and saying,
    "Mommy's got your nose."

But time doesn't wait for anyone,
Aladdin's lamp may not exist.
And the time we spent when you were young,
Now are precious memories in the mist.

So, I'll focus on the beauty of the joy you bring today,
The beautiful woman you are, and your truthful spirited way,
The dedication you show to all in everything you do,
Your generous kind and loving heart, I am so very proud of you.

Where ever your road may lead you, whatever
*   you do in this world,*
You have always been and always will be "my beautiful baby girl."

Yes, if I could have three wishes,
One wish for me would be.
To go back when you were a little girl,
And you sat upon my knee…Love you, baby girl.

This brings me to the best excursion for zip lining ever! Except for the bride and groom, three of our girls and two of their men, my three granddaughters, several nieces, and a good friend of the family all went on an amazing excursion to this huge park. We did the best zip lining I have ever experienced yet! The first zip line took you through a river and then you had to swim in to the guide and he would undo your zip line. But the best part was that you were sitting in a hammock type seat. Incredible fun for sure! The next zip lines got higher and longer and they were all different scenarios. But they saved the best for last, or the worst, whichever way you would look at it. Let's just say it took forever to get to the top of this zip line. Just as we are climbing this high tower (which was also on a hill), it started to rain. As we got closer to the top it started pouring one of those sideways rains that pelts your face and soaks your body. My daughter Charlie asked the guide if it was safe to go across in this weather and he says, "Oh, yes, my lady, no problem. Best time to go in rain!" Holy crap, this is just crazy, but I knew the longer we stood there the more we wouldn't do it. But before I could say something, our two young granddaughters were on the zip line seat together and saying, "See you on the other side!" We had no other choice now but to follow them. The guide put my daughter and me on the same seat because we needed the weight to get across. My daughter was in the front of me and she was shitting bricks. I of course (the brave one) proceed to tell her we were safe and it would be a blast. Oh, it was a blast, all right. My daughter was being pelted with the rain and I was tucked behind her so I wouldn't get pelted. The only time I got pelted was when I would move my face beside her face to see where we were going and it was hard to see anything in front of us. It was a pure adrenaline ride! Holy crap, were we really doing this in the pouring rain high above the park? That ride beat all rides I have ever tried in my life and it was worth it. We all survived and talked about it for the rest of the day.

Okay, you know how I am claustrophobic and don't like closed-in spaces? Well, on this excursion you also got to go down into the caves in this one area and paddle a raftlike boat through the caverns. Sounds okay but they had rain the day before and just walking to this area we were walking in a foot of water which meant the water in the cavern area was above it's normal height. Not a good swimmer, I say, and not good in small spaces. I gave myself a good positive talk while walking through the winding pathway down to the caverns. I was sweating bricks but I was determined as I watched my granddaughters brave it to face my fears. We got to our destination and two by two we got on the small boats. They told us the water had risen so there would be areas where we would have to duck so we wouldn't hit our heads on the ceiling which was made of rock and crusty looking stalactites. So off we went. Except for the ducking in a few places, I told myself to enjoy the beauty that I saw. And it truly was a magical sight. It was surreal actually to me. Between the beautiful aqua green water and the amazing crystal-like stalactites coming down from the rock above us it was something I had never seen before and I was in awe of this little piece of heaven. If I had just said to Michael, "I can't do it, you go without me," I would have missed out on something I may never see again. And not to mention I did that so many times in my life that I would regret not doing these special things with Michael and my family. So, I have the joy of smiling when I think of our daughter's wedding not only for her stunning wedding but also for all the activities I was blessed to do.

And then when I least expected it, our daughter Ava and her husband Joshua came to visit us one day and gave me a bag to open and said it was to thank me for something I didn't quite understand. But then when I looked in the bag I saw a tiny little Thanksgiving T-shirt that said "My first Thanksgiving" and my jaw dropped open and I jumped up and said something like, "Oh my goodness, are you kidding me? Yahoo, oh my goodness, I am so excited!"

Then Michael said, "What's going on? What's in the bag?" I passed him the bag and he just smiled from ear to ear and said, "Congratulations, guys!"

Holy crap, my baby was having a baby. Didn't see that coming so soon! I was over the moon happy! What a nice surprise! And so on October 24, 2014, Ava and Joshua had a beautiful baby boy! We couldn't be happier. The count was now three beautiful granddaughters and three handsome grandsons! They named him Scooter. Just kidding, they named him Luca. He was cuddly like Sampson and it was such a joy to hold him and welcome him into our family. Whenever I looked at Luca I could see Ava as a little girl and of course I could see Joshua too but the resemblance of Ava was very strong. My heart was so in love with this little guy. Our family grew bigger and bigger over the years and we just opened our hearts and our arms to all of our four girls, our sons-in-law, and our six grandchildren. Our house was full and I was and always will be the proud mom and nanny.

And so, just when you think life is going great, of course something comes along that shakes you up again. Only this time it wasn't happening to me, it just affected me in a very sad and helpless and angry way. You see, my friend Kevin (Tat's husband) hadn't been feeling very well for a few months. He was going back and forth to the doctors and having tests done with no answers. And then in December of 2014, three days before Christmas, he was diagnosed with stage 4 terminal lung cancer. What the fuck? Kevin and Tat did not tell anyone at Christmas as they were in shock and dealing with it the best they could and they wanted to enjoy their Christmas as best they could. Kevin told me that one of the tests he had gone for they were looking in his stomach area and noticed something at the bottom of his lungs. The next thing you know, he was told this devastating news. When we were told this news, both Michael and I felt so sick inside. Kevin and I always joked about being long lost brother and sister. He would always tell me I am the sister he never wanted and I tell him the same. Kevin was always the jokester out of the four of us and he always kept us laughing. All these years, all these wonderful vacations together and family gatherings couldn't stop now. Oh, God, dear God, no, please. This can't be happening to Kevin. I cried and prayed hard to God for him to help Kevin. I reached out to my church and my good friends and got them praying. All of Kevin's friends and relatives who believed in prayer would pray for Kevin and his family. And maybe those who didn't believe in prayer actually prayed too, I don't know. What I do know was that it couldn't hurt to pray.

Then the strangest thing happened. I got a call from Tat and she said the second CAT scan or MRI came back showing that the tumor in Kevin's lungs was gone. What? What the hell is going on? We didn't care what was going on, all we cared about was that they had diagnosed the wrong problem. Although there was something seriously wrong, he wasn't terminal. We were over the moon happy when we got that news. Those of us who prayed and believed in the power of prayer knew in our hearts that God had something to do with it. But wait the story isn't over. Through a few weeks of more tests and blood work, they finally diagnosed him (still not 100 percent sure) with non-Hodgkin lymphoma. Okay, still cancer, but now there was more hope than there was with the news of terminal lung cancer. Now they had somewhat a diagnose and knew they had to get him started on chemo. And Kevin's hard and sometimes torturous journey with chemo began.

It was heart-wrenching to hear how he was doing through Tat. She was his biggest supporter and was with him every second of every day making sure he was okay. As hard as it was to be positive when Kevin had days and days of sickness that turned into months of sickness, he still hung on. It was not an easy journey to go through. With

Tat and his daughter Melanie at his side he did the best he could. He had days where he couldn't get out of bed and days where he could get as far as the couch. But he still had a sense of humor as he would dye his hair bright yellow or some other vibrant color. When he started losing most of his hair, Tat just shaved the rest of it off. Kevin had shaved his head before when Daniel (his brother-in-law) was sick with his cancer. Having no hair was the least of his worries. He became well known at the hospital and always joked with the nurses. He tried very hard to be upbeat but there were times when you knew he was having a very tough time. And then there were several times when he had to go into the hospital because his counts were so low he needed blood transfusions. After the blood transfusions, he always felt better for a few days. After his chemo sessions, he would feel terrible by several days later and felt like death warmed over. Eventually he had to stop having the chemo for several weeks because he was so weak. And of course just when he was feeling half normal again then they started the chemo again. I would visit when I could and Michael and I would go to the hospital to visit him. I would send funny cards to Kevin to try and pick up his day even for just a few minutes. I would call Tat every several days to check in on them. I wanted to be there for her as she was for me. I would try so hard to be up for her and positive and tell her I was always there for her to talk to. Tat is a very strong-willed person and for her to lean on someone is very seldom. She did not want to cry at all because she was afraid if she started to cry that she would never stop and she needed and wanted to be strong for Kevin. God bless her for all the hours of sleepless nights and worry for Kevin. She kept him on his toes and would not even let him think any negative thoughts. Sometimes she was tough on him but that was her way of dealing with it and helping him get through it. I admired her strength and was very proud of her coping skills. I still wanted her to get help for herself and talk to someone but that didn't really pan out. She always says I am stubborn, but you haven't seen stubborn until you've seen Tat in action. Love you, Tat.

Kevin went through months and months of chemo every two weeks and it took a huge toll on him, but thank God he didn't give up. Tat went through months and months of the chemo too. Even though it wasn't in her body, it was in her every thought watching Kevin slide in and out of misery. They stood by each other even through moments of exhaustion and anger and counted every day that brought them closer to the end of the chemo treatments. And then the chemo was over. He lived through all the treatments and hospital visits and feeling like he was near death. He came to the other side. He still had to get through the things he got because of the chemo. He had to deal with diabetes from the chemo which eventually he got in order. He also had a tumor behind his one eye during all this and they gave him radiation to shrink the tumor. Thank goodness it worked, but it affected his eye so bad that he will need to have an operation on his eye to get it back to normal. But it's okay, he is still here for us to pick on and love. He just had his three-month tests and everything came back normal. Thank God he is cancer free. Now if only they could help him with his other abnormal problem, his brain. Kevin will smile when he reads that last line because it wouldn't be us if we didn't pick on each other. I love you, Kevin and Tat, and wish you many more happy years of life together. My life has been much better having the two of you in it. God bless you both.

 ## MY THOUGHTS

I have a plaque in my hallway upstairs that I see every morning and this is what it says:
    Faith is being sure of what we hope for and certain of what we do not see. (Hebrews 11:1)

You know by now obviously that I have a great faith in God. Sometimes people get very nervous or even angry when the word

God is brought up. I understand that, truly I do, especially with all of the Isis shit and all of the evil people before Isis that use God as an excuse for killing innocent people. So, I get it. I have so many questions myself and I believe that someday when I do leave this earth I will get those answers. I believe there is life after death. Surely, after living with all the hell that a lot of us go through there is something waiting for us on the other side. Just what is waiting for us I do not know? But what I do know is that my whole life I have felt something in my heart and soul that leads me to believe that something beautiful is waiting for me. I have walked around most of my life with so much darkness around me and now I walk around most of my days with faith, trust and light because I choose to. And this may sound weird but I believe that there is hell right here on earth. Just look around us. All the evil and horrendous things that happen to good people, it doesn't make sense. And where does God come in? I believe he comes to us when we ask him to help us through our worst nightmare. I don't have the answers to why bad things happen to good people but I don't believe the God I love sits on a throne and says, "Okay, let's see, I think today we will let little five-year-old Mary be brutally murdered," or "Well, now, those five hundred people on the airplane will die today." I cannot believe that the God I love would be so cruel. So, until I know different (which will be the day I die), I choose to believe that God does love us very much and does cry when something horrible happens to the people we love and even the people we do not know.

I saw a movie this year (2016) called *Miracles from Heaven* with my good friend Karen. It was a true story about a ten-year-old girl who had a rare incurable disease called pseudo-obstruction motility. She had to use feeding tubes for nutrition and her stomach would bloat up and she was weak and sick to her stomach most of the time. She had a strong faith in God because she was raised in a family who believed in God and went to church faithfully. But after the little girl gets very ill the mother has a hard time with her faith and stops going to church. She concentrates on getting her daughter the best care she can and so she goes on a quest to save her daughter which was hard on the family but necessary. The story has a lot going on in it but the main focus is this little girl and how she has faith but also wonders why God is not helping her. Eventually the little girl climbs a three-story tree in their yard and falls down into the hollow part of the tree head first. Everyone is mortified. The ambulance arrives and the fire trucks come, and even though everyone believes she was surely dead the mother finally goes to the tree and kneels down to pray to God for her child. Then her husband joins her and their other children and then everyone who was there put their heads down and pray. It is a beautiful moment in this movie and touches your heart. But to make a long story short, they finally bring the little girl up through the tree. They take her to the hospital and she survives this fall to the head which was a miracle in itself. A few weeks later, they start to notice that the big lump in her stomach was going down. She started to fit into her clothes and the mom noticed she had more energy and was amazed at how her little girl was so happy. The mom takes her to the specialist and they do tests and lo and behold they find out that the disease she had was gone. She is miraculously cured of her disease. It was totally gone. She was now a very healthy little girl. The medical specialists are mystified. But that's not all that happened. The little girl makes a comment one day to her parents that she wasn't afraid anymore because He told her she would be okay. Her parents asked her who said she would be okay. And she said so sweetly and innocently something to the effect of, "God told me I would be okay, I saw him in the tree." Then the daughter proceeded to tell her parents what she saw while she was in the tree and how she wanted to stay there because it was a happy place but she had to leave. This little ten-year-old girl had a near-death experience. The mother shared their story in their church and the rest is history. But my point about all of this is not only to show you that a power does exist in our universe (to me that's God) but also this is just one of many, many true spiritual stories. Among the answers I don't have are why some people get miracles and others don't. That is something I do not understand but I have faith that I will know some day, but in the meantime, I will not question the unconditional love that I know God has for me. Does this mean that my life is stress free or perfect? No, it doesn't. I go through stresses and life challenges just like anyone else but I know for me that I can get through my life challenges a whole lot better with my faith in God than I could without it. My God is my strength.

CHAPTER 31

And that story will bring us to our most recent vacation which was in February of 2015 at Punta Cana, Dominican Republic. Michael and I had never stayed in Punta Cana, Dominican Republic, and we were very impressed with the beautiful white sandy beaches. The resort was perfect and we had amazing quality time with our families. Michael and I decided we wanted to spend a lot of time at the resort this time and maybe do one excursion. We were blessed to have some of our family members come and our dearest of friends. Tat and Kevin and their adult children Christopher and his wife Crystal and their daughter Melanie came. Kevin's brother and wife from B.C. met us there. My brother Brad and my sister-in-law Christine and their two daughters (and their oldest daughter's boyfriend Ray) met us there. Our daughter Charlie, son-in-law Jacob, and their three daughters came. We had lots of dinners together when we could and lots of swimming in the pools together. There was a lot of laughing together. And the times we weren't together was not a problem at all. There was so many of us sometimes we just needed space and that was okay too. That's the beauty of going away with others you just go with the flow.

The one and only excursion I did was to go parasailing! I finally had the opportunity to go and I wasn't going to back out this time. Michael, my brother and a few others passed on this excursion but they watched us from the beach until they couldn't see us anymore. So, there was myself, my daughter Charlie, Tat, Kevin, their daughter Melanie, my sister-in-law Christine, her two daughters Josie and Julie, and Julie's boyfriend Ray. It was crazy, to say the least. We all had to jump, literally jump into a rocking speed boat on the beach and the driver pushed us out further into the water. He takes us out to a bigger boat which we had to be careful as the waves were really rocking that day as we got into the bigger boat. Then there were other people who got on too, which was great. The more the merrier. When Tat and Kevin got on the double seat we were all cheering them on. Not only because this was Kevin's first trip two weeks after his last chemo treatment! But also because he had beaten cancer and a year before this trip we didn't know if this would happen. As the instructor raised them higher and higher they leaned over to each other and kissed. All of us were so emotional. I had tears in my eyes.

The stranger beside me noticed and said, "Aww, that was so sweet."

I said, "You have no idea how sweet it is. They just beat cancer together and to see them here parasailing is such a miracle to us."

I wiped my tears and thanked God for that moment which filled my heart with so much love and hope for my dearest, oldest friends. They did it, they beat cancer together, how inspiring it was for me to see them flying high above the water laughing and smiling together.

I watched my sister-in-law and her youngest daughter Josie have their turn and they loved it. Then Julie and her boyfriend Ray went up and enjoyed it too. This was all new to all of us except Tat and Kevin who did it in the Bahamas on their twenty-fifth wedding anniversary. And then it was my turn. I did not have one bit of fear to speak of. I was more than excited and thrilled to get on the three-seater with my dear niece Melanie and my dear daughter Charlie. Together the three of us yelled, "Yahoo!" Of course the crew had a little bit of trouble getting us up out of the water apparently because of the wind but once they got us up it was incredible to us. It was so quiet up there. You could see for miles and we just floated above it all. I loved it. I would do it again in a heartbeat. I felt like I could do anything when I was up there. I thanked God again for the beauty I could see and the peace I felt. I thought about the time I missed out on parasailing when Michael and I were in the Bahamas many years ago. I knew I would not miss out on this or anything else that I really wanted to do again. I knew I was well into being free of anxiety and all that it took from me through my whole life. I could have floated forever with the peace and freedom I felt at that moment in my life. Freedom of the fear that threatened to keep me locked up in my house, freedom of the fear that laughed at me when I succumbed to the fear, and freedom of the fear that kept me from living the life I was meant to live. I read somewhere in my Attacking Anxiety program that fear means "false evidence appearing real." This is a wonderful way to describe fear. It takes the fear out of our fear if that makes any sense.

The rest of the trip was so much fun! I was still on a high from parasailing and found a new step in my walk. I got to spend so much quality time with people I love and then go home feeling proud and hopeful for myself.

As I come to the end of my story I would like to take the time to share how proud I am of my family. Michael and I are very blessed to have such a close, healthy and loving relationship with each other and our four daughters. Our daughters have brought us so much joy, laughter and love and we couldn't be more proud to be their parents. They have chosen amazing husbands whom we love like sons. Our soninlaw's are very good to us and the love and respect they show us is wonderful to see. And of course the creme de la creme, our Six grandchildren! Three granddaughters and three grandsons so far. They are all unique and gifted and give us so much joy and love! And we have a lot more love to give any other grandchildren that may come in the future. Just saying. Family means the world to me and I have an amazing family that keeps me young. Lucky me!

Can I still get anxiety or panic? Yes, but not to the extreme that I lived with on a daily basis for many years. I immediately or eventually use the tools I was taught and just breathe and tell myself it is just anxiety, it is not going to hurt me and I am okay. I soothe myself with my positive self-talk and I remind myself that I am not going to die or lose my mind. I tell myself that I will be okay in a few minutes and if it takes longer, then so be it, but I will not let the panic take total control of me anymore. And the one thing I always tell myself is that I am not alone, God is with me and I am totally okay. Lucinda Bassett says in one of her tapes that she stepped through that wall of fear and I am following her footsteps and I don't allow the fear to spoil my day especially when I accept that I am in control of any thoughts that go into my head. For many years I lived with sadness, anger, hopelessness, and fear. I worked through so much shit and came to the other side every time. I had faith in God and eventually I had faith in myself. I learned to look in the mirror and love myself despite my bad choices. God put the right things in my path and it was up to me to pick it up and follow it. I am grateful for all the things and people that came into my life and helped me to help myself. I am grateful for my amazing husband and my beautiful family and friends. My life is filled to the brim with good things and positive things and when life happens to be stressful with down times I get through it the best I can and I never give up. I may get down but I never give up. I refuse to work through all this just to go back to my old way of thinking. I am worth more than I ever thought I could be. I deserve to have the things I have in my life. I fought hard to get to where I am today. So look out, negative thoughts, because a new thought pattern is in town and she is not a pushover anymore. I am no longer haunted by the darkness for I have been graced by the light, the light that has always been in me, I just needed to let it shine.

Once upon a time I truly was a lost girl and now because of God's amazing grace I am found. Thank you, God.

The Oak Tree

(Written by Johnny Ray Ryder Jr.)

A Mighty wind blew night and day.
It stole the oak tree's leaves away.
Then snapped its boughs and pulled its bark
until the oak was tired and stark.
But still the oak tree held its ground
while other trees fell all around.
The weary wind gave up and spoke,
"How can you still be standing Oak?"
The oak tree said,
I know that you can break
Each branch off in two,
Carry every leaf away,
Shake my limbs and make me sway.
But I have roots stretched in the earth,
Growing stronger since my birth.
You'll never touch them, for you see
They are the deepest part of me.
Until today, I wasn't sure
Of just how much I could endure.
But now I've found with thanks to you,
I AM STRONGER THAN I EVER KNEW.

🦋 MY THOUGHTS

The purpose of this book is to help someone else to overcome obstacles in their life that has kept them living in darkness with no hope instead of taking a step forward into the light. The light that has saved me from drowning in the depths of darkness that eats away at your soul until there is nowhere left to go. We all have a choice.

It is ours to make, nobody else's. I chose to step into the light and I hope you will too. The choice is yours. There is a light within all of us. For some it may shine bright, for some it may be a spark, and for some the light is waiting to be lit. This light is a gift from God that shines for us through Jesus, God's only son, our Lord. This light is filled with many gifts such as strength, courage, peace, joy, forgiveness, faith, hope, and most of all, love.

ABOUT THE AUTHOR

The author was born and raised in a small city in the province of New Brunswick, Canada. Her mother instilled in her the stories of God and taught her to say her prayers every night before bedtime. When she was a little girl, she loved to hear the "Once upon a time" stories and believed in the happy endings. But the author was not to have a happy ending anytime soon and eventually moved to another small city in the province of Ontario with her two small children. Amidst everything that was happening around her, she held onto her relationship with God and her love of poetry and writing. The author has always believed that every one of us has a story to tell. One of her dreams was to write a book about her life and how she managed to push through her tough times, so she could help someone else get to the other side with faith, trust and hope. And last but not least, the author believes that her story turned out amazing because of her faith in God.

CPSIA information can be obtained
at www.ICGtesting.com
Printed in the USA
LVOW08s1507060617
537124LV00003B/383/P